Political Transition and Inclusive Development in Malawi

Malawi is among the few countries in sub-Saharan Africa that has witnessed significant improvements in relation to meeting the Millennium Development Goal (MDG) targets. It exhibits some of the main challenges facing African democracies while they attempt to consolidate the benefits of democratisation.

Political Transition and Inclusive Development in Malawi critically analyses opportunities and constraints related to the impact of democracy on development in one of the world's poorest countries. The book explores how, and to what extent, processes related to democratic and economic governance can be strengthened in order to make political and administrative authorities more responsive to development needs. It also considers characteristics of successful implementation of public policy and the effective and timely delivery of basic services in local contexts; increased citizen participation and dialogue with local government authorities; factors that enable civil society organisations to hold political and administrative officials to account; and better utilisation of academic research for improved evidence-based policy formulation and implementation.

This volume will be of great interest to scholars in development studies, African studies, politics, law and anthropology, as well as policymakers and those interested in democracy, governance, human rights and the implementation of anti-poverty programmes, development administration and decentralisation.

Dan Banik is Professor of Political Science and Research Director at the Centre for Development and the Environment, University of Oslo, Norway. He is also a Consulting Scholar at the Center on Democracy, Development and the Rule of Law at Stanford University, USA.

Blessings Chinsinga is Professor at the Department of Political and Administrative Studies at Chancellor College, University of Malawi, Malawi. He is also Deputy Director of the University of Malawi's Centre for Social Research.

Routledge Studies in African Development

Self-Determination and Secession in Africa
The post-colonial state
Edited by Redie Bereketeab

Economic Growth and Development in Africa
Understanding global trends and prospects
Horman Chitonge

African Youth and the Persistence of Marginalization
Employment, politics and prospects for change
Edited by Danielle Resnick and James Thurlow

HIV and East Africa
Thirty years in the shadow of an epidemic
Janet Seeley

Development Discourse and Global History
From colonialism to the sustainable development goals
Aram Ziai

Higher Education and Capacity Building in Africa
The geography and power of knowledge under changing conditions
Hanne Kirstine Adriansen, Lene Møller Madsen and Stig Jensen

Gender and the Political Economy of Conflict in Africa
The persistence of violence
Meredeth Turshen

Social Innovation in Africa
A practical guide for scaling impact
Ndidi Okonkwo Nwuneli

Political Transition and Inclusive Development in Malawi
The democratic dividend
Edited by Dan Banik and Blessings Chinsinga

Political Transition and Inclusive Development in Malawi

The democratic dividend

Edited by Dan Banik and
Blessings Chinsinga

Routledge
Taylor & Francis Group

LONDON AND NEW YORK

First published 2016 by Routledge

2 Park Square, Milton Park, Abingdon, Oxfordshire OX14 4RN
711 Third Avenue, New York, NY 10017

Routledge is an imprint of the Taylor & Francis Group, an informa business

First issued in paperback 2017

British Library Cataloguing-in-Publication Data
A catalogue record for this book is available from the British Library

Library of Congress Cataloging-in-Publication Data
Names: Banik, Dan, 1969- editor. | Chinsinga, Blessings, editor.
Title: Political transition and inclusive development in Malawi : the democratic dividend / edited by Dan Banik and Blessings Chinsinga.
Description: New York, NY : Routledge, 2016.
Identifiers: LCCN 2016000882 | ISBN 9781138925212 (hb) | ISBN 9781315683898 (ebook)
Subjects: LCSH: Malawi--Politics and government--1994- | Malawi--Economic conditions. | Democracy--Malawi. | Economic development--Malawi.
Classification: LCC DT3237.3 .P65 2016 | DDC 968.97042--dc23
LC record available at http://lccn.loc.gov/2016000882_

ISBN: 978-1-138-92521-2 (hbk)
ISBN: 978-0-8153-5928-9 (pbk)

Typeset in Goudy
by Saxon Graphics Ltd, Derby

Contents

Figures

Tables

Notes on contributors

Dan Banik is professor of political science and research director at the Centre for Development and the Environment, University of Oslo. He is also a consulting scholar at Stanford University's Centre on Democracy, Development and the Rule of Law and a visiting professor at China Agricultural University in Beijing. Prof. Banik has conducted research in India, China, Bangladesh, Malawi, Uganda, Ethiopia, Tanzania, South Africa and Mexico, and directs the interdisciplinary research program 'Poverty and Development in the 21st Century (PAD)' at the University of Oslo. He has previously served as the head of the Norwegian–Finnish Trust Fund in the World Bank for Environmentally and Socially Sustainable Development (TFESSD) and on the Board of the Norwegian Crown Prince and Crown Princess's Foundation. His books include *The Legal Empowerment Agenda: Poverty, Labour and the Informal Economy in Africa* (2011, Ashgate), *Poverty and Elusive Development* (2010, Scandinavian University Press) and *Starvation and India's Democracy* (2009, Routledge).

Michael Chasukwa is a Senior Lecturer and former Head of the Department of Political and Administrative Studies, Chancellor College, University of Malawi. He holds an MA (Political Science) and BA (Public Administration) from the University of Malawi. His research and teaching interests include development aid, political economy of development, agricultural policies as they relate to land, youth and development, local government, governance and decentralization. He is currently a PhD candidate in development studies in the School of Politics and International Studies at the University of Leeds. Mr Chasukwa has published in peer-reviewed articles in several international journals including *International Journal of Public Administration, Journal of Development Effectiveness, Africa Review* and *Journal of Asian and African Studies*.

Blessings Chinsinga is an experienced academic, researcher and consultant currently based at the Department of Political and Administrative Studies, Chancellor College, University of Malawi, where he is a Professor specializing in political economy of development, governance and democracy, public policy analysis, rural livelihoods and local level politics. He is also Deputy Director of the Centre for Social Research (CSR) – the research arm of the

University of Malawi's Faculty of Social Science. Prof. Chinsinga is a prominent media commentator and a much sought-after consultant on development-related issues in Malawi.

Asiyati Lorraine Chiweza is an Associate Professor and an expert on local governance in the Department of Political and Administrative Studies at Chancellor College, University of Malawi. She holds a PhD from Curtin University, Western Australia (2007), a master's degree in public administration from Dalhousie University, Canada (1995) and a bachelor's degree in social science from the University of Malawi (1988). Dr Chiweza has written extensively on matters of decentralization and local government in Malawi.

Boniface Dulani is a lecturer in Political Science at Chancellor College, University of Malawi. Dr Dulani, who received his PhD in political science from Michigan State University, also doubles as the Fieldwork Operations Manager for Afrobarometer, a pan-African research network that conducts public opinion surveys on democracy, governance, market reforms and related issues in Africa. His research on presidential succession and elections has been published in *African Affairs*, *Electoral Studies* and other journals.

Lewis B. Dzimbiri is a Professor of Public Administration at Chancellor College, University of Malawi. He studied at Keele University for a PhD in industrial relations and has held teaching positions at Galilee International Management Institute (Israel), Midlands State University (Zimbabwe) and the University of Botswana. His areas of interest include public service human resource management, industrial relations, organisation theory and management, organisation development, public policy and administration and strategic planning and management. Prof. Dzimbiri's publications include four books, numerous refereed journal articles and book chapters, and over one hundred conference papers and consultancy reports. He has functioned as a postgraduate Programme Coordinator, Head of Department, Dean of the Faculty of Social Science, Vice Principal and as member of numerous committees and boards within and outside the university.

Fidelis Edge Kanyongolo is an Associate Professor of Law at the University of Malawi, with a particular research interest in the interplay between law and politics. Dr Kanyongolo combines academic work with human rights activism, in which role he has served as a trustee of the Media Institute of Southern Africa (MISA), a member of the Advisory Board of the Africa Programme of ARTICLE 19 (Global Campaign for Free Expression) and a member of the Board of Directors of the Open Society Initiative for Southern Africa (OSISA). He co-edited *Democracy in Progress: Malawi's 2009 Parliamentary and Presidential Elections* (2009), and has authored a number of governance assessment reports including *Malawi: Justice Sector and the Rule of Law* (2006) and *The State of the Judiciary Report: Malawi 2003*.

Happy Mickson Kayuni is Associate Professor and Head of Department of the University of Malawi's Political and Administrative Studies Department. He holds a PhD in political science from the University of Western Cape, South Africa. Apart from the University of Malawi where he is currently employed, Dr Kayuni has also taught political science and public management at the University of the Western Cape and Cape Peninsula University of Technology in South Africa. Taking into consideration the multidisciplinary nature of public administration, Happy Mickson Kayuni has authored (or co-authored) thirty-two peer-reviewed journal articles and book chapters as well as over sixty consultancy reports or conference papers in the areas of gender, public policy and administration, management, politics and development.

Nandini Patel is a Professor of Political Science at the Catholic University of Malawi. She has taught political science for over 25 years in India and Malawi and is the Chairperson of the Institute for Policy Interaction, a local think-tank. Dr Patel's research interests include political institutions in emerging democracies with particular focus on elections in the SADC region. She has conducted academic research on the topic as well as undertaken several consultancies.

Kizito Tenthani has worked in the area of democracy and governance for 15 years. His work has focused on empowering rural communities on civil and political rights. In 2003, he joined the Netherlands Institute for Multiparty Democracy (NIMD) as a National Coordinator for Malawi. With support from NIMD, he spearheaded the formation and establishment of the Centre for Multiparty Democracy (CMD) in Lilongwe in 1995, where he is currently Executive Director. Among other duties, Mr. Tenthani is involved in coordinating an interparty dialogue platform for political parties in addition to facilitating dialogue between the Electoral Commission of Malawi and various political parties. He holds a degree in public administration from the University of Malawi and a master's degree in public and development management from the University of the Witwatersrand. Mr Tenthani is currently pursuing a PhD in development studies, and his research focuses on Malawi's development experience from a political settlement perspective.

Acknowledgements

This volume is the first of a series of publications resulting from the research collaboration between the Department of Political and Administrative Studies at the University of Malawi's Chancellor College and the Centre for Development and the Environment at the University of Oslo. The Norwegian Agency for Development Cooperation (Norad) has provided generous funding to the project under the auspices of the Norwegian Programme for Capacity Development in Higher Education and Research for Development (NORHED).

For useful discussions and advice on a wide range of issues that have helped shape this book, we thank Vibeke Kieding Banik, Benedicte Bull, Michael Chasukwa, Henry Chingaipe, Larry Diamond, Boniface Dulani, Gitte Egenberg, Øyvind Eggen, Asbjørn Eidhammer, Francis Fukuyama, Bjarne Garden, Kikkan Haugen, Rafiq Hajat, Nikolai Hegertun, Erik Jensen, Edge Kanyongolo, Happy Mickson Kayuni, Stephen Krasner, Xiaoyun Li, Desmond McNeill, Wilma Nchito, Jorun Nossum, Progress Nyanga, Sidsel Roalkvam, John Saka, James C. Scott, Erik Solheim, Kristi Anne Stølen, Richard Tambulasi, Lixia Tang, Raphael Tenthani, Ernest Thindwa, Silje Vevatne, Robert Wade, Ola Westengen, Tanja Winther and Øyvind Østerud.

For excellent research and administrative assistance, we thank Anja Bergersen, Peter Beza, Kaja Elise Gresko, Manhar Harmansen, Maren Olene Kloster, Joan Phiri, Ernest Thindwa, Kristoffer Ring, Terje Røysum and Marie Thörnfeldt.

We are grateful to three referees, who prefer to remain anonymous, for their extremely helpful comments and suggestions on our initial proposal, and Dave Wright. We are particularly pleased to have the opportunity of working with our editors at Routledge, Khanam Virjee and Margaret Farrelly. Thanks goes also to our copy editor Chris Shaw and production manager Dave Wright. The main credit for this volume goes to our co-authors, who deserve special thanks for their contributions and for willing to be a part of this project.

1 Introduction

Dan Banik and Blessings Chinsinga

The debate on the relationship between democracy and development has become increasingly complex. The emerging scholarship on the topic has begun questioning the dominant western orthodoxy that good governance and democracy are not simply desirable, but also essential conditions for development in all societies. Indeed, recent scholarship in many parts of the world has raised important questions about the implied positive causal relationship between democracy and development. The broad conclusion from the resulting studies is that the institutional characteristics and requirements for development, and those for stable and consolidated democracy, essentially pull in opposite directions. This conclusion is supported by the fact that countries that are widely considered as promising development success stories across the African continent (e.g. Rwanda, Ethiopia, Angola and Mozambique) are not democracies in the classical sense. These countries are characterized either by a dominant party with consensual decision-making tradition or an organic bureaucracy insulated from the political process (Booth, 2011; Kelsall, 2012).

The emerging scholarship on democracy and development has revived interest in the seminal work of Seymour Martin Lipset. Some argue that the introduction of democracy in a country enhances the prospects of it achieving transformative and sustainable development. The case for democracy is further reinforced by Sen (1999), who defines development in relation to the extent of freedom enjoyed by individuals and groups in society. Thus, in addition to economic indicators, Sen argues that freedoms of various kinds and social opportunities are essential ingredients in the development process. Consequently, the democratic process is intrinsically valuable and policy decisions can potentially be made in an inclusive, participatory, transparent and accountable manner that broadly represents different societal interests. Studies by Przeworski (2005), however, do not conclusively assert whether and to what extent democracy is good for development. Although the development track records of dictatorships and democracies are not distinctively different, democracies are substantially better off as dictatorships exhibit great variations in development performance. This apparent variability in performance is attributed to the fact that policymaking and implementation of development programmes in non-democracies are considerably dependent on the personal preferences and whims of the ruler.

Those that remain sceptical about the overall efficacy of democracies in promoting development argue that the good governance agenda is totally misleading on the prerequisites for fundamental economic transformation in Africa (Henley and Van Donge, 2012). This resonates well with an emerging strand of scholarship that advocates for a shift from the preoccupation with good governance to 'political settlement' as the basis for understanding contemporary challenges in developing countries in general, and Africa in particular (Khan, 2005; Hickey, 2012). Political settlement, thus understood, refers to the formal and informal agreements between contending groups over the organization of power in society and the rules of political engagement (Khan, 2005). Consequently, differences in political settlement can explain the overall quality and extent to which institutional structures in developing countries function. Such a framework can further help identify relevant governance reforms that, if implemented properly, can promote development as well as provide a framework for understanding how political settlement patterns change in different local, regional and national contexts. Moreover, the political settlement approach draws attention to the fact that political, economic and social institutions, both formal and informal, interact with each other to shape the distribution of wealth and power in society.

The character of political settlement may explain the quality of policy processes and the nature of the resultant policies. There is thus a particular emphasis on the role of context in shaping development outcomes, as achieving development entails not just identifying concrete outcomes, but also paying attention to the nature and quality of the process through which these outcomes are achieved. Andrews (2013) argues against a pre-set toolkit of best practices or blueprints of institutional reforms largely promoted by international development agencies. The argument is that functional reforms aimed at facilitating sustainable development can only be achieved by using a problem-driven iterative approach, rooted in context specific understandings of problems as an entry point for change. Andrews concludes that the current set of reforms promoted by western donor agencies, under the banner of good governance, cannot deliver effective and sustainable development mainly because such reforms are aimed at providing developing country governments a modicum of legitimacy in the eyes of the donor community.

It is against this backdrop that this volume revisits the question of whether certain regimes are better able and equipped to promote economic growth and eradicate poverty than others, which has preoccupied academics and policymakers alike for several decades. We are essentially concerned with better understanding the relationship between democratic consolidation and development. Influenced by the work of Atul Kohli and others, we understand development as a deliberate movement of societies towards a situation of more liveable life conditions (Banik, 2010). Three critical elements of such liveable conditions are economic growth, some redistribution of growth and democracy for the redistribution of the benefits of growth. Development is thus a process where these goals are to be maximized even though there may be trade-offs in the process. Development, thus broadly understood, entails the transformation of society that goes beyond economic growth (Stiglitz, 2002) to also include social dimensions such as improvements in literacy, distribution of income and life expectancy at birth – variables captured in the UNDP's human development index as well as the redistribution of wealth.

Our volume is motivated by the fact that, despite strong claims about the limitations of the good governance agenda, many western countries continue to argue that developing countries must democratize if they are to develop. And, acting in their role as providers of foreign aid, these countries and their development agencies continue to highlight the key role that elections play in the democratization process, often making aid conditional upon the holding of free and fair elections and improvements of civil and political rights. Many development actors also readily criticise the recent trend by many emerging country nations (e.g. China, Brazil, India, Taiwan and South Korea) to provide generous grants and loans to African countries without tying up such development assistance to good governance and the promotion of human rights. The impression given is that democracy, or at least its introduction, will save poor countries from falling further into the trap of poverty. As noted earlier, democracy, apart from being intrinsically valuable, is largely viewed by many development actors as further promoting an important instrumental goal, namely development.

Political developments during the so-called 'Arab Spring' in 2011 ushered in new optimism of Africa's potential of accelerating democracy and development. However, recent events in the continent (including the dramatic military coup in Egypt) indicate that the initial optimism of increased democratization is slowly being tempered down. In relation to economic growth, however, the picture looks much brighter and there has been considerable talk of 'Africa Rising' and 'Emerging Africa', with several countries (e.g. Rwanda and Ethiopia) being highlighted as major successes despite limited evidence of democratization within their borders. Thus Radelet (2010) highlights five set of factors that characterize the successful development stories in emerging Africa:

- more democratic and accountable governments;
- more sensible economic policies (market friendly, with budget and fiscal discipline);
- a new relationship with the international community upon the end of the debt crisis;
- the spread of new digital technologies that foster business and political accountability;
- a new generation of policymakers, civic activists, and business leaders.

Several chapters in this volume therefore discuss broad theoretical and practical assumptions on the relationship between democracy, development and poverty reduction. They also highlight selected sets of mechanisms for achieving reducing poverty in the context of democratization, including a critical look at national policies as well as development policy advice provided by bilateral donors and international development organizations. Many of these initiatives have not achieved intended goals and objectives, despite the economic rise of Africa.

The apparent dismal track record of development and poverty reduction interventions invariably raises serious questions about the relationship between growth and distribution. This is underscored by recent waves of protests across the continent where large groups of people have voiced their concerns over deepening socio-economic disparities. Thus, we examine why democracy has not fully delivered on development and poverty reduction. We argue that the emphasis on 'governance', and not necessarily on 'politics', has resulted in disproportionately formalistic approaches that do not pay adequate attention to incentives available to the political leadership. Thus there is limited attention to the dynamic interaction between policy and politics in shaping development and poverty reduction outcomes.

Revisiting the democracy and development relationship is also interesting, timely and relevant given the increased use of the concept of 'good governance', 'pro-poor governance' and 'democratic governance' by western donors and multilateral institutions when they impart advice to aid-recipient countries. Yet the evidence linking democracy and development in one way or another remains inclusive and highly contentious (Przeworski, 2005). It is in this context that Malawi provides an illustrative example of some of the challenges a relatively young democracy faces in strengthening civil and political rights on the one hand while ensuring the protection and promotion of economic, social and cultural rights on the other. Moreover, we consider Malawi as an ideal case to shed further light on the democracy and development debate for two reasons:

- First, Malawi is widely considered as a successful case of democratic transition achieved largely outside the international limelight and underpinned by a progressive constitution.
- Second, Malawi has held five consecutive democratic elections since the transition to democracy in the early 1990s, and all of these elections have been classified as free, fair and credible.

The democratization project that Malawi embarked upon in 1993 appeared initially to promise good democratic governance that would translate into effective management of the economy for growth, development and poverty reduction. And the events that followed in the aftermath of the establishment of democracy in the country raised the hopes of Malawians of being able to take centre stage in public affairs, and consequently becoming the targets and beneficiaries of development interventions through active participation in national and local decision-making processes. The neo-liberal agenda that was subsequently adopted further gave the impression that Malawians would no longer be relegated to playing a peripheral role in issues of political, economic and social governance. However, nineteen years down the line, all available evidence indicates that the initial promises and goals of the national democracy project remain largely elusive. Participation and actual influence in public affairs, including business transactions, remain the privilege of a small group of elites. Moreover, poverty remains deep, severe and widespread. According to the 2012

Integrated Household Survey (IHS), poverty in Malawi declined marginally from 52.4 to 50.7 per cent between 2005 and 2011. The proportion of the ultra poor increased from 22 to 25 per cent, the majority residing in rural areas. While urban poverty declined from 25 to 17.3 per cent, rural poverty increased from 55.9 to 56 per cent. And the Gini coefficient – which provides an indication of the extent of inequality in a country – increased from 0.39 in 2005 to 0.45 in 2012, providing further evidence of the widening gap between the rich and poor.

One of the problems we highlight in this volume relates to the impact of a political culture of informality on Malawi's democratization and development agendas. Indeed, Malawi's democratization project remains fragile and is constantly threatened by prospects of reversal, if not complete breakdown, despite concerted efforts to establish a functioning democratic regime in the past two decades. This is in line with Hyden's (2006) contention that the interface between formal and informal institutions is critical in shaping political, economic and social development outcomes – and that Africa is an ideal starting point to fully grasp these dynamics. Consequently, some scholars have claimed that the main challenge for the democratization project is that Malawi has experienced transition without transformation. Indeed, throughout the volume, we argue that while Malawi has embraced a gamut of institutions of democracy, they do not function as expected because the one-party political culture, deeply wedded to the ethos of informality, remains squarely intact in the country.

The volume

This volume focuses on how, and to what extent, processes related to democratic and economic governance can be strengthened in order to make political and administrative authorities more responsive to the development needs of Africa. In other words, how can countries in the region consolidate democracy given the dominance of a one-party political culture? Additional topics of general interest covered in this volume relate to the characteristic features of public policy implementation, the nature of citizen participation and dialogue with various levels of government and the factors that enable civil society organizations to hold political and administrative officials to account for failing to provide efficient delivery of public services. Our goal is to synthesize the results of on-going academic research with the aim of achieving improved and evidence-based policy formulation and implementation.

It is against this background that we aim to critically analyse opportunities and constraints related to the impact of democracy on development in one of the world's poorest countries. While a focus on Malawi may appear too narrow for general consumption, we believe the timing for doing so is opportune as the Malawian case exhibits some of the main challenges facing African democracies while they attempt to consolidate the benefits of democratization. There are very few good scholarly works on the topic that covers Malawi, and we believe that the studies in this volume on the Malawian experience provide a sound basis for comparing democratic experiments in other African countries. Further, recent studies by international organizations show that Malawi is among the few countries in sub-Saharan Africa that has witnessed significant improvements in relation to meeting the Millennium Development Goal (MDG) targets.

This volume is the product of a long-term collaboration between the editors and their institutions in Norway and Malawi. The impetus for this publication came from a research project entitled 'Strengthening capacity for democratic and economic governance in Malawi', funded by the Norwegian Agency for Development Cooperation (Norad) under the Norwegian Programme for Capacity Development in Higher Education and Research for Development (NORHED). The main goal of the project is to enable Chancellor College to help build a critical mass of more and better-qualified Malawians who can effectively engage with political and economic elites and policymakers, and thereby positively influence decision-making processes related to democratic and economic governance.

The contributors to this volume – with a background in the social sciences and law – represent some of the most influential voices on political development in Malawi, and include academics, practitioners, media commentators and activists.

The volume is structured around three broad parts:

- Part I: Democratization and political culture;
- Part II: Governance and policy implementation; and
- Part III: Activism, aid and accountability.

The chapters in each of these parts examine whether and to what extent Malawi's democracy has progressed, stagnated or been threatened with reversal.

Part I consists of three chapters that examine the extent of institutional consolidation in the country and its impact on civil, political, economic and cultural rights. In particular, the focus is on political parties, the parliament and the judiciary.

In Chapter 2, Boniface Dulani examines the five election cycles in Malawi, including the latest elections that were held in 2014 which marked two decades of uninterrupted democracy. The euphoria of change that characterized the landmark democratic elections of 18 May 1994 has since been replaced with critical reflection of the nature and overall trajectory of the country's nascent democracy. Dulani examines whether Malawi's democracy has progressed, stagnated or been threatened with reversal. Has the pessimism over economic performance translated into a questioning of the democracy itself? Based on a critical examination of the political developments in the two decades between 1994 and 2014, Dulani argues that, despite a myriad of challenges, democracy appears to have taken root in the country and the passage of time is lowering the odds for democratic reversal. He analyses micro-level data from public opinion surveys conducted by Afrobarometer, which further demonstrates high levels of public commitment to democracy even though many Malawians are disappointed with how the political elites have failed to perform to the expected standards. Using a demand and supply analysis of survey data, he argues that prospects for progress remain high against a background of consistently high demand for democracy, even if the evidence suggests low levels of its supply. Dulani concludes by asserting that, having overcome numerous episodes that could have derailed it, Malawi's democracy is tilting towards progress and that the passage of time is increasingly reducing the likelihood of democratic stagnation or even reversal.

Kizito Tenthani and Blessings Chinsinga examine the relationship between political parties, political settlement and development in Chapter 3. Despite their flaws, political parties are considered to be the lifeblood of a multiparty democracy – a political system that if harnessed properly has the potential of ushering in economic development and poverty reduction in a country like Malawi. Tenthani and Chinsinga begin by providing an overview of the history, development and operation of political parties in the country before critically examining the nature of political settlements that have characterized both national and local politics. A specific focus on the legal framework offers explanations of how political parties are formed, how the party system is regulated and the extent to which parties serve the interests of voters. The general conclusion is that political parties in Malawi have failed to reach a level and type of political settlement that can facilitate sustainable development.

In Chapter 4, Edge Kanyongolo studies the linkages between political parties and the judiciary and what he terms as the 'judicialisation' and 'informalisation' of politics in Malawi. Since the early 1990s, the Malawian judiciary has played a growing role in the mediation and arbitration of political relations. Kanyongolo analyses this role in the context of debates over the interplay between the institutional framework of politics and the institutionalization of democratic governance. Using the regulation of political parties as a case study, and applying critical legal theoretical approaches, he examines supply-side and demand-side factors that influence the potential of the judiciary to facilitate the institutionalization of the democratic principles of participation, accountability, the rule of law and human rights in Malawian political culture and practice. Kanyongolo argues that the potential of the Malawian judiciary to contribute to the institutionalization of democratic governance is constrained by a number of conceptual, jurisdictional, procedural and substantive factors that obstruct courts from sufficiently integrating the realities of informalization of politics into the jurisprudence of political party regulation. He further argues that the obstructive effect of these factors is a function of the dominance of formalism in Malawian legal theory. Enhancing the contribution of the judiciary to the democratization of Malawian politics therefore requires a reorientation of judicial discourse on political parties away from the dogmatic dichotomization of law and politics, which the formalism of classic legal positivist theory currently establishes and perpetuates.

Part II focuses on governance and policy formulation and implementation. While the first two chapters in this section highlight the formal and actual linkages between various levels of elected and non-elected officials, the third chapter highlights the specific case of agricultural policy aimed at generating youth employment.

In Chapter 5, Lewis Dzimbiri discusses the Malawian public service, a key institution that the government uses to implement national policies aimed at promoting economic and social development. While a well-functioning public service is crucial in enabling a government to function and deliver on its mandates, it is also widely accepted that an effective public service depends on a good interface between the political and administrative leadership to ensure that polices are formulated and implemented properly. Dzimbiri examines the role ministers (as elected leaders) and principal secretaries (as the highest ranked bureaucrats in ministries) play in the recruitment, promotion, demotion, transfer and disciplining of public servants. The aim is to better understand how these roles impact on the functioning of the public service machinery. Dzimbiri notes that politics and administration in Malawi are inseparable, and there is considerable integration of the roles of ministers and principal secretaries in policy processes. The entire process is moreover characterized by considerable political interference in the appointments, promotions, transfers, etc., of public servants, which in turn adversely affects public service morale and contributes to ineffective service delivery. Dzimbiri nonetheless concludes on an optimistic note, arguing that current proposals for reform, if properly implemented, have the potential of addressing many of the current challenges.

Asiyati Lorraine Chiweza's focus in Chapter 6 is local government and the political economy of local level politics. In the international development discourse, decentralization is frequently advocated as a tool for improving the efficiency and effectiveness of public service delivery and for promoting participatory democracy and decision-making. Thus, donors and policymakers viewed Malawi's adoption of a democratic decentralization policy in 1998 as a logical conclusion of the transition to the national democratic agenda that started in 1994. There was considerable hope that policy reforms would institutionalize political, administrative and fiscal decision-making powers and authority in local governments, and that the local governments would pursue development policies on the ground based on the principles of accountability, transparency and participation. Chiweza examines the impact of politics on local government paralysis in terms of ensuring accountable, transparent and participatory decision-making and service delivery. Her study – which focuses on the politics of representation, district decision-making and oversight processes in district councils – concludes that the scope for realizing the commonly advocated goals of improved service delivery, governance and poverty reduction goals has remained elusive.

Youth unemployment is a rapidly growing problem not only in Malawi but in large parts of the African continent. Blessings Chinsinga and Michael Chasukwa examine the problem in Chapter 7, with a particular focus on the agriculture sector, which continues to be the largest employer in Malawi. Like in the rest of Africa, Malawi has witnessed a disproportionate increase in youth unemployment, which is now a major social problem. It is therefore natural to expect the country's largest employment sector to address the issue of rising youth unemployment. Thus, Chinsinga and Chasukwa examine the extent to which the youth have featured in the country's agricultural policy and how the agriculture sector features in the government's national youth policy. They argue that, despite several attempts to promote youth development in Malawi since 1994, agriculture has been grossly neglected in these efforts. Indeed, politicians do not view the sector as providing adequate incentives for strong patronage networks, which in turn explains why youth unemployment is not accorded a policy priority in what is possibly the sector with the greatest potential for generating employment.

Part III discusses the role and impact of activism and foreign aid on holding the government to account. The three chapters in this section examine the role of the media, the legislature, civil society organizations and providers of foreign aid.

In Chapter 8, Nandini Patel discusses government accountability and the oversight role of governmental and non-governmental bodies. There is a direct functional relationship between the legislature and constitutional bodies such as the Human Rights Commission, the Ombudsman, the Director of Public Prosecutions and the Anti-Corruption Bureau. A vibrant and adversarial legislature can effectively interact with and enhance the role, power and influence of these institutions. However, legislatures in many developing countries are weak and 'rubber stamp' legislation leading to the executive amassing power amidst a culture of impunity. Such practices often result in the growth of autocracy and corruption. The prevalence of neo-patrimonialism within the modern state is thus a significant challenge to oversight bodies playing their rightful roles, although not the sole challenge. Patel examines the performance and contributions of the oversight bodies, with the aim of exploring whether these bodies have now developed the capacity to face these constant political and economic challenges and can sustain themselves. She finds that the gradual and systematic rise of watchdog institutions in Malawi was dealt a severe setback during the years 2009–2011, when democracy was under siege. The legislature's role in general was reduced and its oversight role was particularly thwarted. Appointments of officials to the independent bodies were based on patronage and their independence was severely constrained. Despite a host of challenges, Patel argues that the Malawian parliament – especially through its various committees – has demonstrated that it has the potential, and can be an effective mechanism, for ensuring accountable governance.

Malawi's economy is heavily dependent on western foreign aid, which funds almost 40 per cent of the national budget. However, China is increasingly supporting a wide range of projects (from infrastructure and health to education and agricultural technology) that appear to complement western efforts to promote development and reduce poverty. In Chapter 9, Dan Banik and Michael Chasukwa critically analyse and highlight the impact of ideas, values and tangible benefits resulting from China's engagement in Malawi. Rather than providing budget support to governments, and conditioning aid on support for democracy and gender equality, the Chinese model has consistently emphasized the principles of 'win–win', 'mutual respect', 'friendship' and 'non-interference'. Despite the rhetoric often found in western media outlets, Banik and Chasukwa do not find substantial evidence to indicate that western donors and the Chinese are competing in Malawi. They further conclude that, although Chinese aid is making important contributions to development and employment generation in tune with local needs, there are numerous challenges looming in the horizon. These relate primarily to future availability of adequate capital given the recent slowdown of the Chinese economy and growing dissatisfaction with Chinese traders in rural areas.

The post-1994 democratization period witnessed a growing interest in bringing about realistic participation of women in Malawian politics. In preparation for the 2009 general elections, the quest for increased female political participation took a more organized approach under the banner of the 50–50 campaign – relying heavily on the media. In Chapter 10, Happy Mickson Kayuni examines the role of the media in shaping political views and social behaviour in relation to gender equality. He argues that, although the media may have contributed to enriching democracy by facilitating debates on female representation in parliament, the entire 50–50 campaign was based on a politically unsustainable premise. Kayuni also finds that the media's approach to gender issues in Malawi has been too narrow, over-simplistic and oriented towards the short term.

In the final chapter of this volume, we briefly summarize some of the main arguments presented by our co-authors and identify a set of political and development issues that require the urgent attention of policymakers and the international community in order to highlight realistic ways of making democracy count for transformative, inclusive and sustainable development.

It is our hope that this volume provides an important source of knowledge about political transformation and inclusive development in one of the world's most impoverished nations. We would be delighted if this volume proves to be useful as a tool of analysis for researchers, teachers and undergraduate and post-graduate students in politics, law, sociology, geography, anthropology, economics, law, history, philosophy, development and area studies, and as a guide to policy for decision-makers. This volume should appeal to those interested in democracy, governance, human rights, state action and the implementation of anti-poverty programmes, development administration and decentralization. In addition to specific case studies from Malawi, we also hope the volume will provide theoretical and comparative insights for cross-cultural extensions.

References

Andrews, M. (2013) *The Limits of Institutional Reform in Development: Changing Rules for Realistic Solutions*, Cambridge: Cambridge University Press.

Banik, D. (2010) *Poverty and Elusive Development*, Oslo: Scandinavian University Press.

Booth, D. (2011) 'Introduction: Working with the Grain? The Africa Power and Politics Programme', *IDS Bulletin*, 42(2): 1–8.

Henley, D. and Van Donge, J. K. (2012) 'Policy for Development in Africa: Learning from Southeast Asia', *DRA Policy Brief 1*, available at: http://www.institutions-africa.org/filestream/20120318-dra-policy-brief-01 (accessed 11 February 2016).

Hickey, S. (2012) 'Investigating the Politics of Inclusive Development: Towards a Relational Approach', *ESID Working Paper No. 1*, Manchester: ESID.

Hyden, G. (2006) *African Politics in Comparative Perspective*, New York: Cambridge University Press.

Khan, M. H. (2005) 'Markets, States and Democracy: Patron-Client Networks and the Case for Democracy in Developing Countries', *Democratization* 12(5): 705–25.

Kelsall, T. (2012) 'Neo-Patrimonialism, Rent-Seeking and Development: Going with the Grain?' *New Political Economy*, 17(5): 677–82.

Przeworski, A. (2005) 'Democracy as an Equilibrium', *Public Choice* 123: 253–73.

Radelet, S. (2010) *Emerging Africa: How 17 Countries are Leading the Way*, Washington, DC: Center for Global Development.

Sen, A. (1999) *Development as Freedom*, Oxford: Oxford University Press.

Stiglitz, J. E. (2002) *Globalization and its Discontents*, New York: W. W. Norton & Company.

Part I

Democratization and political culture

2 Progress or stagnation?

Twenty years of democracy

Boniface Dulani

Introduction

Within a span of two decades, Malawi has undergone five democratic election cycles. During the period 1994 to 2014, the country has been served by four presidents: Bakili Muluzi (1994–2004), Bingu wa Mutharika (2004–12), Joyce Banda (2012–14) and Peter Mutharika (2014–). The euphoria of change that characterized the landmark democratic elections of 18 May 1994 has since been replaced with largely pessimistic reflections on the nature and overall trajectory of the country's nascent democracy (Chirwa *et al.*, 2003; Dulani, 2008, Chirambo, 2009, Svasand, 2011). Within this debate, questions have been raised about the overall strength and durability of the country's nascent democracy. The view that Malawian democracy is on shaky and uncertain ground is summed up most succinctly by Svasand (2011: 20), who notes that the country's democracy indicators show 'stagnation, or in some cases, reversals'.

Previous attempts at assessing the trajectory of Malawi's democracy faced the challenge of insufficient data points given the relatively short duration of the democratic regime. However, as Malawi's democratic experiment hits the twenty-year mark, there are enough data points that make it possible to have a fuller assessment on the overall direction that the country is making in terms of democratic consolidation. Is the country making progress, stagnating or even regressing in its democracy? This is the central question that this chapter will address. Drawing on expert data sources and complimented by public opinion survey data, the findings reveal a rather mixed picture, one that points more towards the stagnation thesis. Numerous international indices of democracy – including the Freedom House scores, Polity Index and Ibrahim index of African governance – show that, beyond the initial gains of the transition years, there has actually been limited progress on the country's democratic trajectory to a higher level. At the same time, there have been a few mild reversals but these have not been sufficiently large enough to take the country significantly backwards. Meanwhile, the evidence from the public opinion data shows similar trends, with modest gains in support for democracy and rejection of authoritarian alternatives. While public attitudes in favour of democracy appear resilient to economic downturns, the empirical evidence suggests that major political events, such as former president Bakili Muluzi's attempts to remove the constitutional clause limiting presidents to serving a maximum of two terms in office, can erode public expressions of support for democracy in ways that undermine the viability of the regime.

Although support for democracy has since increased, a significant minority – mainly women, rural residents, people with lower educational attainments and people who are either unemployed or engaged in unskilled work – consistently expresses preference for one of three forms of non-democratic regimes: one-party, military and one-man rule. Ultimately, although support for democracy is wide, it is at the same time shallow in the sense that a number of Malawians say that they support democracy but are at the same time willing to countenance authoritarian modes of government. When demand for democracy is measured against perceived supply, the conclusion is similar – as one of stagnation, where demand for democracy appears to be in equilibrium with perceived supply at levels suggesting consolidation of a hybrid regime; one that is neither fully democratic or regressing back to authoritarian rule. Based on both the expert-driven and public opinion data sources, I conclude by asserting that Malawi's democracy is tilting towards stagnation at hybrid levels. Put differently, Malawi faces little risk of sliding back to authoritarian rule as a large proportion of the public reject authoritarianism, yet, at the same time, commitment to democracy is not very strong, suggesting that there is limited appetite among the populace for further democratic reforms. This state of affairs suggests that the public would resist any attempts to remove the democratic gains made thus far but will, at the same time, not pressure leaders to introduce additional democratic reforms. This scenario leads to the consolidation of a hybrid type of regime, one that is neither fully democratic nor authoritarian.

Conceptualizing democracy consolidation

The debates on the viability of Malawi's democracy appear to be informed, at least in part, by the literature on democracy consolidation, which suggests that transitions from authoritarian rule do not always result in consolidated democracies. Instead, democratic regimes typically face the risk of collapse and reversal to authoritarian rule (Linz and Stepan, 1979; Wallerstein, 1980; Cohen, 1994; Bermeo, 2005; Diskin *et al.*, 2005; Bratton and Gyimah-Boadi, 2015).

With the literature suggesting that the likelihood of democratic reversal is higher in poorer countries than wealthier ones (Przeworski and Limongi, 1993; Przeworski *et al.*, 1996), the discourse on Africa's third-wave democracies has shifted from the democratic transitions themselves to consolidation. While there are multiple meanings attached to democratic consolidation, including those that place emphasis on institutions (Schedler, 2001) and on political alternation (cf. Huntington, 1991), I draw primarily from the literature that looks at attitudinal measures to assess the extent to which democratic values have been internalized among the general citizenry. Several works on democracy consolidation inform this position. O'Donnell (1996), for example, argues that democracy consolidation should be reflected in measures that imply expectations of regime continuity especially when faced with socio-economic and political challenges. Accordingly, democracy is consolidated when the system endures during times of socio-economic and political hardships and there exists no significant political anti-system parties (O'Donnell, 1996). Przeworski (1991) echoes this view and places emphasis on the internalization of democratic attitudes and values among citizens. He thus contends that 'democracy is consolidated when under given political and economic conditions a particular system of institutions becomes the only game in town; when no one can imagine acting outside the democratic institutions, when all losers want to do is to try again within the same institutions under which they have just lost' (Przeworski, 1991: 23).

The attitudinal view of democratic consolidation is further expounded by Schedler (2001), when he relates democracy consolidation to the absence of anti-democratic behaviour and attitudes between the both political actors and the public at large. Under this scenario, 'democracy appears to be safe if all relevant players conform to the basic rules of the democratic game' (Schedler, 2001: 70). Schedler's citizen-centric view of democracy consolidation is echoed by Linz and Stepan (1996) when they contend that democracies can be considered consolidated when democracy becomes 'behaviourally, attitudinally and constitutionally' internalized. The authors go on to contend that from a behavioural angle, democracy is consolidated when 'no significant political groups seriously attempt to overthrow the democratic regime or secede from the state', (Linz and Stepan, 1996: 15). The attitudinal dimension meanwhile places emphasis on the attitudes of a majority of ordinary citizens keeping faith in democracy even when faced with 'severe political and economic crises' (Linz and Stepan, 1996: 15). Thus in order to ascertain whether a democracy has consolidated or not, public opinion measures should, in the words of Linz and Stepan (1996: 16), show that 'a strong majority, even in the midst of major economic problems and deep dissatisfaction with incumbents, hold the belief that democratic procedures and institutions are the most appropriate way to govern collective life, and when support for anti-system alternatives is quite small or isolated from pro-democratic forces'.

The literature on institutions has further highlighted the important role that 'critical junctures',[1] play in the survival of democracy (Przeworski, 1991; Capoccia and Kelemen, 2007; Linz and Stepan, 1996). Understanding the fate of Malawi's democracy thus also requires a detailed examination of what happens during times that qualify as 'critical junctures'. In the two decades since the arrival of democracy in the country, there have been numerous critical junctures that have had the potential of shaping the trajectory of the country in either positive or negative directions. Three such events stand out:

- the unsuccessful bids by President Bakili Muluzi to seek a third term in office in 2002 and 2003 by changing the constitution;
- the increasing authoritarianism tendencies exhibited during the second term of Bingu wa Mutharika's presidency; and

- the death in office of President Mutharika in 2012, which was marked by an unconstitutional attempt by the deceased president's loyalists to install the President's brother, Peter Mutharika, as president over the then Vice-President, Joyce Banda.

Some authors have contended that generally poor economic performance, in a context where the democratic transition was founded on the belief that it would deliver better development prospects for ordinary citizens, presents a continuing threat to the survival of democracy in the country (Dulani, 2005; Chirwa *et al.*, 2003). The revelation of a major corruption scandal in late 2013, locally dubbed as 'Cashgate',[2] threatened to further diminish public confidence in democratic politics in ways that could further derail the democratic regime.

A model of regime consolidation

To ascertain the status of Malawi's democratic consolidation, the study adapts a model of regime consolidation proposed by Bratton and Mattes (2009). The model, which is designed to draw from public opinion data, uses a demand and supply framework to gauge whether a regime is consolidating as a democracy, an autocracy, a hybrid regime or one that is still in transition. Demand for democracy, once again, is an index based on the proportion of respondents who express support for democracy and reject three non-democratic forms of government. Supply of democracy, on the other hand, is a composite index that captures the proportion of respondents that perceive extensive democracy and at the same time express satisfaction with it. The model is illustrated in Figure 2.1.

| **DEMAND FOR DEMOCRACY** | | **SUPPLY FOR DEMOCRACY** |

| **REGIME CONSOLIDATION** |

Low Level Equilibrium ➡ Autocracy

Mid- Level Equilibrium ➡ Hybrid Regime

High Level Equilibrium ➡ Democracy

Figure 2.1 Model of regime consolidation
Source: Adapted from Bratton and Mattes (2009)

The model suggests three possible outcomes. A regime can consolidate as:

- an autocracy (demand and supply in low equilibrium);
- a hybrid regime (mid-level equilibrium) or
- a democracy (high level equilibrium).

For a regime to consolidate as an autocracy, demand for democracy and perceived supply should be in equilibrium at low levels. Hybrid regimes are those where demand and supply are in equilibrium at moderate levels. For a regime to consolidate as a democracy, however, demand and supply should be at high level equilibrium. But there is also a fourth scenario, one where demand and supply are in a state of disequilibrium. In this case, it can be argued that the regime is one in transition, and that it can move towards a democracy, or an autocracy, or end up as a hybrid.

Data

To answer the question on whether Malawi's democracy has made progress or stagnated, I use two different sources of data. The first includes democracy indices developed by experts – Freedom House, Polity Index and the Ibrahim Index of African Governance (IIAG). In order to demonstrate the behavioural and attitudinal dimensions of democracy consolidation in Malawi, I also draw on a second source of data: public opinion data gathered by Afrobarometer[3] in Malawi between 1999 and 2014. The data are then used to develop a demand and supply framework that sheds greater light on popular attitudes and commitment to democracy measured against popular perceptions on the supply of democracy (Bratton and Mattes, 2009). Demand for democracy is a scale constructed from four questions measuring support for democracy and the rejection of the three authoritarian alternatives. Respondents who say they both prefer democracy and also reject all three non-democratic alternatives are held to demand democracy.[4] The logic of the scale is that effective demand requires 'more than lip service [i.e. expressed support] to democracy; it also implies that people abandon attachments to old autocratic [modes of governance]'(Bratton, 2012). To measure the supply side of democracy, an index is developed from two indicators that measure citizen's judgements of the extent of democracy[5] and their expressed satisfaction with democracy in practice.[6]

Findings

Democratic trends in Malawi

All three measures of Malawi's democratic trajectory reveal an initial period of progress, followed by an interim phase of regression that has since been replaced by stability at low democratic levels. The first draws from Freedom House Index, which measures democracy along two dimensions of political rights and civil liberties.[7] However, to capture the positivity scores of higher values, I have opted to reverse the scores, such that a score of 1 is reversed to 7 while the score of 7 is reversed to 1 and the same with the middle categories (see Figure 2.2)

Although the aggregate indicators suggest an initial period of progress – characterized by relatively high scores that placed Malawi in the 'full democracy' category between 1994 and 1998 – this was followed by a period of decline between 1999 and 2002, when the reversed average scores for the country dropped from 11 to 8, bringing the country into the realm of partially free or the partially democratic category. Despite a slight increase in the average scores in 2010, Malawi has, since 1999, firmly remained in the partially free category, a finding that suggests stagnation rather than progress.

A similar picture of stagnation at low democratic levels is reflected in Polity Index Scores for Malawi between 1994 and 2013 (the year when the latest scores are available; see Figure 2.3). The Polity Index, which dates back to the 1800s,

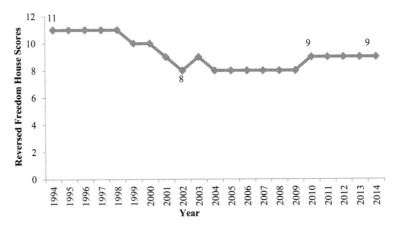

Figure 2.2 Freedom House scores for Malawi (reversed Freedom House scores, 1994–2014)

Source: Freedom House, https://freedomhouse.org/report/freedom-world/freedom-world-2015

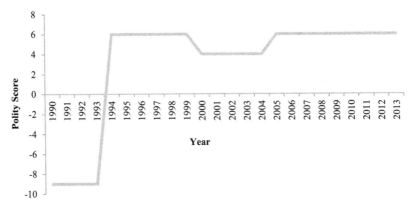

Figure 2.3 Polity index scores for Malawi, 1990–2013

Source: Polity IV project, www.systemicpeace.org/polity/polity4x.htm

measures democracy on a −10 to +10 scale, where −10 represents the most extreme form of autocracy and +10 indicates the most democratic states.[8] In terms of actual measures, the Polity Index compares factors such as competitiveness of political participation, competitiveness of executive recruitment, openness of executive recruitment and constraints on the chief executive.

The Polity Index scores in Figure 2.3 capture the effects of the democratic transition of 1994, which pushed the country from the ranks of an autocracy to a democracy. However, between 2000 and 2004, which coincided with Bakili Muluzi's attempt to manipulate the constitution to seek additional terms in office, Malawi fell out of the category of democracies and into one of 'open anocracy'.[9] However, after 2004, the country's scores improved again and have remained consistent at an average of 6 since then, a finding that is consistent with the stagnation noted in the Freedom House scores above. The drop in the Polity Index score for the period 2001–2004, which we discuss below, suggests that major political events, such as those that threaten to reverse democratic trends, as was the case with Muluzi's third term quest, can have a major impact on Malawi's democratic trajectory. And this very episode also had important effects in diminishing public attitudes toward democracy. As with the Freedom House scores, the evidence from the Polity scores fails to suggest any progress beyond the initial jump in 1994. Since then, Malawi's average Polity Index scores have been 5.5, supporting yet again the picture of stagnation noted in the Freedom House score findings.

The third measure I use is the Ibrahim Index of African governance. This index, which was first introduced in 2007, combines over 100 variables based on four conceptual categories:

- safety and rule of law;
- participation and human rights;
- sustainable economic opportunity; and
- human development.

The scores range from zero for the poorest performing countries to 100 for the best. The high number of variables that is accounted for means that, when compared to the other two indexes, the Mo Ibrahim Index is more likely to track even minute changes in governance, whether positive and negative. Figure 2.4 provides Malawi's MIIAG scores for 2007–2014.

Although the IIAG does not date back very far, the evidence again suggests stagnation, as there is very little variation in the scores for Malawi in the eight cycles for which data were available. In particular, it is telling that, according to the IIAG, Malawi's governance peaked with a score of 63.9 in 2008, a year prior to the fourth democratic election of 2009. However, by 2010, Malawi's state of governance had fallen to its lowest levels at 52.33, before gradually picking up to trend upwards. The precipitous decline in 2010 arguably captures the socio-economic decline during the second half of Bingu Mutharika's presidency, which was further compounded by increasing authoritarian tendencies. However, in

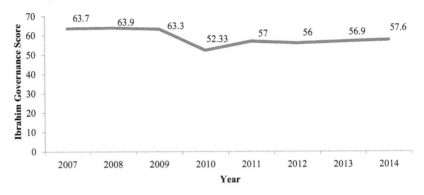

Figure 2.4 Malawi Ibrahim index of African governance scores, 2007–14
Source: Ibrahim Foundation index or African governance annual reports (various)

recent years, Malawi's governance performance has recovered slightly, especially following the death in office of President Bingu Mutharika in April 2012. However, the positive trend was not sustained, as it did not recover to the high levels of 2007–9. Instead, Malawi's governance scores have remained more or less static in the post-2010 period, neither trending upwards or downwards. This period coincided with Mutharika's second term, which was characterized by the suppression of opposition voices and generally poor political and economic governance (Dionne and Dulani, 2013). Although Mutharika's sudden death in April 2012 brought an end to the period of poor political and economic governance, his successor, Joyce Banda, only addressed the political governance issues. On the economic front, Banda failed to introduce sound economic governance principles, as evidenced by the theft of large sums of public funds under her watch in what has come to be known as the 'Cashgate scandal'. Thus, although Banda presided over a relatively calm period in terms of political governance, the corruption scandals during her presidency cancelled out the political gains, such that the country's overall governance scores remained stagnant.

Perceived quality of democracy as viewed by ordinary Malawians

While the expert assessments suggest stagnation in the trajectory of Malawian democracy, we now turn to examining the perceived extent of democracy. Drawing on the views of ordinary citizens allows us to gauge and test the expert assumptions that Malawian democracy has stalled. It is particularly interesting studying the proportion of Malawians who express the view that the country is a full democracy or one with only minor problems. An additional measure of satisfaction with democracy is also examined to get a fuller picture on whether Malawians consider the new political regime meaningful or not. The results are presented in Figure 2.5.

Consistent with the findings on the expert measurements discussed above, the evidence from the Afrobarometer surveys show that Malawians believe that their

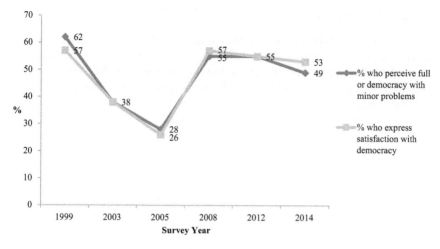

Figure 2.5 Support for and perceived extent of democracy, 1999–2014
Source: Afrobarometer

democracy peaked in 1999, a year when just about two-thirds of the country's citizens perceived the country to have been a democracy. In the years 1999–2005, Malawians, just like the international experts, were of the view that the country's political trajectory was heading away from democracy. Once more, this period coincided with the national campaign by the Muluzi administration to remove presidential term limits. Although the perceived extent of democracy picked up again in 2008, the numbers have not recovered to the 1999 peak. If anything, there is a perception in 2014 that the country is sliding backwards, albeit marginally. Meanwhile, public satisfaction with democracy appears to mirror the perceptions of its extent. Yet again, support for democracy and satisfaction with it among the public, was at its lowest level in 2005, creating a possibility that Malawians might have been tempted to look elsewhere for an alternative regime type.

The overall picture, from the expert-based democracy indicators and the perception data, is thus one of stagnation. From the two indicators for which data from 1994 are available, the overall picture is that the 1994 transition was an important event in Malawi's democratic trajectory, marking the highest level of the democratic experience. After an initial period of high scores, there followed a period of regression, precipitated by Muluzi's attempt to remove the term-limit clause from the country's constitution in the first few years of the twenty-first century. Although the democracy began to recover after 2005, poor economic and political governance, especially in the second term of Bingu Mutharika's presidency, has meant that the country's democracy has failed to recover fully to its peak levels of the mid- to late 1990s. As a result, Malawi remains stuck in a phase of stagnation.

Demand for democracy in Malawi, 1999–2014

Although both expert and survey data suggest that Malawi's democracy has stagnated, we must also address whether a comprehensive assessment of consolidation requires that the study further consider whether the observed stagnation is impacting on public attitudes towards democracy. This is in keeping with the democracy consolidation literature, which suggests that democracy can only be considered consolidated when there is an absence of anti-democratic behaviour and attitudes among both political actors and ordinary citizens. In other words, a consolidated democracy requires that citizens internalize democracy and refuse to support non-democratic modes of governance.

To measure the extent of democratic commitment, I examined the Afrobarometer survey data to ascertain trends in demand for democracy. Where democracy has been fully internalized, and thus consolidated, citizens would be expected to maintain support for this particular regime type and while simultaneously refusing to contemplate the introduction of authoritarian alternatives, even if democracy is considered to be failing (Bratton and Mattes, 2009). Subsequently, a scale was developed from the Afrobarometer survey data to measure demand for democracy. This scale was constructed from four questions: do you support democracy, and do you reject each or any of the three authoritarian alternatives of one-party, military and one-man rule. Respondents who say they both prefer democracy and also reject all three non-democratic alternatives are held to demand democracy.

Since 1999, a majority of Malawians have expressed support for democracy. With the exception of 2005, support for democracy has been on an upward trend. Thus, support for democracy has increased by 11 percentage points (i.e. from 65 per cent to 76 per cent). As the duration of the country's democratic experience increases, support for the regime has also correspondingly increased. This would seem to at least suggest that democratic attitudes are consolidating, with

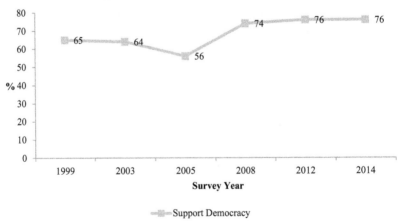

Figure 2.6   Support for democracy in Malawi, 1999–2014
Source: Afrobarometer

Malawians refusing to offer support for other alternatives. This would, on the surface, suggest that democracy is becoming the only game in town.

However, in order to fully understand the depth and commitment towards democracy, it is important to move beyond mere expressions of support for a democratic regime. As Bratton (2012) has argued, effective demand for democracy requires more than lip service (i.e. expressed support) for democracy. Instead, genuine demand indicates that people both support democracy *and* abandon attachments to old autocratic modes of governance. It is important to test both as individuals are liable to say they support democracy whilst at the same time countenancing non-democratic forms of government. The findings on the proportion of Malawians that have rejected three authoritarian forms of government in the period 1999–2014 are presented in Figure 2.7.

Figure 2.7 shows that a majority of Malawians reject, by a large margin, the three authoritarian forms of government. However, there remains a sizeable minority of Malawians for whom democracy has not become the only game in town. In particular, support for authoritarian forms of government is higher among rural Malawians, women and those with lower levels of education. Malawians who are unemployed, young (18- to 24-year-olds) or elderly (those aged 65 and above) also tend to have relatively higher acceptance levels for authoritarian regimes (Table 2.1).

The descriptive statistics show that, of the three forms of authoritarian rule, Malawians are more nostalgic for one-party rule. This suggests that twenty years of democracy have not completely erased memories of the one-party era from the minds of some Malawians. Indeed, the proportion of Malawians rejecting one-party rule has fallen from 76 per cent in 1999 to 69 per cent in 2014. It is interesting to note that the proportion of Malawians that reject one-party rule in 2014 is almost identical to the 64 per cent that voted in favour of multi-party competition in the referendum of 1993. It could thus be argued that the passage of time has not won over those Malawians who consider multi-party democracy as a better form of government.

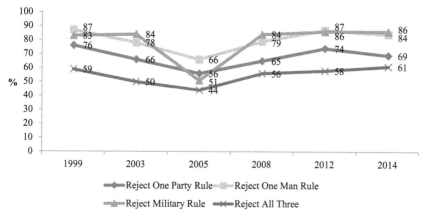

Figure 2.7 Rejection of non-democratic alternatives in Malawi, 1999–2014
Source: Afrobarometer

Table 2.1 Approval of authoritarian rule among different socio-economic groups in Malawi, 2014

		Proportion approving one-party rule	Proportion approving military rule	Proportion approving one-man rule
Gender	Male	19	8	8
	Female	34	11	16
Rural/Urban locality	Rural	27	11	13
	Urban	20	4	8
Age categories	18-24	30	10	12
	25-34	25	8	11
	35-44	24	12	14
	45-54	27	11	10
	55-64	20	9	8
	>65	27	11	12
Education levels	No formal Schooling	37	16	22
	Primary	30	12	14
	Secondary	17	4	5
	Post-Secondary	9	4	1
Employment status	Unemployed	27	10	12
	Employed	17	11	10
Lived Poverty Status	Non-Poor	21	10	10
	Moderately Poor	27	9	12
	Extremely Poor	30	12	12

Source: http://afrobarometer.org/data/malawi-round-6-data-2014, accessed 26 February 2016

Although rejection of authoritarian forms of government has remained high and has been growing over the years, there is evidence to suggest that critical events can potentially undermine confidence in democracy, thus demonstrating some fragility in the democratization process. This is evident in the low rejection rates of authoritarian alternatives in the 2005 survey, where less than half (44 per cent) of Malawians rejected all three authoritarian forms. These results followed the attempts by President Bakili Muluzi's attempts to change the constitution in order to seek a third term in office.

However, since then, rejection of all three authoritarian forms has picked up and is steadily growing, suggesting that the events of 2002–4 did not have long-lasting effects in democratic attitudes among Malawians. In keeping with Bratton's (2012) contention that effective demand for democracy requires individuals to both express support for democracy and reject all three authoritarian forms of government, we will further examine the proportion of respondents who can be termed true and committed democrats. Using the very strict measure of effective demand outlined in Figure 2.8, the proportion of Malawians who can be said to be true and committed democrats was then calculated and illustrated in Figure 2.9.

Between 1999 and 2012, less than half of Malawians appear to have been effective and committed democrats. The overall low level of democratic demand

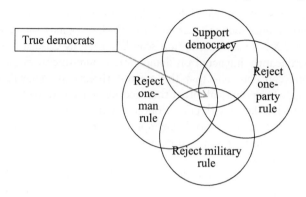

Figure 2.8 Modelling true democrats

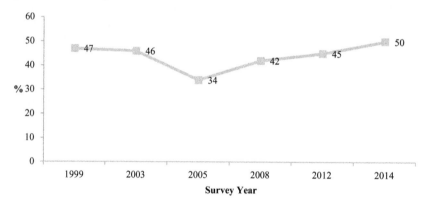

Figure 2.9 Demand for democracy in Malawi, 1999–2014
Source: Afrobarometer

suggests that the country's democracy remains very fragile. The claims of democratic support among Malawian citizens thus remain shallow as, at best, no more than half of the country's citizens express support for democracy while disavowing the three non-democratic alternatives. In other words, a substantial proportion of the population, at times more than half, have failed to make 'democracy the only game in town' by completely rejecting one-party rule, military rule and dictatorship. This scenario is likely to render the country's path towards democracy consolidation bumpy and susceptible to elite capture with little likelihood of popular resistance. This is the scenario that prevailed between 2004 and 2009, when large majorities of Malawians expressed support for the performance of Bingu Mutharika, despite him exhibiting increasing authoritarian tendencies.[10]

Although the proportion of Malawians who express support for democracy and disavow all three non-democratic forms of government has remained low, it compares favourably with continental trends.[11] With just around one-third of Malawians qualifying as committed democrats in 2005, the evidence once more suggests the earlier observation that Bakili Muluzi's quest for a third term in office posed the greatest threat to Malawi's democracy. Yet it appears that poor economic performance such as occurred during the later years of Bingu Mutharika's presidency in 2009–12 and corruption scandals, such as Cashgate of 2013–14, have not significantly impacted on democratic commitment. From this angle, therefore, one can conclude that the greatest threats to Malawi's democracy originate largely from political rather than economic factors; in other words, it is more resilient when faced with poor economic performance.

In order to explore the socio-demographic origins of demand for demand in Malawi, the study further analysed demand for democracy across a number of attributes(see Table 2.2).

The results tracking the socio-demographic characteristics of Malawians who demand democracy reveal a number of interesting characteristics of Malawians who can be labelled as 'committed democrats'. The northern region has, at 62 per cent, by far the largest proportion of individuals qualifying as committed democrats. By contrast, less than half of Malawians residing in the central and southern regions express support for democracy and also reject all three authoritarian forms of government. Yet again, this is in keeping with results of the 1993 referendum, when the northern region had the largest proportion of individuals who voted in favour of introducing multi-party rule.[12] However, the most worrisome result in this regard relates to Malawians who live in the southern

Table 2.2 Demand for democracy among socio-demographic groups in Malawi, 2014

Socio-demographic characteristic		Proportion of effective democrats (%)
Region	Northern	62
	Central	49
	Southern	46
Location	Rural	47
	Urban	59
Gender	Male	60
	Female	39
Age	18–24	44
	25–34	53
	35–44	53
	45–54	48
	55–64	56
	65+	40
Education	No formal education	26
	Primary education	45
	Secondary education	67
	Post-secondary education	71
Employment status	Employed	48
	Unemployed	54
Lived poverty status	Non-poor	55
	Moderately poor	50
	Extremely poor	43

Source: http://afrobarometer.org/data/malawi-round-6-data-2014, accessed 26 February 2016 region, where only 46 per cent qualify as effective democrats. Yet, in 1994 84 per cent of people in this region had voted in favour of multi-party rule. This suggests a possibility that the people in this region are not as committed to democracy as they were in 1993.

Consistent with the broader democratization literature (Bratton and Mattes, 2001; Dulani, 2008), the findings presented in Table 2.2 also demonstrate that urban populations are more committed to democracy than their rural counterparts; that women are less committed compared to men; and that more educated individuals tend to have a stronger attachment to democracy compared to those with low educational attainment. Employed Malawians, as well as citizens that experience no or moderate lived poverty, are stronger democrats compared to the unemployed and extremely poor citizens. The effects of age, on the other hand, suggest a curvilinear relationship: effective demand for democracy is low at the lower age brackets, but increases before beginning to decline again after age 44. The low demand for democracy among the 18- to 24-year-olds is particularly concerning about the overall fate of democracy in the country, given that young people make up a large proportion of the Malawi populace. However, given the positive effects of education on demand for democracy, this situation is not as dire as it might initially appear, as the younger category of democrats is flexible and more likely to change their positions over time.

Does poor economic performance affect demand for democracy?

The literature on democracy consolidation highlights the important fact that democratic attitudes should remain resilient, even in the face of poor economic conditions (O'Donnell, 1996; Przeworski, 1991; Przeworski *et al.*, 1996; Schedler, 2001). When faced with economic and other political changes, committed democrats should not lose confidence in democracy itself but, instead, use it to choose a calibre of politicians that can turn things around (Dulani, 2005; Bratton and Gyimah-Boadi, 2015). Given that Malawi is almost perennially experiencing poor economic performance, the study explored the relationship between three measures of economic evaluations[13] from the 2014 edition of the Afrobarometer survey (see Table 2.3).

Table 2.3 The effects of economic performance on demand for democracy, 2014

	Positive rating (% demanding democracy)	Negative rating (% demanding democracy)	t-score	P-value
Overall country direction	48	50	1.67	0.048
Evaluation of country's economic condition	45	50	5.30	0.000
Evaluation of own economic condition	46	50	4.61	0.000

Source: http://afrobarometer.org/data/malawi-round-6-data-2014, accessed 26 February 2016

The results tracking the effects of economic performance on demand for democracy show that there is no significant difference between the proportion of Malawians who demand democracy based on their overall assessment of the general direction of the country. Thus, holding negative or positive views on the overall direction of the country has no effect on attitudes toward democracy. However, interestingly, a relatively higher proportion of Malawians who held negative views about the economic situation in the country, and their own, were more likely to demand democracy than respondents that held positive evaluations. The differences in both cases were statistically significant. This means that negative evaluations of economic performance might be helping to strengthen faith in democracy rather than undermining it. Although further analysis is needed to determine causality, the preliminary evidence appears to suggest that democracy in Malawi might actually be strengthened by perceptions of poor economic performance rather than being undermined by it. This would seem to point towards consolidation to the extent that Malawians might be looking at democracy as the better form of government that would give them, in the near future, opportunities to solve their and the country's economic problems.

Demand and supply of democracy in Malawi

Applying the demand and supply framework outlined earlier in this chapter, the evidence suggests that demand for democracy among ordinary Malawians has remained consistently higher than the perceived supply (Figure 2.10).

With very few exceptions, demand and supply of democracy in Malawi appear to be at the mid-level equilibrium point – in other words, medium demand and medium supply. At these equilibrium points, citizens perceive moderate democracy being supplied but also demand moderate levels. Thus there is no pressure on political leaders to supply more democracy, resulting therefore in the status quo where democracy neither progresses nor regresses. This scenario, it can

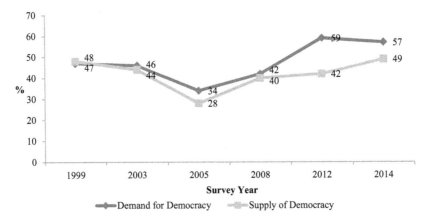

Figure 2.10 Demand and supply of democracy in Malawi, 1999–2014
Source: Afrobarometer

be argued, explains the findings on stagnation revealed by the expert and public opinion data above.

On a positive note, it would appear that since 2012 the supply and demand lines have begun to diverge, creating a situation of disequilibrium where demand is beginning to outstrip supply. The disequilibrium situation creates a new period of transition, marked by uncertainty. However, the fact that demand exceeds supply, suggests that Malawians will pressure the regime to introduce further democratic reforms while standing up against any attempts to undermine the existing democratic gains. It is thus not surprising that the period since 2008 has been marked by numerous anti-government protests and demonstrations, the most notable of which were demonstrations mounted by civil society organizations in July 2011 aimed at forcing the late Bingu Mutharika to honour the country's democratic institutions. Similarly, in 2014, Joyce Banda, whose government had been embroidered in the Cashgate scandal, was voted out of office in favour of Peter Mutharika.

Conclusion

Democracy is considered consolidated when it has become internalized by the citizens and become the only game in town. Even in times of major political and economic upheavals, citizens in a consolidated democracy should remain confident in the regime, even if they are displeased with the calibre and performance of the politicians in power. From the analysis of both expert and public opinion data, the findings of this chapter suggest that Malawi's democracy is stuck in a period of transition, neither consolidating as a democracy nor regressing to the era of authoritarianism. From the data from expert sources, the evidence points towards an initial period of progress between 1994 and 1999 that was followed by a period of regression from 2000 to 2005. The period of regression coincided with president Bakili Muluzi's attempt to remove the presidential limit clause from the constitution, making this one of the most critical junctures in Malawi's twenty-year democratic history. Although the trajectory of Malawi's democracy began to trend upwards again after 2005, the evidence suggests that it is yet to recover fully to its pre-2000 heights. Instead, the period after 2009 in particular, appears to be one of stagnation, where the country is not making progressive either positively or negatively.

The above findings are further supported by public opinion data, with Malawian citizens expressing support for democracy even if some say so while simultaneously saying sometimes authoritarian rule can be preferred. This suggests that democratic attitudes are still not fully embraced, a finding that once more suggests that even if a large proportion of Malawians support democracy, it is still yet to become the only game in town, reinforcing the picture of a transition that is yet to fully consolidate as a fully fledged democracy. Further analysis of the survey data using a demand and supply framework suggests that the stagnation phase might be evidence of a different type of consolidation, namely as a hybrid regime instead of a democracy. In other words, the country might have been getting comfortable with moderate levels of democracy. Under this scenario, democracy would neither be progressing or regressing. However, there is also some emerging evidence to suggest that demand for democracy is beginning to outstrip supply, which might create a disequilibrium favouring grassroots pressure for further democratic reform. There is thus cause for cautious optimism that democracy in Malawi will rise again even though it is currently in a period of stagnation.

Notes

1 This chapter adopts the definition of critical junctures suggested by Capoccia and Kelemen (2007: 348), who define them as 'relatively short periods of time during which there is a substantially heightened probability that agents' choices will affect the outcome of interest'. In this case, the outcome of interest is democracy.

2 Cashgate refers to the occasion between 2012 and 2013 when 'perpetrators exploited the weaknesses in the Integrated Financial Management System (IFMIS), through collusion, to transfer funds from government bank accounts to vendor accounts for goods and services that were never supplied and then deleted these transactions from the IFMIS system' (Baker Tilly, 2014: 1–2).

3 The Afrobarometer is a comparative series of public attitude surveys that measure citizen attitudes on democracy and governance, the economy, civil society and other related topics. At the time of writing this chapter, a total of six survey cycles had been done in Malawi, the first in 1999, then 2003, 2005, 2008, 2012 and 2014. The first four surveys had national sample sizes of 1,200, giving a margin of error of ±3%. The most recent surveys (2012, 2014), had sample sizes of 2,400, giving a margin of error of ±2% at the 95% confidence interval.

4 To measure support for democracy, survey respondents were asked to indicate which of three statements were closest to their opinion:
   • Democracy is preferable to any other kind of government.
   • In some circumstances, a non-democratic government can be preferable.
   • For someone like me, it doesn't matter what kind of government we have.
   Democracy supporters were those respondents that chose the first statement. To measure rejection of authoritarian alternatives, respondents were asked to indicate whether they would disapprove or approve of three non-democratic forms of government, namely, one-party rule, military rule and one-man presidential rule.

5 Respondents were asked 'In your opinion, how much of a democracy is Malawi today?' Responses ranged from 'A full democracy', 'A democracy but with minor problems', 'A democracy with major problems', and 'Not a democracy'. Respondents who perceived extensive democracy were those who said 'a full democracy' or 'a democracy but with minor problems'.

6 Respondents were asked: 'Overall, how satisfied are you with the way democracy works in Malawi today'? Responses ranged from 'Very satisfied', 'Fairly satisfied', 'Not very satisfied', and 'Not at all satisfied'. Satisfied respondents were those who said they were 'Very satisfied' or 'fairly satisfied'.

7 On each of the two dimensions of the Freedom House scores, the index ranges from 1 to 7. A score of 1 represents the highest possible score, i.e. very democratic, while a score of 7 represents the least democratic. The two indicators are often averaged to come up with country scores that are in turn classified on three dimensions: an average score of 1–2.5 are considered free; average scores of 3.0–5.0 are partly free and a score of 5.5–7.0 are tabbed as not free.

8 Countries in the Polity Index are grouped into five categories: Full Democracies (score of 10); Democracies (scores of 6–9); Open Anocracy (1–5); Closed Anocracy (−5–0); Autocracies (−6–−10).

9 An 'anocracy' is defined as a regime that is characterized by inherent qualities of political instability and ineffectiveness, as well as an 'incoherent mix of democratic and autocratic traits and practices'.

10 See 'African viewpoint: Is Malawi reverting to dictatorship?' available online at http://www.bbc.com/news/world-africa-13266263, accessed 18 February 2016.

11 For example, demand for democracy among 31 African countries, Malawi inclusive, in 2014 was 49 per cent. This was almost identical to Malawi's figure of 50 per cent.

12 Some 89 per cent of northerners voted for the introduction of multiparty rule. This compares to 85 per cent southerners and 32 per cent of people in the central region.

13 The indicators include respondents to a general question that asks respondents to indicate their evaluations of the overall direction of the country; to indicate their perceptions of the general economic situation of the country; and to measure the respondent's own perceived economic situation.

References

Baker Tilly (2004) 'Report on Fraud Mismanagement of Malawi government Finance,' London: Baker Tilly Ltd.

Bermeo, N. (2005) *Ordinary People in Extraordinary Times: The Citizenry and the Breakdown of Democracy*, Princeton: Princeton University Press.

Bratton, M. and Gyimah-Boadi, E. (2015) 'Political Risks Facing African Democracies: Evidence from the Afrobarometer,' Afrobarometer Working Paper Number 157.

Bratton, M. and Mattes, R. (2001) 'How People View Democracy: Africans' surprising Universalism,' *Journal of Democracy*, 12(1): 107–121.

Bratton, M. and Mattes, R. (2009) 'Neither Consolidating nor Fully Democratic,' Afrobarometer Briefing Paper No. 67.

Capoccia, G. and Kelemen, D. (2007) 'The Study of Critical Junctures: theory, Narrative and Counterfactuals in Historical Institutionalism,' *World Politics*, 59(3): 341–69.

Chirambo, R. (2009) 'Democracy as a Limiting Factor for Politicised Cultural Populism in Malawi,' *African Spectrum*, 44(2): 77–94.

Chirwa, W., Patel, N. and Kanyongolo E. (2003) *Democracy Report for Malawi*, International Institute for Democracy and Electoral Competition. Available at: www.idea.int/publications/sod/upload/Malawi.pdf (accessed 29 February 2016).

Cohen, Y. (1994) *Radicals, Reformers and Reactionaries: The Prisoner's Dilemma and the Collapse of Democracy in Latin America*, Chicago: The University of Chicago Press.

Dionne, K. and Dulani, B. (2013) 'Constitutional Provisions and Executive Succession: Malawi's 2012 Succession in Comparative Perspective,' *African Affairs*, 112(146): 111–37.

Diskin, A., Diskin H. and Hazan R. (2005) 'Why Democracies Collapse: The Reasons for Democratic Failure and Success, *International Political Science Review*, Vol 26(3): 291–309.

Dulani, B. (2008) 'Consolidating Malawi's Democracy? An Analysis of the 2004 General Elections in Malawi,' in Adar, K.G. Hamdok, A. and Rukambe, J. (eds), *Electoral Process and the Prospects for Democracy Consolidation: Contextualizing the African Multiparty Elections of 2004*, Pretoria: Africa Institute of South Africa, pp. 71–92.

Dulani, B. (2005) 'Three Cheers for Democracy? Democracy, Governance and Development in Malawi,' in Jacques G. and Lesetedi G. (eds), *The New Partnership for Africa's Development: Debates, Opportunities and Challenges*, Pretoria: Africa Institute.

Huntington, S. (1991) *The Third Wave: Democratisation in the Late Twentieth Century*, Norman, OK: University of Oklahoma Press.

Linz, J. and Stepan A. (1979) *The Breakdown of Democratic Regimes*, Baltimore: John Hopkins University Press.

Linz, J.J. and Stepan, A (1996) 'Toward Consolidated Democracies', *Journal of Democracy*, 7(2): 14–33.

Bratton, M. (2012) 'Trends in popular attitudes to multiparty democracy in Africa, 2000–2012,' *Afrobarometer Briefing Paper No. 105.*

O'Donnell, G. (1996) 'Illusions about Consolidation', *Journal of Democracy*, 7(2): 34–51.

Przeworski, A (1991) *Democracy and the Market: Political and Economic Reforms in Eastern Europe and Latin America*, Cambridge: Cambridge University Press.

Przeworski, A. and Limongi, F. (1993) 'Political Regimes and Economic Growth', *Journal of Economic Perspectives*, 7(3): 51–69.

Przeworski, A., Alvarez, M., Cheibub, J. and Limongi, F. (1996) 'What Makes Democracies Endure?' *Journal of Democracy* 7(1): 39–55.

Schedler, A. (2001) 'Measuring Democracy Consolidation,' *Studies in Comparative and International Development* 36(1): 61–87.

Svasand, L. (2011) 'Democratization in Malawi: Moving forward, stuck on transition or backsliding?' *Forum for Development Studies*, 38(1): 1–24.

Wallerstein, M. (1980) The Collapse of Democracy in Brazil: Its Economic Determinants, in *Latin American Research Review*, 15(3): 3–40.

3 Political parties, political settlement and development

Kizito Tenthani and Blessings Chinsinga

Introduction

Malawi achieved independence from Britain in 1964. However, the country slid into a one-party dictatorship immediately after independence, and multiparty politics was barred for over three decades. The country became a democracy in 1993, when multiparty politics were reintroduced, and currently Malawi boasts over 50 registered political parties. This chapter traces the evolution and consolidation of four major political parties: Malawi Congress Party, United Democratic Front, Democratic Progressive Party and the People's Party. The aim is to examine the various political settlements that these political parties negotiated and the impact of such settlements on economic and political development (or lack of it) in the country.

We begin by providing a brief historical overview of the development of the party system in the country before outlining a conceptual framework within which political parties in Malawi will be interrogated. Thereafter, we address the question of political ideologies, by examining how far parties are guided by ideological orientation. This is undertaken by presenting a study on party ideologies that was conducted by the Centre for Multiparty Democracy (CMD – Malawi) based in Lilongwe. We conclude by arguing that political parties in Malawi are not playing their rightful role of championing social economic transformation, and that they are largely to blame for the lack of economic development of the country.

The political history of Malawi: An overview

The modern political history of Malawi can be traced to 1893, when so-called Nyasa districts were formally named as British Central Africa Protectorate with the headquarters situated in Zomba. At that time, and until 1907 – when the country was renamed Nyasaland with the formalization of colonial structures in a constitutional framework called the Nyasaland Order in Council – politics was dominated by the European settlers. An early attempt at an Africa-led political organization to agitate for some special interest issues was led by John Chilembwe in 1915. Using his influence as a Church minister, Chilembwe mobilized a protest movement against the inhuman treatment of the local population by European settlers, and the recruitment and use of Nyasa soldiers against the Germans in East Africa. The revolt was, however, crushed and Chilembwe was killed.

After the collapse of the Chilembwe uprising, the Nyasaland African Congress (NAC) led a more organized political organization with a greater national appeal in 1944. While the initial intention of the NAC was to coordinate the native associations and other groups within Nyasaland (Ross, 2009), the declaration of a Federation of Rhodesia and Nyasaland in 1953 changed the game plan in that the fight against the Federation and the push for self-government became the principle agenda of the NAC. During the time when the NAC was formed, Hastings Kamuzu Banda, a prominent Nyasa (as Malawians were then called), had spent nearly four decades outside the country, for the most part in the USA and United Kingdom, and briefly in Kumasi, Ghana. He was following the political developments in Malawi closely and became an ardent supporter of the NAC. When Banda returned to Malawi in 1958, he assumed the leadership of NAC and immediately went on a drive to mobilize people to agitate for the end of the Federation of Rhodesia and Nyasaland. His arguments and rallying points were that Nyasaland was not benefiting from the federation arrangement as it was merely considered to be a source of cheap labour for developing economies such as that of Rhodesia. This stirred so much unrest that in 1959 the NAC was banned and its leaders including Banda were arrested. During this period, the Malawi Congress Party (MCP) emerged to replace the NAC and continued to agitate for independence. And when the first parliamentary elections were organized in 1961, the Malawi Congress Party won all contested seats, apart from the seats that were reserved for the white minority (Chirwa, 2014). The MCP became the dominant political force, and held 22 of the 28 seats in the legislative council (Banda, 2014).

The poor showing of most political parties in the 1961 elections notwithstanding, Malawi attained independence as a multiparty democratic state in 1963. The MCP, however, dominated the April 1964 elections once again. And with the remaining political parties disintegrating, a new constitution was enacted in 1966, which declared Malawi as a single party state (Mariyamkono and Kanyongolo, 2003). Why would a political party that benefited from a multiparty system turn against the very system that provided space for it to thrive? As has been argued elsewhere (Ross, 2009), the MCP came into being after the Nyasaland Africa Congress was banned. The MCP was therefore formed when Hastings Banda – himself a late addition to the top echelons of the NAC politburo, despite being an influential and dominant figure – was in detention.

The party was fortunate to be well endowed with potential leaders who drove the agenda of the NAC and later the MCP itself when Banda was in jail. Most notable among these leaders were Orton Chirwa (who presided over the transition of the NAC into the MCP), Henry Chipembere (an intelligent and charismatic orator) and Dunduzu Chisiza (an independent-minded and foresighted leader) (Lwanda, 2009). Some have argued that the MCP's aversion for multiparty politics stemmed from a desire to accelerate development (Cammack and Kelsall,

2010). Given the numerous developmental challenges the country faced, there appeared to be a need in some circles to rally behind a strong leader rather than waste time with opposition politics. Another, and perhaps a more plausible, motivation for the country to slide into a one-party dictatorship was what subsequently came to be known as a 'cabinet crisis' that erupted only weeks after the country gained independence in 1964.

The cabinet crisis arose after the ambitious and mostly youthful ministers in the cabinet began noticing the dictatorial tendencies emerging from Hasting Banda's rule. For example, the President was seen to be undermining the day-to-day functions of his ministers and his unilateral decision to accept the Skinner Report (Skinner, 1964) (which purportedly gave lower wages to Africans for the same job) was another bone of contention. Several of Banda's ministers, moreover, did not subscribe to the regime's foreign policy, especially Banda's alignment with apartheid-tainted South Africa. Yet another source of dissatisfaction was Banda's proposal to levy hospital fees on rural Africans (Baker, 2001; Lwanda, 2009).

Despite growing discontentment, Banda persevered and survived all challenges to his power. As would later become typical of his rule, his strategy included a reliance on the MCP grassroots machinery for political support, and he portrayed revolting ministers as evil. Banda continued to successfully employ his 'divide and rule' tactics and propelled some loyal followers such as Gwanda Chakuamba, Aleke Banda, Albert Muwalo and John Tembo to the highest echelons of power and influence, effectively replacing Orton Chirwa, Henry Chipembere, Yatuta Chisiza and others who were the leaders of the cabinet revolt (Baker, 2001). These loyalists, who were swiftly promoted in the power structure, also turned out to be the foot soldiers that in 1966 championed and advanced the quest for the country to become a one-party state. This situation prevailed from 1966 to 1994.

The original Constitution of 1964, which was drafted by the British Colonial Office, had an entrenched Bill of Rights that guaranteed a wide variety of civil and political rights and freedoms – including freedom of speech, assembly and association. This encouraged the formation of numerous political parties. However, the Bill of Rights was removed from the subsequent Republican Constitution of 1966, which went on to declare that the Malawi Congress Party would be the only party allowed to operate within the country. With the removal of the Bill of Rights, political parties were not the only casualties. Indeed, all fundamental rights of citizens were under threat as there were no effective safeguards from arbitrary decisions of the Banda regime. What followed was a state of tyranny and oppression. Banda's opponents either disappeared or were detained without trial, and the justice system was severely undermined while there was a general shrinking of space for political discourse. The MCP and the government became synonymous, and the period 1966–94 was characterized by authoritarianism, paternalism, repression and economic domination and exploitation (Mhone, 1992).

A summation of the ills of the one-party dictatorship that followed were well espoused in 'Living our Faith', a pastoral letter written by the Catholic bishops of Malawi, which arguably put the last nail in the dictatorship's coffin and paved the way for more open challenges to Banda's hitherto undisputed power. The letter argued for the need for the respect of basic human rights and freedoms (including the right to free speech and association), and was hence a direct attack on the 1966 Constitution that was in force. The letter also specifically mentioned that every constitution ought to have a bill of rights, as a way of safeguarding human dignity, and went on to denounce the infringement of rights of the critics of Banda's rule. A major criticism levelled against the regime by the pastoral letter was the accusation that the education sector not only continued to be underdeveloped, but was also actively being undermined by the MCP (Mhone, 1992; Mitchell, 2012). As a result, the majority of the population was forced to join the underpaid labour market in order to service the growing commercial agriculture sector (mainly the production of burley tobacco), which was controlled by business elites directly or indirectly linked to the political establishment of the MCP.

The one-party dictatorship that developed post-1966 was defined by ruthless suppression of dissenting views: detention without trial, political disappearances, political assassinations, and suppression of academic, religious and artistic freedoms. Trade unionism was prohibited and the civil society arena was stifled. And only international development NGOs such as Save the Children were allowed to operate in the country. Schools were not allowed to teach or discuss politics, apart from in courses on 'civics', a compulsory subject in primary school aimed at socializing school children and brainwashing them with the regime's emphasis on four so-called cornerstone principles: unity, discipline, loyalty and obedience. Not surprisingly, these principles were actively used as tools for further oppression and subjugation (Mhone, 1992; Divala, 2007). The sole alternative for people to participate in the political sphere was through attendance of MCP rallies and the purchase of the compulsory party 'membership' card. Anyone who refused to toe the party line was severely dealt with by the ever-present youth leaguers or the notorious Malawi Young Pioneers (MYP).[1] The political norm was set by the MCP apologists, often using the name of Hastings Banda, and any deviation from that set norm, real or imaginary, was taken to be an act of treason punishable by imprisonment without trial (Mpasu, 2995; Kasambara, 1998).

Another significant dimension of the one-party rule was the grip the MCP had on the national economy. Malawi's economy is largely agriculture-based, and tobacco has dominated the agriculture sector for decades. The new political elites that emerged after independence saw the tobacco sector as an effective instrument for extracting rents. The political and economic systems were systematically planned and state interventions conducted in a manner that benefited those who were close to the centre of power in the party (Mhone, 1992). Thus the political structure was used to underpin, propagate and perpetuate its own domination in the economy by using a variety of state-driven tactics, such as ensuring a steady supply of cheap labour, and state monopoly in the agriculture marketing boards. The state was regulating the production and marketing of barley tobacco. The Press Corporation conglomerate ensured the extraction and appropriation of rents to the politically connected elites in support and perpetuation of the MCP machinery (Van Donge, 2002b).

The ensuing political settlement that emerged during the one-party era was defined largely by a heavy-handed authoritarian system that had a stranglehold on the only productive sector of the economy: estate agriculture (Van Donge, 2002a; Cammack, 2011). Thus, the political elites and others well connected to the political establishment were extracting rents through participation in the regulated economy, especially the estate sector. While economic analyses from the 1980s show that Malawi was a success story despite widespread patrimonialism, (World Bank, 1981), the political settlement was built on a foundation based on an underlying set of economic contradictions (Mhone, 1992).

The economic system was designed to favour and benefit the elite – the small group of individuals and families that were politically connected to the centre of power in the MCP. These were politicians, civil servants, traders and businessmen, and estate owners. Through the organization and regulation of the economy, the elites extracted rents by getting preferential and subsidized credits, where resources from business were diverted to politics and where for political expediency, market price signals were constantly ignored (Van Donge, 2002a). The elites who were beneficiaries of this system were merely supporters of the existing political establishment, and not of the long-term development needs of the country. Thus, there was the emergence of an extractive political settlement where the elites pursued short-term goals at the expense of long-term developmental goals that could have been more beneficial to Malawi (Khan, 2010).

Scholars argue that a political settlement results in positive development outcomes when the cost of maintaining it is favourable to the elites and when it is inclusive and not predatory (Acemoglu et al., 2004; Khan, 2010). Such was not the case for Malawi. The political settlement reached was not broad based and hence resulted in widespread discontentment. The political centre that used a strong and ruthless state–party machine to crush opposition and dissent was getting weak. The authority that used its highly centralized executive to implement its development policy (including centralization of the production and distribution of rents and ensuring compliance while rewarding loyalists) could no longer hold. And the whole settlement faltered on its own weight (Cammack, 2011). The prevailing settlement was also increasingly challenged by external economic shocks and the growing popularity of opposition parties, which in turn ushered in a new political dispensation of multiparty politics.

Malawians found themselves in another struggle for independence in 1992, but now in a fight for freedom from the dictatorship of the one-party state. Just as in the struggle for independence, the struggle in 1992 was not only a political one, but an economic one as well, with the multiparty politics advocates promising more economic freedom, which would translate into the realization of comprehensive economic rights (Oloka-Onyango, 1995). This resonates well with the Nobel laureate Amartya Sen's well-known conception of 'development as freedom', where the process of development requires the removal of major sources of 'unfreedoms' (Sen, 1999). Thus, the fight for freedom was in fact the struggle for development since the lack of substantive freedoms had only perpetuated poverty and denied Malawians the enjoyment of basic rights to food and shelter.

The transition to multiparty democracy in 1993 was therefore considered to be an opportunity that would not only lead to political emancipation, but also a new environment where the role and functions of political parties in Malawi were broadened to include being agents of change and sustainable transformation. However, after more than two decades following the transition to democracy, the Malawian political system remains highly fragile (Cammack, 2011). The fragility of the country's democracy was particularly heightened during the last years of President Mutharika's term in office. Malawi experienced tremendous political, economic and social challenges, which were rooted in serious lapses in governance and the systemic failures to invoke checks and balances as provided in the country's Constitution. This culminated in a series of protests in July 2011, leading to the death of twenty individuals as Malawians across all walks of life rose to reclaim the ideals of the democratic dispensation they fought for in the early 1990s. These protests also showed to the rest of the world that ruling elites continued to maintain their grip on power despite not enjoying widespread popular support. Indeed, the mass protests of July 2011 aptly summed up general public disappointment with the achievements of the multiparty system since the elections that were held in May 1994. The performance of successive governments is hardly inspiring when assessed against the expectations the transition to a multiparty political dispensation initially raised. According to Van Donge (1995), Malawians enthusiastically embraced democracy as a magic wand that would solve the political, economic and social ills that they had endured for at least three decades under the authoritarian rule of Hastings Banda – a regime that not only actively used political oppression but also did not officially recognize the existence of poverty!

The record of Malawian political parties as primary agents in building up a viable democratic dispensation in the country is not very inspiring. Indeed, all political parties in the country have failed to meaningfully play their role in spearheading fundamental and sustainable democratic and structural transformation. While transition from a one-party to a multiparty democratic dispensation has taken place, it has not been accompanied by discernible transformation, particularly in terms of how the day-to-day governance activities in various spheres are conducted.

Thus, the popular diagnosis of the political system is that political parties are unable to drive and preside over a visionary political, economic and social agenda because they are not strongly grounded in ideology. None of the parties have adequately reflected on what they stand for and how they differ from each other. Consequently, it is invariably difficult for political parties to justify their existence beyond serving as vehicles for contesting state power once every five years. This makes it extremely difficult for parties to envision the world as it should be and specifying acceptable means of attaining social, economic and political ideals.

Understanding political parties

Providing a universally accepted definition of political parties is a futile exercise, as parties must be understood within a given context, specific ideology and specific cultural settings. Ranny and Kendall (1956) define political parties as autonomous groups with an aim of making nominations and contesting in elections for the purposes of controlling people and policies in government. Thus, the raison d'état of political parties is their use as vehicles for winning elections and to influence public policies.

A political party, in the definition advanced by Shively (2008: 247), is defined as 'a group of officials or would-be officials who are linked with a sizable group of citizens into an organization; a chief object of this organization is to ensure that its officials attain power or are maintained in power'. Such a definition points to the need for parties to have meaningful linkages with the citizenry from which they can derive their legitimacy. Further, the definition asserts the need for attaining power or being maintained in power, which can also be extrapolated to mean that small but significant political parties can actually influence the use of power even if they do not form the government or are the main opposition parties. Examples of such parties are those with strong grassroots linkages and community-based organizations and civil society organizations. However, not all such entities have higher-level national agendas, as many so-called street-level parties profess a localized agenda and may thus not be interested in contesting national offices (Ogunwa, 2012). A political party, moreover, must articulate an explicit ideology, expressed in a programme or manifesto, which will allow it to build a platform in the quest for political power. Thus, it needs to develop and sustain a structure that is constantly engaging with the citizenry and trying to drum up support in order for it to make a meaningful impact on the polity.

One of the core functions of political parties is to aggregate and represent the interest of citizens (Key, 1964). Thus, a political party must have in-built mechanisms for capturing the real interests of citizens, which are often varied and at times competing, and attempt to propose policy alternatives that best serve the maximum number of its supporters. In doing so, Key observes that political parties may have to take into account views of other interest groups within the society, thereby establishing regular contact with civil society. Others have suggested that 'political parties articulate and aggregate interests, in pursuit of their electoral and policymaking functions' and 'represent citizens who have interests' (NIMD, 2004: 9). Thus, it is inconceivable that a political party will not attempt to influence, and, in the process, most likely be influenced by, some civil society organizations such as business associations and unions (NIMD, 2004: 9).

As parties engage the citizenry and advance their policy agendas, they also begin to generate awareness and educate citizens on political issues (Katz and Crotty, 2006). Upon galvanizing the interests of the people and processing them into policy alternatives, political parties become interlocutors between the citizens and the state.

Perhaps one of the most pronounced functions of political parties is that of identifying, recruiting, screening and popularizing potential leaders. Through the party establishment, leaders are nurtured and prepared to take up leadership roles within the political party itself, as well as in national and local legislatures, and broadly in government (Key, 1964; Katz and Crotty, 2006). And, through these leaders, parties play other important functions – running the government should they win an election or assuming the role of the opposition party and holding the ruling party and government to account.

There have been numerous accounts documenting the declining role and dysfunctional nature of political parties. One line of argument is that politics is no longer noble or relevant and that parties are weak (or 'hollow shells'), unable to discharge their democratic obligations to their supporters or the electorate (Vongdouangchanh, 2006). Others argue that parties have largely failed to meet the expectations of citizens or simply failed to provide bold alternatives to social challenges. Still others claim that parties are facing enormous challenges in mobilizing their supporters given the weakening roots of their political base in local communities.

While there is a general distrust and low rating of political parties, however, no other alternative has been identified for an effective and functional democracy to emerge and be sustained. Indeed, parties are indispensable in performing checks on the arbitrary power of government. They are also instrumental in providing leaders that, at least on paper, represent the interest of the citizenry;– leaders who are able to articulate and package the needs and aspirations of the citizenry into policy alternatives.

Political parties in Malawi

The Constitution of Malawi, section 40 (1), makes reference to political parties by spelling out the rights of people to establish, and become members of political parties, while section 40 (2) provides for public financing of parties based on specific criteria for entities that qualify to receive such funding.[2] A more detailed guidance to the creation and operation of political parties is found in the Political Parties (Registration and Regulation) Act (PPRRA) of 1993. The PPRRA was enacted 20 days after Malawians opted to revert to a multiparty democracy model in a referendum that was held on 14 June 1993. It is not surprising that many scholars and commentators have identified numerous shortcomings of the PPRRA, given the sheer speed with which the legislation was enacted. For example, one would have expected that the PPRRA would be formulated in the spirit of the Constitution to reflect and be in tandem with the liberal democratic principles such as transparency and accountability. The Act does not, however, make any implicit or explicit reference to guidelines for parties to, for instance, embrace internal democratic practices.

The PPRRA provides for the creation of the Office of the Registrar of Political Parties as an interim arrangement. And, until such time as this Registrar is appointed, it provides that the Registrar General shall act as the registrar of political parties. Almost two decades after the PPRRA's enactment, the position of Registrar of Political Parties is yet to be filled, and no attempt whatsoever has been made to fill this position. Moreover, an examination of the interim functioning of the office of the Registrar General finds that the ruling party and its leaders considerably influence the office. Two incidents in particular point in this direction. First, although it is relatively easy to register a party in Malawi, some parties have in reality struggled to get themselves registered. In 2003, President Bakili Muluzi – leader of the United Democratic Front (UDF) party – fell out with his staunch supporter, the influential Brown Mpinganjira, who subsequently went on to establish his own party – the National Democratic Alliance (NDA). Mpinganjira, however, struggled to get his organization registered amidst pressure exerted on the Registrar General by the President. Also, in 2010, President Bingu wa Mutharika – leader of the Democratic People's Party (DPP) – found himself at odds with the Vice-President and fellow DPP member Joyce Banda. When Banda finally left the DPP to form the People's Party (PP), she found it difficult to get the organization registered. And registration was only possible after the intervention of the judiciary.

In terms of the criteria that an aspiring political party should meet in order to be registered, the Act stipulates that at least 100 individuals must endorse the application. The Act does not stipulate the backgrounds of these individuals or who qualify to endorse an application. As a result, Malawi has witnessed a dramatic rise in the number of parties registered – from the 7 political parties that contested the 1994 elections to the current tally of 55.

The PPRRA is also silent about the private financing of political parties, and as a result parties are under no obligation to declare their funding sources. Further, the parties are not required by the Act to declare their assets. Many individuals and organizations therefore find it puzzling that ruling parties always appear to be extremely well-endowed with resources while opposition parties find it difficult to generate funds for party activities. The problem has come to light in the recent Cashgate scandal when the Director of Public Prosecutions, while commenting on the actions of an indicted official, remarked that political parties and their agents have aspired for the control of government in order to use that as a means of appropriating wealth to themselves (*The Nation*, September 2015). They either award their supporters and loyalists with lucrative contracts or they tend to directly siphon off funds from the state.

After proving this brief overview of the framework within which political parties operate in Malawi, the ensuing sections will examine why political parties appear to have failed to function as agents of fundamental and sustainable socio-economic transformation in one of the poorest countries of the world. We will focus on the four major parties – MCP, UDF, DPP and PP – and assess them in relation to three sets of interrelated issues: corruption and patronage, weak or absent ideological platforms and persistent leadership struggles.

The emergence of four 'major' parties

It is challenging to determine a criterion for categorizing political parties as major or minor. It is even more challenging to do so in the case of Malawi because of the absence of a criterion for registering and tracking members of political parties. Notwithstanding such challenges, we will apply two main criteria in this chapter. First, we will consider a party as being major if it has been in government (i.e. has been a ruling party). In Malawi, this would imply that the party participated in the presidential elections and succeeded in sponsoring a candidate to the presidency. Second, we will use the number of parliamentary seats that the party has in the national assembly to classify them into major and minor categories. Table 3.1 indicates that of the 54 registered political parties that Malawi had as it went to the tripartite elections[3] in 2014, only 17 participated in the parliamentary elections. And out of these 17 political parties, only 4 – MCP, DPP, UDF, PP – fielded candidates in over 30 per cent of parliamentary seats. These were also the same parties that won a significant number of seats. Indeed, only two other parties, AFORD and CCP, won representation in the National Assembly, with 1 seat each. Thus, for all practical purposes, the MCP, UDF, DPP and PP are considered the major parties in the Malawian context.

Malawi Congress Party (MCP)

The MCP is the oldest of all the political parties in Malawi, having been established in 1959 and with the aim of replacing the Nyasaland Africa Congress (NCA). There was widespread unrest in 1959 when the country was agitating for cessation from the Federation of Rhodesia and Nyasaland, and the NCA had been banned. Orton Chirwa, MCP's founding president, was in effect a caretaker leader, keeping the position warm for Dr Hastings Kamuzu Banda, who was at that time incarcerated by the colonial administration at Gweru Prison.

Upon release from prison, Banda assumed leadership of the MCP and, in the first elections held in 1961, the party won all the contested seats[4] (Chirwa,

Table 3.1 Participation of parties in parliamentary elections, 2014

Party	No. of candidates (Total: 193 constituencies)
MCP, UDF, PP and DPP	160
PPM	47
NASAF	27
UIP	17
AFORD	12
NARC	7
CCP	6
NCP	5
NLP, MAFUNDE, UP, PETRA	4
MPP, PDM	1

Source: Compilation from Malawi Government Gazettes and Malawi Electoral Commission (various years)

2014). Banda was appointed Prime Minister, and, after Malawi achieved independence in 1964, the party faced its first major challenge – the 'cabinet crisis' that we discussed earlier. This crisis forced the party to find unorthodox ways of consolidating their hold on power, and in 1966 the party machinery successfully advocated the repeal of the constitutionally provided Bill of Rights, which made it the only political party allowed to operate in Malawi. MCP enjoyed a stranglehold on power from 1966 to 1993, when a referendum was held and the country voted to revert to multiparty politics. In the ensuing 1994 general elections, the party won only 56 seats and its candidate (Kamuzu Banda) went on to lose the presidency to the United Democratic Front. The party has since remained the country's strongest opposition party by winning 66 seats in the 1999 elections and 56 in the 2004 elections. Its lowest point was in 2014, when it won a mere 27 seats. In the latest election held in May 2014, the MCP emerged with 48 seats (see Table 3.2 for comparison with the performance of the other political parties).

The United Democratic Front (UDF)

The UDF began as a coalition of business people and former politicians and civil servants who had either fallen out of grace with the MCP or become disillusioned with Banda's stranglehold on power. The party rode on the wave of change, joining the Alliance for Democracy, and became a formidable pressure group agitating for change after the 1992 Catholic Bishops pastoral letter. UDF was registered as a political party in 1993, and contested the 1994 general elections. Bakili Muluzi, UDF's leader and presidential candidate, triumphed in the elections and ended the dominance of MCP in Malawian politics.

Apart from winning the presidency, the UDF also won a large majority of seats in the National Assembly in 1994, getting 85 seats out of 177. The party's popularity under President Muluzi ensured yet another election triumph in 1999, when it increased its parliamentary strength to 93 seats. After two terms in office, and following a failed attempt at securing a third term, President Muluzi and his party began to lose its grip on the electorate. Muluzi nominated Bingu wa Mutharika as the UDF's presidential candidate (hoping to retain control of the party and the government), but the party won only 49 seats in the 2004 elections. And although the party won the presidency, it suddenly found itself sitting on the opposition benches when the presidential candidate they successfully sponsored,–

Table 3.2 Results from parliamentary elections, 1994–2014

Party	1994	1999	2004	2009	2014
AFORD	36	29	6	1	1
DPP	N/A	N/A	N/A	112	50
MCP	56	66	57	28	48
PP	N/A	N/A	N/A	N/A	26
UDF	85	93	49	17	14

Source: Compilation from Malawi Government Gazettes and Malawi Electoral Commission (various years)

Bingu wa Mutharika,– ditched the UDF and formed his own political party – the DPP. Thus, with a mismanaged succession in 2004 the numbers continued to dwindle for the party, and in the 2014 elections it was able to win a mere 14 seats.

The Democratic Progressive Party (DPP)

As discussed above, Bingu wa Mutharika became President of Malawi on a UDF ticket following an impressive campaign funded and orchestrated by two-term president Bakili Muluzi. However, Mutharika was not content at being Muluzi's puppet, and literally ran away with the presidency when he formed the DPP with breakaway factions of the UDF. The creation of the DPP was helped by the absence of constitutional provisions that address a situation whereby a president, upon winning the elections, resigns from the party that sponsored him into office. Thus the DPP was formed from within parliament: MPs elected on UDF tickets or independents crossed the floor and formed a new political outfit. This renewed a debate on floor crossing as enshrined in section 65 of the Constitution, which states that members who defect from one party to join another party represented in the House are deemed to have crossed the floor, and consequently they will lose their seats.

The UDF and MCP pushed for the implementation of the floor-crossing provision, to declare vacant the seats of the MPs who had defected. However, a series of court injunctions obtained from the members who believed they would be affected by the provision effectively tied the hands of the Speaker of the National Assembly and no seat was declared vacant. The DPP only managed to get 'its own' MPs following by-elections that were held in December 2005, when it won all the five contested seats.

Bingu wa Mutharika's and DPP's first term in office was filled with political tensions in Parliament, as the party faced the combined wrath of the UDF (who felt cheated) and the MCP (who actually thought they had won the elections by securing the majority of seats in Parliament). Indeed, UDF and MCP commanded a formidable opposition block that managed to frustrate the DPP's attempts to govern the country as it saw fit. The most prominent of all debates that defined this period (from 2005, when the DPP was formed, to 2009) included the issue surrounding the floor-crossing provision, popularly known as section 65 in the Constitution and the passing of the annual national budget. The UDF and the MCP managed to frustrate and punish the DPP by declaring that they would only support the national budget if members of parliament who were deemed to have crossed the floor had their seats declared vacant, a move which could have possibly led to the collapse of the DPP administration since it could have lost almost all its members except the five who had won seats through a by-election.

The DPP for its part used a range of tactics to avoid discussing the floor-crossing issue: it regularly sought court injunctions, refused to fund parliamentary sittings (since in Malawi, for Parliament to convene, the Speaker has to first consult the President and obtain consent)[5] and prorogued parliament in order to prevent debates on section 65. Thus, when the opposition tied the passing of the budget to the implementation of the floor-crossing provision, it forced Mutharika and the DPP to pursue such policies as infrastructure development and subsidy programmes as a way of connecting to the people (Cammack, 2011).

The DPP launched a massive propaganda drive telling the public that the opposition's actions in blocking the budget proceedings would cause much hardship. For example, the party claimed that the government would not be able to pay civil servants, provide drugs in the hospitals and, perhaps the most effective propaganda piece, –implement the hugely popular farm input subsidy programme (FISP). The party, exercising control over public broadcasters, targeted primarily the rural population with low literacy levels and generally poor, hence more vulnerable to manipulation than urban groups. Sections of civil society were also roped in, and the country witnessed a spirited campaign by civil society organizations in support of the government and argued that politicization of national issues was causing more harm to poor and vulnerable groups. The above set of strategies worked well for the DPP, and opposition parties were severely punished in the 2009 elections. Bingu wa Mutharika not only won the presidency, but the DPP won a landslide victory with 113 MPs winning seats (the highest a single party had ever amassed in the post-1993 era) against a miserable 27 for the MCP and a meagre 17 for the UDF.

Soon after gaining such overwhelming support in an election that drastically weakened the power and influence of the opposition parties, the desire of the DPP to impress the masses with tangible development interventions became less urgent (Cammack, 2011). The period also witnessed growing intolerance and autocratic tendencies of the Bingu wa Mutharika administration. In particular, President Mutharika, perhaps aware of his age and failing health, began to actively promote the idea of his younger brother – Peter Mutharika – as his successor and hence the next president of Malawi. Thus, the DPP – just like its rival the UDF in previous years – continued the tradition of succession politics. As Cammack (2011) observes, increased allegations of corruption began to surface coinciding with a worsening of the general social and economic situation of the country. Tobacco prices during this period were at their lowest, and the country faced a severe scarcity of fuel, foreign exchange and basic necessities. Such problems provided the background for mass protests that were held in various parts of the country in July 2011. As fate would have it, President Mutharika died unexpectedly while in office and a period of political instability ensued. The automatic choice to succeed Mutharika was the Vice-President, Joyce Banda, but the DPP leadership had other plans, as Banda had previously been expelled from the DPP and had gone on to establish her own political party – the People's Party. The DPP had already appointed the late President's brother– Peter Mutharika– as party president, and a group of senior leaders tried to seek the support of the judiciary and the military to have a new Mutharika assume the presidency. Such attempts did not bear fruit, and Joyce Banda took over as the first female President of Malawi. The DPP suddenly found itself relegated to the opposition benches with the People's Party becoming a de facto ruling party and attracting floor-crossing MPs from other parties, including the DPP.

Banda's popularity, however, was short lived, as we discuss below, and the DPP fared much better in the 2014 elections (securing 50 seats in Parliament, and its candidate won a closely fought contest for the presidency).

The People's Party (PP)

The People's Party was founded in 2011 by Joyce Banda who was at that time the Vice-President of Malawi, having contested the 2009 elections as a running mate for Bingu wa Mutharika on a DPP ticket. Between 2009 and 2011, Banda and President Mutharika began disagreeing over numerous issues, and a range of circumstances (which we will discuss later in this chapter), resulted in her expulsion from the DPP. With no constitutional mechanism providing for the resolution of such situations, Joyce Banda continued to serve in her post as Vice-President (just as Bingu wa Mutharika did upon first being elected on a UDF ticket and later switching to a newly formed party), despite being fired from the party on whose ticket she was elected to the vice-presidency.

Following the sudden death of Bingu wa Mutharika, Joyce Banda ascended to the presidency in April 2012 to serve out the former president's term, and her PP became the de facto ruling party. Despite being a very young and inexperienced political entity, the PP had to hit the ground running as it came into office at a time when Malawi's economy was in serious trouble. The party not only had to try and resolve immediately economic problems, but it also had to lay the foundations and prepare for a general election that was to be held within the short span of two years. The PP's tasks appeared insurmountable and the party not only won a mere 26 seats, its candidate (Joyce Banda) lost heavily in the presidential elections, coming in a distant third.

Ideological malaise of political parties in Malawi[6]

An ideology is a worldview or a lens through which one sees the world. It is a framework through which one can interpret various social problems that a society faces. Thus, an ideology often provides the foundational basis for political action. It is difficult to provide a universal definition of an ideology because of the very nature of the concept. As Heywood (1997: 141) observes:

> no one sees the world as it is [since] all of us look at the world through a veil of theories, presumptions and assumptions [such] that when we look at the world, we are also engaged in imposing meaning upon it.

A recent study (Chinsinga, 2013) finds that political parties in Malawi cannot be firmly distinguished from each other on the basis of their ideological orientations. Indeed, the study finds that justification given by informants (MPs and other leaders) for either joining or quitting political parties do not qualify as issues that can be tested and defined along the ideological spectrum. Rather, four sets of interrelated factors determine the formation and functioning of political parties in Malawi – patronage, clientelism, ethnicity and tribalism. In the ensuing sections, we will examine the professed ideological foundations of the four major political parties in the country. This will help further deepen our understanding of the policy formation dynamics within political parties and examine whether the policymaking processes are informed by any particular ideological leaning. The empirical basis is formed by the debates and discourse during the annual conventions that these four parties have held in recent years.

The Malawi Congress Party (MCP)

The MCP held a convention in November 2008, just before its election manifesto was finalized. However, prior to the convention, MCP had mooted the idea of reworking its election manifesto justified as a strategy to develop a crop of leaders, party agents, values and ideals.

The 2008 convention passed resolutions on the basis of the party president's opening speech. These included:

- delegates unanimously endorsed John Tembo as party president;
- delegates unanimously endorsed Tembo as the party's presidential candidate for the May 2009 elections;
- the party's vice-presidential candidate for the 2009 elections should be elected by the National Executive Committee (NEC);
- if elected to power, the MCP will prioritize implementation of the universal fertilizer subsidy programme;
- a government formed by the MCP will not take revenge for the atrocities inflicted on the party or its leadership by other parties;
- a government formed by the MCP will give top priority to agriculture, extension services and irrigation programmes;
- a government formed by the MCP will prioritise equitable distribution of development resources throughout the country;
- a government formed by the MCP will work with other parties with similar policies, while allowing these parties to maintain their individual identities;
- the MCP will pursue a well-designed youth policy with a view to engaging the youth in national development; and
- leaders of the MCP will be elected by the people and not imposed on the people by the party leadership.

Following these resolutions, the convention conducted elections to fill the vacant positions of Vice-President, Secretary General and Treasurer General. However, contrary to one of its resolutions of ensuring that the party's leadership is popularly elected, the delegates mandated the party president to appoint 'deserving people' to the remaining positions in the NEC. The MCP eventually produced an election manifesto but argued that 'the convention had little or no influence at all in the framing of the manifesto because the policy resolutions which were made were based on the president's speech' (Chinsinga, 2013: 39). Nonetheless,

MCP officials argued that 'the convention was part and parcel of the process of developing an election manifesto because delegates, through the resolutions that were passed, had directed the shape and issues to be addressed in the manifesto'.

The United Democratic Front (UDF)

The UDF held its latest convention in November 2012, having held the previous one four years earlier. Both conventions were largely held to endorse the party's presidential candidates for the May 2009 and 2014 elections, respectively. The major difference between the 2008 and 2012 conventions was that the latter included the election of new office bearers in addition to endorsing the presidential candidate for the May 2014 elections.

In 2008, there were no calls within the party for an election manifesto although the party president's speech to the convention contained a range of policy statements that would be typical of such a document. Indeed, the leader promised a new manifesto whose development would be highly participatory 'in determining and validating the type of development agenda that will meet [our] aspirations for a better Malawi after May 2009' (Chinsinga, 2013: 38).

By not holding a party conference, the party's constitutional provision – empowering the party conference to decide on its election programme – was effectively ignored. Moreover, the 2008 convention lasted only for a day. No documents were circulated in advance, and no delegate spoke on any of the issues on the agenda. The same procedure was repeated at the 2012 convention. There were no substantive discussions on the party's policy platform, apart from endorsing Atupele Muluzi as the UDF's presidential candidate and filling up some NEC positions. The newly appointed presidential candidate, however, promised to hold a policy convention before the May 2014 general elections and this was done, making the UDF the only party to have held such an *indaba* aimed at discussing future public policy.

The Democratic Progressive Party (DPP)

Since it was founded in February 2005, the DPP has held two conventions – in 2009 and 2013. The 2009 convention had only one agenda item: the adoption of the party's parliamentary candidates and former president Mutharika, the party's founder, as its presidential candidate for the May 2009 elections. Moreover, until the April 2013 convention, none of the party's office bearers had ever been elected to their positions. All decisions regarding party positions were taken either by the party leader or those very close to him.

DPP officials have on several occasions indicated to scholars that their National Governing Council (NGC) is responsible for the development of party policies and programmes. However, we found that most officials of the party did not possess even a rudimentary understanding of how the party develops its policy positions. Rather, we found that the DPP's election manifesto was developed by a team of officials appointed by President Mutharika, in a process lacking transparency. As a member of the manifesto team remarked, 'Most of us learnt about the manifesto when it was released during the campaign, and we did not know who had developed it and how it was developed' (Chinsinga, 2013).

We find that, on paper, the party's NGC plays a critical role in formulating policies. In reality, however, the NGC does not meet quarterly as it is supposed to. An official observed that the NGC 'meetings are hugely ad hoc, and few of us understand how the NGC operates' (Chinsinga, 2013). Other officials claimed that 'most of the critical party and policy decisions are taken by the party's central executive committee, which is a sub-committee of the NGC . . . And the central executive committee essentially means the party president since most of the members are very loyal to him' (Chinsinga, 2013). Thus, neither the DPP's governing statutes nor the 2009 election manifesto were endorsed by the party convention despite the party constitution stipulating structures through which these processes are supposed to take place.

The major focus of the April 2013 convention was the election of office bearers for the NGC. Apart from the acceptance speech by the former president's brother, Peter Mutharika, as the party's torchbearer in the May 2004 elections, the convention did not discuss or debate the party's policy priorities. There was no indication at all whether a policy specific *indaba* would be held to discuss the party's policy messages ahead of the May 2014 elections.

The People's Party (PP)

The PP held its inaugural convention in August 2012. While the original plans were to organize a one-day event, a decision was taken to extend it by an extra day in order to meet logistical challenges. The convention had two main agenda items:

- to elect office bearers; and
- to adopt the party's election manifesto.

Despite the extra day, the convention did not manage to adopt the manifesto. While some party members claimed that the party did indeed have a specific manifesto, others dismissed such claims. Those who indicated that the PP did possess a manifesto argued that 'a party of its calibre cannot exist without one; whatever President Joyce Banda says and does is a reflection of PP's manifesto'.

The functioning of parties in Malawi

The implication of the above findings is that, while all major political parties express a desire to engage with their members in the process of developing party platforms and policies, they fail spectacularly to translate this commitment into practice. Indeed, Malawian parties fail 'to function according to their own constitutions' (Chinsinga, 2013: 40) mainly because of deficiencies in intra-party democracy that subject parties to the suffocating grip of their leaders or founders.

Our discussion above demonstrates some of the challenges that political parties in Malawi face, although such challenges are not particularly unique to Malawi. Other empirical studies of party manifesto development indicate deficiencies in internal democracy and allude to the fact that the process of manifesto development is strongly controlled by the political elites (Cohen, 1999; Scarrow, 2000). Thus, in spite of many opportunities for inputs and feedback from the rank and file party members and lower levels in party organization, the party elites in most countries nevertheless almost always dominate the process. Scarrow (2000: 136) argues that 'electoral leadership will seek to curtail the power of party congresses over policy by reducing the frequency with which they are held [and by simply putting such items off the agenda]'. The situation appears particularly relevant to Malawi where control of the manifesto remains in, or passes into, the hands of the electoral leadership.

Notwithstanding the numerous challenges of developing manifestos across parties in Malawi, there are even further challenges in communicating the manifestos to voters. The primary function of a manifesto is to inform the electorate of what the parties stand for especially since the expectation is that 'voters will make up their mind about who to vote for, at least partly, based on the party programme' (Chinsinga, 2013: 40). This assumes or, indeed, presupposes a seamless flow of information from the parties to the electorate. However, our study finds this to be a huge challenge in Malawi, where parties are seldom concerned with effectively communicating with their followers, mainly due to the entrenched culture of secrecy and suspicion that exists in the political system. For example, none of the four major parties have websites with information on party programmes, and even the rudimentary information available on these sites is seldom updated. Indeed, it is extremely difficult to acquire a hard copy of a manifesto during the election campaign, even at a party's official headquarters, as parties and their leaders are wary of getting their ideas 'stolen'. Hence, as one official observed, 'we prefer to keep our manifestos close to our chests; we only release them when we are absolutely sure that our competitors will not have adequate time to photocopy them for their own purposes.'

As a result of the weak or absent ideological foundations, Phiri (2000) and Mpesi (2009) argue that political parties in Malawi have the following characteristics:

- parties lack long-term vision and are largely preoccupied with securing short-term survival and protecting the immediate economic interests of their constituents;
- parties often fail to successfully manage internal conflicts, which results in the formation of splinter groups or their leaders frequently switching loyalties with ease and without any sense of shame; and
- party leaders deliver inconsistent messages even during crucial national events.

Thus, the apparent ideological deficit among political parties in Malawi has resulted in a multiparty democratic system in which political power and control are built around personalities that centre on the 'big man' syndrome and their networks rather than organizations with clear ideologies and programmes. And as Mpesi (2009) argues, regionalism, ethnicity and a culture of hand-outs have become de facto guiding principles for ordinary Malawians when it comes to choosing between political parties.

Conclusion

This chapter set out to trace the development of political parties in Malawi with the aim of examining various political settlements that political parties have negotiated over the years. The goal was to assess the impact of such settlements on economic and political development (or lack of it) in Malawi. Malawians embraced democracy in 1993–94 in order to escape from the political, economic and social ills that they had endured for three decades under the authoritarian one-party rule of Hastings Banda. Thus, the struggle in 1993, just as in the independence struggle in the 1950s and 1960s, was not only a struggle for political emancipation but also a struggle for general improvements in the quality of life. Over two decades after the arrival of democracy, poverty levels remain alarmingly high and inequality is rising in the country (GoM, 2012).

The current legal framework has led to the opening of political space, with an exponential growth in the number of political parties, from 3 in 1994 to 55 by the time the country was holding its fifth general election. However, political parties in Malawi have not been able to function as drivers of economic and social transformation. Considering that political parties are a central unit of governance in any democratic system of government (Maiyo, 2008), Malawians expected their parties to take control and drive the country towards a more assured future based on a specific and well-defined agenda of development (Mpesi, 2009). This has not happened. In the period between 1966 and 1994, the Malawi Congress Party created a clientelist political settlement that only benefited ruling political elites and their cronies. This state of affairs did not improve with the reintroduction of multiparty politics. While the country is witness to clientelistic party competition and maintains formal institutions of democracy (Khan, 2010), the fundamental political behaviours have remained the same (Cammack, 2011). All parties that have come to power in Malawi have perpetuated clientelistic behaviour, forging settlements within which the political elites and those well connected to the political establishment have benefited at the expense of national development. Political parties as critical actors in the policymaking processes have thus not provided an adequate forum through which the general populace can provide input in the policy discourses. Political parties have by and large been used to promote personal or sectional interests at the expense of a collective national good.

Notes

1   The Youth League, was a youth branch of the MCP and was used to drum up support primarily through coercion and intimidation. The Malawi Young Pioneers (MYP), on the other hand, was a paramilitary wing that operated as a political militia, aimed at compliance enforcement and intelligence-gathering, though it also performed certain civilian functions in developing agricultural and other entrepreneurial skills amongst young people.
2   Section 40 (2) reads: 'The State shall provide funds so as to ensure that, during the life of any Parliament, any political party which has secured more than one-tenth of the national vote in elections to that Parliament has sufficient funds to continue to represent its constituency.'
3   In 2014, for the first time, Malawi simultaneously conducted local, parliamentary and presidential elections.
4   The Legislative Council had 28 seats, 20 seats were on the lower roll while 8 were on the higher roll. MCP won all the seats on the lower roll and 3 on the higher roll. The rest (5) were reserved for the United Federal Party (see Banda, 2014).
5   See section 59 of the Malawian Constitution.
6   This section borrows from, and presents an overview of, findings of an assessment pertaining to the status and practical feasibility of political ideologies as the basis for political engagement and development in Malawi (Chinsinga, 2013). The Centre for Multiparty Democracy commissioned the study.

References

Acemoglu, D. and Robinson, J. (2012) *Why Nations Fail: The Origins of Power, Prosperity and Poverty*. London: Profile Books.

Acemoglu, D., Johnson, S. and Robinson, J. (2004) *Institutions as the Fundamental Cause of Long-Run Growth*. National Bureau of Economic Research. Working Paper No. 10481. Available at: http://www.nber.org/papers/w10481.pdf (accessed 26 February 2016).

Baker, C. (2001) *Revolt of the Ministers: The Malawi Cabinet Crisis 1964–1965*. London: I.B. Tauris.

Banda, H.C. (2014) *Malawi Parliament: Origins, Reforms and Practices*. Lilongwe: Pan African Publishers.

Cammack, D. (2011) 'Malawi's Political Settlement in Crisis'. ODI: Africa Power and Politics. Background Paper, November.

Cammack, D. and Kelsall, T. (2010) *Developmental Patrimonialism? The Case of Malawi*. Working Paper 12. London: Africa Power and Politics Programme.

Chinsinga, B. (2002) 'The Politics of Poverty Alleviation in Malawi: A Critical Review', in Englund H. (ed.) *A Democracy of Chameleon: Politics and Culture in New Malawi*. Uppsala: Nordiska Afrika Institutet.

Chinsinga, B. (2013) *Searching for a Holy Grail: Exploring the Feasibility of Political Party Ideologies in Malawi*. A study conducted by the Centre for Multiparty Democracy, Balaka: Montfort Media.

Chirwa, W. (2014) *Malawi: Democracy and Political Participation*. Rosebank, SA: OSISA.

Cohen, J. (1999) 'Deliberation and Democratic Legitimacy', in Bohman, J. and Rehg, W. (eds.) *Deliberative Democracy: Essays on Season and Politics*. London: MIT Press.

Divala, J. (2007) 'Malawi's Approach to Democracy: Implications for the Teaching of Democratic Citizenship'. *Citizenship Teaching and Learning*. 3(1): 32–44.

GoM (2012) *Integrated Household Survey 2012*. Zomba: National Statistics Office (NSO).

Heywood, A. (1997) *Politics*. Basingstoke: Macmillan.

Kasambara, R. (1998) 'Citizenship education in Malawi since 1992: an appraisal', in Ross, K. and Phiri, K. (eds.) *Democratisation in Malawi: A Stocktaking.* Blantyre: CLAIM.

Katz, R. and Crotty, W. (eds.) (2006) *Handbook of Party Politics.* London: Sage.

Key, V. (1964) *Politics, parties, & pressure groups,* 5th edn. New York: Thomas Y. Crowell Co.

Khan, M. (2010) 'Political Settlements and the Governance of Growth-Enhancing Institutions'. SOAS, London: Mimeo, available at: http://eprints.soas.ac.uk/9968/ (accessed 14 February 2016).

Lwanda, J. (2009) *Kamuzu Banda of Malawi: The Study in Promise, Power and Legacy.* Zomba: Kachere.

Maiyo, J. (2008) *Preaching Water, Drinking Wine? Political Parties and Intra-Party Democracy in East Africa: Considerations for Democratic Consolidation.* Paper presented at a seminar on Intra-Party Democracy at the Africa Studies Centre, Leiden University on 9 September. Available at: www.ascleiden.nl/pdf/paper20080909.pdf (accessed 28 February 2016).

Mariyamkono, T.L and Kanyongolo, F.E. (eds) (2003) *When Political Parties Clash.* Eastern and Southern African Universities Research Program (ESAURP). Dar es Salaam: TEMA Publishers.

Mhone, G. (1992) 'The Political Economy of Malawi: an Overview' in Mhone, G.Z. (ed) *Malawi at the Cross Roads: The Post Colonial Political Economy.* Harare: SAPES Trust.

Mitchell, M. (2012) '"Living Our Faith:" The Lenten Pastoral Letter of the Bishops of Malawi and the Shift to Multiparty Democracy, 1992–93'. *Journal for the Scientific Study of Religion* 41(1): 5–18.

Mpasu, S. (1995) *Political Prisoner 3/75 of Dr. H. Kamuzu Banda of Malawi.* Lilongwe: Pan African Publishers.

Mpesi, A. (2009) 'Political Parties and their Manifestos: Inferring Political Party Ideologies in Malawi since 1994', MA Thesis: Chancellor College, University of Malawi, Zomba.

NIMD (2004) *A Framework for Democratic Party-Building.* The Hague: NIMD.

Ogunwa, S. (2012) 'Problems and Prospects of the Opposition Parties in Nigeria's Political System', *Ilorin Journal of Sociology* 4(1).

Oloka-Onyango, J. (1995) 'Beyond the Rhetoric: Reinvigorating the Struggle for Economic and Social Rights in Africa'. *California West International Law Journal,* 26: 1.

Phiri, K. (2000) 'Reflections of Party Ideologies and Programmes', in Phiri, K., and Patel, N. (eds.) *Malawi's Second Democratic Elections: Process, Problems and Prospects,* Blantyre: CLAIM.

Ranny, A. and Kendall, W. (1956) *Democracy and the American: Party System.* New York: Harcourt, Brace and Company.

Ross, A. (2009) *Colonialism to Cabinet Crisis: A Political History of Malawi.* Zomba: Kachere.

Scarrow, S. (2000) *Political Parties and Democracy in Theoretical Perspectives: Implementing Intra-Party Democracy.* Washington, DC: National Democratic Institute of International Affairs.

Sen, A. (1999) *Development as Freedom.* New York: Oxford University Press.

Shively, W. P. (2008) *Power and Choice: An Introduction to Political Science,* 9th edn. New York: McGraw Hill Higher Education.

Skinner, T. M. (1964) 'The Report on the Commission to Examine the Salary Scales and Conditions of Service of Local Officers', Nyasaland Government Establishment Circular No. 148. Zomba: Government Printer.

Van Donge, J. (1995) 'Kamuzu's Legacy: The Democratization of Malawi', *African Affairs,* 14: 227–57.

Van Donge, J. K. (2002a) 'Disordering the Market: The Liberalization of Burley Tobacco in Malawi in the 1990s'. *Journal of Southern African Studies*, 28(1): 89–115.

Van Donge, J. K. (2002b) 'The Fate of an African "Chaebol": Malawi's Press Corporation after Democratisation', *Journal of Modern African Studies*, 40(4): 651–81.

Vongdouangchanh, B. (2006) 'Political parties in state of deep decline, political operatives say', *The Hill Times*, 6 March.

World Bank (1981) *Accelerated Development Sub-Saharan Africa: an agenda for action (Berg report)*. Washington, DC: The World Bank.

4 Judicialisation and informalisation of politics in Malawi

Implications for inclusive development

Fidelis Edge Kanyongolo

Introduction

There is a considerable amount of literature that describes and analyses the role of the judiciary in the development of democratic politics in Malawi, especially since 1994, when Malawi adopted a predominantly liberal democratic Constitution. However, despite the vastness of the literature and the depth of insights that they provide on the process of democratisation and its impact on development, studies of the institutional framework and dynamics of the processes pay little attention to the position and role of the judiciary. To the limited extent that the judiciary features in the literature, its analysis is limited to a formalistic nature and functions, with little attention paid to its contribution to the construction and reproduction of the framework of informal institutions. Given the relevance of informal institutions to development, the limited analysis of the role of the judiciary in the literature in Malawian politics and development limits scholarly and policy understanding of the totality of institutional drivers of development and its specific imperatives such as inclusion.

This chapter seeks to contribute to debates on the institutional drivers of inclusive development in Malawi by critically examining the role of the judiciary in the informalisation of politics and the impact of informalisation on inclusive development. Informed by Helmke and Levitsky's (2006: 5) definition of informal institutions as 'socially shared rules, usually unwritten, that are created, communicated and enforced outside officially sanctioned channels', this chapter conceptualises informalisation as the process by which institutions are created, located, communicated and enforced outside officially sanctioned channels. Relying mainly on theoretical insights from critical legal scholarship which challenges legal formalism, the chapter grounds its conceptualisation of the nature and functions of the judiciary in the lived reality of the incidence and drivers of the judicialisation of politics in Malawi since 1994.

Grounded in the acknowledgement of the political role of the judiciary, this chapter examines the tension between the doctrinal and practical approaches of Malawi's highest courts to the inclusion of politics in judicial discourse, with reference to the informalisation of politics in the context of 'customary law' institutions, mechanisms of accountability in parliamentary and political party relations and actions of local government and community structures that lack statutory authority. The chapter thus investigates whether judicial discourse on each of these contexts promotes and/or impedes informalisation, and whether the discourse is guided by any consistent and coherent legal principles that reconcile the upholding of constitutional norms of human rights, the rule of law and accountability with the promotion of informal institutions which are either indifferent or antithetical to such norms. In the final section, the chapter makes some general comments about the effect(s) of judicialisation of politics, in so far as it legitimises informal politics, on the prospects of inclusive development in Malawi. This chapter is limited to highlighting the role of the judiciary in contributing to the dialectics of the formalisation and informalisation of politics and, by extension, inclusive development. In conclusion, the chapter suggests certainty and coherence in judicial discourse and practice; increased attention to the political role of the judiciary in academic and policy discourse and development programming; and more scholarly and public debate of the democratic legitimacy of the judiciary's involvement in adjudication of political issues. This will contribute to debunking of the myth of the political neutrality of the judiciary, justify the demand for more political accountability from courts and underline the need to deepen the democratic legitimacy of the judiciary, an institution that is often universally described as 'the least democratic branch of government' (Dickson, 2014: 169).

Inclusive development

The notion of inclusive development is explored in more detail in other chapters of this book. For present purposes, it suffices to highlight aspects of the concept that pertain most directly to the processes of judicialisation and informalisation discussed in this chapter. In this connection, the definition of the term by the United Nations Development Programme (UNDP) is most instructive. In that definition, development is inclusive 'only if all groups of people contribute to creating opportunities, share the benefits of development and participate in decision-making' (UNDP, U/D). For the UNDP, inclusive development is underpinned by the standards and principles of human rights, namely participation, non-discrimination and accountability (UNDP, U/D).

It is the standards and principles that create the nexus between judicialisation and inclusive development in Malawi. This is because, under the country's constitution, it is the judiciary that has the final authority to interpret and enforce the constitution, including its guarantees of human rights. This makes Malawian courts the final arbiters of the scope and limits of constitutional norms of participation, non-discrimination and accountability. This necessarily implicates courts in the dynamics of the promotion or impediment of inclusive development.

Judicialisation of politics

A number of studies have examined judicial involvement in political questions in the context of Malawi. However, they have largely focussed on specific manifestations and specific drivers of the phenomenon, and have not developed an overarching theoretical framework to underpin the practice in Malawi. Among the specific elements on which the literature has focussed are the nature and effect of judicialisation of Malawian electoral politics (Gloppen and Kanyongolo, 2012), the drivers of judicial assertiveness in Malawi in comparison to Zambia (Vondoepp 2005) and the significance of the political environment as a critical factor that threatens judicial independence (Ellett 2008).

The theoretical context

The broader question of the judicialisation of politics has, however, been the subject of significant academic and public debate in other parts of the world. This is not surprising because the phenomenon raises important questions of democratic principle and practice with respect to the limits of the doctrine of the separation of powers, the democratic legitimacy of judicial power and the co-relationship between judicialisation of politics and the dysfunctionality of political institutions. In a number of countries, for example in Asia (Dressel, 2012), Latin America (Ingram, 2015), Africa (Vondoepp 2009), interest in the judicialisation of politics has gained added impetus from the democratic transitions that have resulted in expansion of judicial power as part of the process of enhancing accountability mechanisms and the rule of law. In addition, judicialisation of politics also merits renewed consideration given its potential to impact directly on developmental processes (Gauri, 2015).

Judicialisation of politics is the process by which courts appropriate the final authority to mediate and adjudicate political competition and conflicts by recasting them into legal forms and resolving them using the legal tools and logics. The legitimacy of judicial involvement in political issues is contested by orthodox legal theories, which predicate the law on the absolute dichotomisation between law and politics. This theoretical position is endorsed by courts in many jurisdictions through the development of various exclusionary principles in judicial discourse.[1]

The absolutist dichotomisation of law and politics reflected in the discourses in the cases mentioned above is challenged by a wide range of radical legal theories, which include the critical legal studies movement, as well as feminist and Marxist legal theories (Barnett, 2013; Leiter, 2014; Unger, 2015). The main thrust of the radical critiques is their rejection of legal formalism and objectivism, which posit the law as a phenomenon that exists, and should be analysed and assessed, independently of non-legal factors such as morality or politics (Banakar and Travers, 2014). The radical scholars essentially argue that the formal dichotomisation of the law and politics, for example, does not reflect the reality that, in practice, law and political, economic and social factors are inextricably linked, and that the law generally reflects the power relations that subsist in any particular context.

The practice of Malawian courts

The High Court and the Supreme Court of Appeal in Malawi have also endorsed the dichotomist conceptualisation of law and politics espoused in classic legal positivist theories. On a number of occasions, the courts have stated that the judiciary should not adjudicate questions that are essentially political. In this regard, the High Court has observed that, 'allowing the judiciary and judges into disputes entirely political unduly politicizes the judiciary and we dare say the judges … That erodes the public's confidence in the judges and the judiciary and also their independence.'[2]

In this particular case, the court also highlighted a reason that justifies the dichotomisation of rhetoric, namely that judges lack the competence or mandate to adjudicate non-legal matters such as politics. In the words of the judge:

> judicial officers are not best placed to decide on matters inter alia of politics. The considerations operating in politics are different to those obtaining in the courts…the courts should be slow, very slow in our humble view, to adjudicate on matters that though dressed up as legal are really political disputes.[3]

The dichotomous position has been endorsed in a number of other cases. For example, in the case of *State v The President of the Republic of Malawi, Ministry of Finance ex-parte SGS Malawi Limited*[4] the judge expressed the view that matters involving socio-economic policy and competing policy considerations are not justiciable. In a similar vein, the judge in the case of *The State v The Minister of Finance and the Secretary to the Treasury, ex parte the Malawi Law Society*[5] noted, albeit in passing, that:

> matters of policy…should be left to those best suited to deal with them namely the people's elected representatives and their permanent advisors i.e. the civil servants. We would therefore be the first to wash our hands off this case if it raised issues only of policy or required this court to evaluate socioeconomic policy or allocate scarce economic resources.[6]

Despite its formalist rhetoric, which normalises the separation of law and politics, the judiciary in Malawi does get involved in the adjudication of essentially political questions in practice. Before examining the evidence of such judicialisation of politics from case law, it is important to note some of the factors that encourage the judiciary to engage with such cases. One such factor is the language of provisions of the Constitution, which define the mandate of the judiciary. Some of the sections of the Constitution use language that creates sufficient interpretive space for judges to extend their adjudicative mandate beyond the boundaries of what positivist legal theorists regard as 'law'. The most pertinent provision in this regard is that which stipulates that, 'in the resolution of political disputes the provisions of this Constitution shall be the supreme arbiter and ultimate source of authority'.[7] Since interpretation and enforcement of the Constitution is the responsibility of the judiciary, this provision implicitly authorizes courts to adjudicate political disputes. In any case, it is up to the judiciary itself to decide what matters fall within its mandate and, relying on this rule, judges have the basis on which they may justify adjudicating what are essentially political matters.

The other factor which contributes to the judicialisation of politics in practice, despite the rhetoric of dichotomisation, is the level of judicial activism of the courts themselves. Here, I adopt the understanding of judicial activism used by Kmiec (2004), which includes invalidation of the arguably constitutional actions of other branches, failure to adhere to precedent, judicial 'legislation', departures from accepted interpretive methodology, and result-oriented judging. In that sense, the High Court can be argued to have displayed a significant degree of activism, by invalidating legislation passed by Parliament, disregarding precedent, 'legislating' by establishing rules of law where Parliament had made no such rule and departing from rules of statutory interpretation. In some of the cases, the activism of the High Court has been constrained by the Supreme Court of Appeal, which has overruled the decisions of the former.

This is not to say that the Supreme Court itself has not performed an activist function. On the contrary, in one of the most significant cases decided in Malawi since 1994,[8] the court appeared to have disregarded accepted interpretive methodologies and engaged in result-oriented judging when it invoked 'the doctrine of necessity' to dismiss the appellants' argument that, for as long as their boycott of proceedings of the National Assembly subsisted, Parliament could not pass any legislation because it was inquorate. The court rejected the argument partly on the ground that to uphold it would result in legislative paralysis, although the logic of the decision was difficult to justify on the basis of precedents and judicial interpretive methodology (Chirwa, 2007: 27–32).

The combination of the permissive constitutional framework and rising judicial activism has led the judiciary in Malawi to contradict its own rhetoric of formalist dichotomisation and become quite activist in resolving what are essentially political disputes. Within an environment conducive to the judicialisation of politics, the country's highest courts have, in a significant number of cases, engaged in adjudication of what are essentially political questions. The questions the courts have addressed include: whether the relationship between a Member of Parliament and his or her constituent is that of delegate or agent;[9] whether the leader of one faction of a political party enjoyed the overwhelming support and loyalty of the party's Members of Parliament while support for his challenger for the leadership of the party existed outside Parliament;[10] and what degree of consultation is required prior to appointment of members of the electoral management body.[11] The courts have also been involved in the judicialisation of politics in the context of disputes over succession to traditional chieftaincies and the legal authority of ad hoc local government and community structures.

Although the judicialisation of politics has attracted some academic interest much of the discussion has not addressed two important questions:

- absence of any development by the courts of principles to guide courts in balancing the legitimate arbitration of political disputes and unjustified judicial encroachment into the constitutional mandates of bodies charged with making political judgments; and
- (of more direct relevance to the aims of this chapter) the effect of the judicialisation of individual political questions on the dialectic of formalisation and informalisation of politics at national level.

Informalisation of politics

Informal institutions may be defined as 'socially shared rules, usually unwritten, that are created, communicated and enforced outside officially sanctioned channels' (Helmke and Levitsky, 2006: 5). Drawing on this definition, this chapter conceptualises informalisation of politics as the process by which informal political institutions are established and operate. The ensuing sections of this chapter addresses the question of the impact of informalisation of politics on inclusive development and argues that the effects of informalisation are not limited to a reconfiguration of institutions, but may extend to the definition of the ability of people to access resources. As Ninsin (2000: 113) notes, informalisation 'produces normative disarray and marginalized or anomic behaviour for a vast majority of members in the society [and] entails the restructuring of access to – and ownership of – the material means for livelihood'.

A growing interest in informal institutions in Malawi has generated a considerable body of literature that identifies the various forms that informal institutions take in various areas of country's political economy (Rakner *et al.*, 2004; Mvula *et al.*, 2014). Although the literature is varied in its conclusions, the most frequently cited characteristics that mark informal institutions in Malawi are neo-patrimonialism and clientilism. These manifestations (and causes) of informality crosscut the institutional terrain of political representation, democratic governance, democratic accountability and the rule of law. This chapter cannot cover the whole institutional landscape and will confine itself to a representative sample of institutions which have a direct impact on democratisation and development. For these purposes, the chapter focuses on the dynamics of judicialisation with respect to their impact on the promotion or constraining of informalisation in relation to the action of political parties (see Chapter 3), Members of Parliament (Rakner *et al.*, 2004) and 'town chiefs' (Cammack *et al.*, 2009).

Helmke and Levitsky (2006) provide a useful framework for analysing the intersection of judicialisation and informalisation of politics. Three aspects of their framework appear to be particularly relevant to the focus of this chapter. The first is the identification of the following key areas in which informality is critical to democratic politics: political representation, democratic accountability, democratic governance and citizenship and the rule of law (Helmke and Levitsky, 2006: 8–13). The second is the recognition that the relationship between informalisation and democratic politics is ambivalent in nature, with informalisation both promoting and impeding democratic politics within the same context.

Viewed from a legal theoretical perspective, Helmke's model presents conceptual challenges in that, unlike in constitutional law theory, it separates 'democratic accountability' from 'democratic governance' and it defines the rule of law almost exclusively with reference to citizenship rights. Nevertheless, it does present a focused and functional framework that is useful for structuring what would otherwise be an incoherent and disjointed narrative. Using Helmke's model in the context of the focus of this chapter, the central question becomes: what is the effect of the judicialisation of politics in Malawi on the processes of political informalisation with respect to political representation, democratic accountability, democratic governance and citizenship and the rule of law? Related to this is the question of whether judicialisation influences the extent to which informalisation facilitates or impedes the development of democratic politics in Malawi?

Answering these questions comprehensively requires in-depth ethnographies of specific manifestations of judicialisation of politics and informalisation of politics that is beyond the scope of this study. Nevertheless, there is ample evidence to indicate that the highest courts in Malawi make a significant contribution to the informalisation of politics by (de)legitimising neopatrimonialism, clientilism and other constitutive features of the character of Malawian politics. The evidence consists primarily of cases in which courts have both promoted and constrained informalisation of politics in judgments that pertain to the aspects of democratic politics identified by Helmke, namely representation, accountability, democratic governance and the rule of law.

The judiciary has contributed to the perpetuation of neo-patrimonialism in at least three ways. The first, and probably most significant, is by reinforcing customary law and its institutions. The term 'customary law' is contested and has attracted critical scepticism from scholars who have argued that it includes a range of norms and institutions, some of which are informal. Because 'customary law' is defined imprecisely, many informal institutions are also included under the umbrella of 'customary law' that the courts uphold. The courts in a number of cases have acknowledged the imprecision of customary law, for example, in *Nyambi v Kambalame*,[12] where the High Court effectively held that 'customary law' is whatever the Chiefs say it is. Similarly in the case of *Banda v Banda*,[13] the High Court acknowledged that 'applicable customary rules may not always be obvious'. The inclusion in 'customary law' of norms and practices that operate outside officially sanctioned channels confirms its character as an informal, or at least hybrid, institution. By definition, the informal institutions that exist outside the formal framework are not subject to control by that framework, which in terms of the Constitution includes guarantees of human rights, including equality under the law. This has implications for the prospects of inclusive development as further demonstrated below.

In upholding customary law, the judiciary contributes to sustaining its informal aspects, such its oral traditions as was acknowledged by the High Court in the case of *Edwin Ingelesi Ganya v James Goodson Ganya et al.*,[14] in which the court stated that 'chieftaincy disputes pose a peculiar adjudicative challenge since they are largely premised on oral tradition'. Similarly, in the case of *Chafumbwa v Village Headman Mkanda et al.*, the court based its decision to disentitle a claimant to a chieftaincy title under 'Chewa custom' on oral evidence of 'local tradition'. In *Mbwana v Kanthiti*,[15] the High Court relied on what it termed 'propositions of good sense and common justice', to guide it in its determination of a dispute revolving around the distribution of matrimonial property following the dissolution of a customary law marriage.

The court has also reinforced customary law by legitimising the informal politics that surround chieftaincy appointments. In the case of *Group Village Headman Kakopa et al. v Chilozi et al.*,[16] the court indicated that, as part of his efforts to protect his right to succeed to the position of a traditional authority, a claimant 'should have taken the initiative, immediately after the present Constitution was adopted, to influence the office of the President to remove late

Dickson Chilozi who was installed Chief Kabudula in 1979'. The court was clearly endorsing executive interference in the process of appointment and removal of traditional authorities, a characteristic feature of Malawi's informal politics.

The second respect in which the judiciary contributes to the informalisation of politics in Malawi is in its establishment of precedents that, directly or indirectly, weaken formal accountability ties between Members of Parliament and their constituents, between members of political parties and their leaders, and between members of political parties and their parties. In a number of precedent-setting decisions made since 1994, the High Court has held that a constituent has no right to compel his or her Member of Parliament to attend parliamentary proceedings;[17] that a member of a political party can be appointed to the Cabinet without the need for his or her party leadership to be consulted;[18] that a Member of Parliament may resign from the political party of which he or she was a member at the time of elections and declare himself or herself to be independent and not lose his or her seat in Parliament;[19] and that the President may determine what constitutes 'consultation' with leaders of political parties represented in the National Assembly for purposes of appointing members of the Electoral Commission.[20]

The decisions contribute to the reduction of the range of formal mechanisms which are available to constituents and members of their political parties and leaders of parties represented in Parliament for enforcement of accountability against Members of Parliament, members and leaders of political parties and the President. The reduced availability of formal institutions of accountability to which the judiciary has contributed through the decisions mentioned above incentivises increased resort to informal ones. It is to this extent that the judiciary promotes the informalisation of politics.

The courts have also promoted informalisation with respect to the rule of law. This is most evident in cases in which the High Court has recognised informal institutions regardless of their lack of any basis in formal law. In addition to upholding the 'power' of informal District Consultative Forums,[21] the High Court has also stated, albeit in passing, that people have an obligation to comply with orders made by 'the traditional leaders who administer land in the affected locality'.[22] This effectively recognised the authority of traditional leaders operating within urban areas despite the fact that Section 3 (5) of the Chiefs Act prohibits chiefs from exercising jurisdiction within cities, municipalities or towns without the written approval of the appropriate council established under the Local Government (Urban Areas) Act, and section 6 of the Local Government Act vests jurisdiction of areas within a district or township to a local council designated under the Act. The statement also indicated judicial promotion of the purported power of traditional authorities to administer land in urban areas despite the fact that statute law vests such powers in a number of formal authorities, including the central and local government authorities.

The judiciary has also promoted informalisation of politics at the expense of the rule of law in at least one other case. In this case,[23] the High Court was asked to decide whether an informal forum established by a local government authority could raise revenue, a function which could be performed lawfully only by elected councillors. In its judgment, the court answered the question in the affirmative. While acknowledging that the forum had no statutory basis, the court nevertheless upheld its decision to raise revenue on the ground that this was necessitated by the unavoidable need for the local government to have resources in order to be able to deliver services to the residents of the city.

However, the contribution of this case to the promotion of informalisation of politics is counterweighed by a case, based on similar facts, in which the court decided that no institution can exercise administrative or adjudicative power in Malawi unless it has specific formal legal authorisation.[24] These two cases exemplify the contradictory contributions of the judiciary to informalisation. In some cases, courts promote informalisation, while in others they constrain it. The High Court has enforced this formalistic view of the law not only in the case of local government structures,[25] but also with respect to community level institutions, which exercise adjudicatory powers without statutory authorisation.[26] The judiciary's efforts to formalise institutions by upholding the outlawing of some informal institutions has not been wholly successful. For example, the prohibition of the institution of adjudication without statutory authority has not resulted in the elimination of the institution. On the contrary, such adjudication continues unabated and is, in fact, supported in official policy as a critical component of the primary justice system.

The High Court has also constrained informalisation of politics by enforcing norms that are antithetical to aspects of the neo-patrimonialism and clientilism which characteristically underlie informal politics. The court has done this mainly through decisions that criminalise certain conduct as corruption, although it may be considered to be acceptable and, even expected, from the point of view of the community.[27] Customary law is subject to the Constitution and cannot override it in cases of inconsistency, thus, for example, it can only limit, and not supplant, constitutional rights.[28] This judicial approach constrains the development of those elements of informal institutions within 'customary law' that are inconsistent with human rights and other stipulations of the Constitution which militate against the relations that characterise informal institutions. Despite the judicial rhetoric, which suggests that courts will review customary law institutions for compliance with human rights, the judiciary continues to uphold 'customary law' institutions under which people are subjects of traditional authorities rather than equal citizens with rights and liberties. Among the institutions which the judiciary has upheld, despite their apparent incompatibility with human rights, are polygamy and hereditary chieftaincy.

The judiciary further constrains informalisation of politics by restricting the freedom of some institutions to regulate themselves. The case of Parliament is illustrative of this judicial approach and its effects on informality. That the Malawian Parliament combines both formality and informality in its organisation and proceedings has been well documented elsewhere (Rakner et al., 2004). The constitutional power of Parliament to regulate its own procedures, therefore, provides it with the opportunity to perpetuate informal aspects of that self-regulation. However, on a number of occasions, the judiciary has limited the scope of Parliament's self-regulation and intervened to subordinate self-regulation, and any informality it includes, to the dictates of formal rules of law.

In the case of *Nseula* v *The Attorney General*,[29] the Supreme Court of Appeal held that courts have the power to intervene in Parliament's regulation of its proceedings if the regulation involves interpretation of the Constitution. Similarly, in the case of *The State* v *Speaker of the National Assembly et al., ex.p. Nangwale*,[30] the High Court held that courts could override the principle of self-regulation of Parliament to enforce the constitutionality of parliamentary decisions and actions. Judicial intervention in these circumstances constrains the informality, which would otherwise thrive under the cover of self-regulation.[31]

From the selection of cases described above, a number of conclusions can be made about the judicialisation of politics in Malawi and how it affects the development of its informalisation:

- the judiciary both facilitates and constrains informalisation of politics;
- the judiciary has not articulated an overarching set of normative principles to guide its involvement in politics and to reconcile the apparent inconsistency between the rhetoric of dichotomisation of law and politics, on the one hand, and the practice of judicialisation of politics on the other; and
- the judiciary further contributes to the informalisation of politics by facilitating it in some respects and impeding it in others.

Noting that a considerable amount of informal political activity remains untouched by judicial activity must preface the analysis of the influence of the judicialisation of politics. The major reason for this is that most Malawians do not have access to the courts for the resolution of their matters. This is largely because of prohibitive financial costs of litigation and long distances that many people have to travel to the nearest court (Schärf et al., 2002). Many of the informal institutions and processes that typify Malawian society, therefore, continue to operate beyond the reach of judicial intervention.

Despite its limited reach into the realm of politics, the judiciary does make a significant contribution to the definition and scope of informal politics in Malawi. In one respect, judicialisation contributes to informalisation by legitimising some forms and practices of informal politics. One example of this is the courts' enforcement of political rights, which entitle citizens to freedom of expression, freedom of association and equality. By upholding these individual liberties and rights, the courts legitimate citizens' actions outside of formal institutional frameworks.

Implications for inclusive development

Despite its promotion in scholarly literature and development practice, inclusive development is neither acknowledged nor promoted explicitly by the country's supreme policy instruments. For example, in over 200 pages of the country's overarching policy framework, the Malawi Growth and Development Strategy (MGDS), the word 'inclusive' appears only five times, and then only in reference to inclusive 'economic' growth. Clearly, this does not capture the totality of the concept of inclusive development, which is not limited to growth and economic transformation, but extends to the question of redistribution of the economic growth dividend (Vom Hau, 2012).

An informed appreciation of inclusive development in Malawi requires an understanding of the institutional dynamics that structure, promote and impede it. Key among such dynamics is the nexus between judicialisation, informalisation and inclusive growth. Judicialisation has causal links with informalisation in that, through the exercise of their adjudicative powers, courts continually shape and reshape political, economic and social relations. Such shaping and reshaping of relations occasionally results in their inclusion or exclusion from the sphere of formal state processes. Thus, for example, by adjudging that a constituent has no enforceable legal right to compel his or her MP to attend meetings of the National Assembly,[32] the courts unwittingly incentivised constituents to find a means of controlling MPs from outside the formal legal framework. In other circumstances, the link between judicialisation and informalisation is more explicit, as is exemplified by situations where courts expressly declare certain relationships and transactions to be outside or within the purview of formal institutional and processes.

By contributing to informalisation of institutions, judicialisation affects inclusive development. As institutions become or remain informalised, access to developmental processes by individuals or groups becomes relative to their possession of informal 'currencies' such as 'time', 'money, 'social status', 'social relations' and 'supernatural powers' (Bierschenk, 2008). Those who lack the currencies become vulnerable to exclusion, as they have no means with which to bargain for entry into the developmental processes. The linear judicialisation–informalisation-inclusive development chain of causation is paralleled by a direct linkage that exists between judicialisation and inclusive development at the normative level. At this level, the judiciary is obligated to promote inclusive development as part of the discharge of its constitutional mandate. In the case of the Constitution of Malawi, for example, the judiciary has the responsibility to enforce norms that promote aspects of inclusive development. Of particular note is the constitutional guarantee (section 30(2)) of the right to development which requires 'The State [to] take all necessary measures for the realization of the right to development [including] equality of opportunity for all in their access to basic resources, education, health services, food, shelter, employment and infrastructure'.

Informalisation of politics has the potential to affect the prospects of inclusive development both negatively and positively. On the one hand, there is evidence that, by reinforcing neo-patrimonialism and clientilism, informalisation of politics creates economic, political and social relations that militate against inclusion of 'clients' in developmental processes. This point is made in a number of other chapters in this book (see also Gaynor, 2010). Suffice it to note at this juncture that informalisation does have an exclusionary effect for people who lack the resources and power to influence decisions made by informal institutions, which are dominated by those who drive the neo-patrimonial and clientilistic order. In fact, there is a strong view among many development theorists and practitioners that the main constraint on inclusive development is the unequal power relations that characterise informal political institutions. Therefore, in so far as the judiciary promotes informalisation, it may be said to be one of the institutional factors that contributes to the impediment of inclusive development in Malawi.

On the other hand, there is evidence from studies conducted elsewhere which suggests that informalisation may be conducive to inclusion because the flexibility it induces creates the space within which disadvantaged social, economic and political groups find it easier to organise, mobilise and take action to demand inclusion in developmental processes than if they attempt to use formal institutions (see e.g. Miraftab, 2006; Lindell, 2010). To the extent that political informality has positive effects on inclusion, the judiciary's contribution may be considered to be desirable and necessary.

Despite the significance of the impact of judicial informalisation of politics on inclusive development, the issue has not been subjected to any systematic jurisprudential analysis in academic literature or case law. This reflects the dominance of classic legal positivism on Malawian legal theory and practice. Predicated on the formal separation of law and politics, classic legal positivism excludes consideration of non-legal factors in legal analysis (Austin and Austin, 1861). Malawian legal theory and judicial discourse reflects such separation of law from extra-legal factors such as the role of the judiciary in the informalisation of politics and, by extension, in the promotion or impediment of inclusive development. The result is that the processes proceed without a complete consideration of the legitimacy of the political role of the judiciary

The immediate implication of this conclusion for development scholars and practitioners is that more attention needs to be paid to the political role that the judiciary plays, including in shaping informal politics. Analyses of the role of the Malawian judiciary in national development should be extended beyond the bounds of institutional formalism and explicitly factor the political role of the judiciary and the influence of courts on the construction and reproduction of informal politics. It should also include a critical analysis of the democratic legitimacy of the judicial involvement in promoting or impeding inclusive development.

In so far as the judiciary can only deal with cases that are brought to it, any positive impact that such engagement may generate for informalisation cannot benefit those who, though willing, are unable to access the courts. The majority of such people are those who lack the resources to enable them to gain such access, for example women and other socio-economically disadvantaged groups, which also face procedural obstacles in an instance of indirect discrimination. One such obstacle is the requirement that the courts can grant a right of audience only to 'legal persons'. This means that only individuals and organisations that are registered by the state can seek the assistance of the courts. The result is that unregistered groups of people cannot apply for judicial remedies in their collective names and for their collective benefit. Given that getting registered by the state has a financial cost and political risk, and that such costs and risks disproportionately affect particular sections of the population such as women, the poor, perceived enemies of the state, the result is that members of such groups are obstructed from benefiting from the positive aspects of judicialisation of politics.

Conclusion

The prospects of attaining inclusive development in Malawi are significantly influenced both positively and negatively by the informalisation that dominates the country's politics. The particular nature of that informalisation and its effects on developmental processes is a function of the specificities of the institutional context that obtains in Malawi. While considerable research has been undertaken to explain the dynamics of the context, it is notable that most of the focus of those studies has been on institutions that have an overtly political character and role. This approach has obscured the equally important role played by institutions, such as the judiciary, which, despite not having an explicit political mandate, have a significant impact on the formalisation and informalisation of politics.

The judiciary in Malawi formally claims to be committed to legal formalist theories which stipulate an absolutist dichotomisation of law and politics, and prohibit courts from involvement in determining political questions. The evidence reviewed in this chapter, however, demonstrates that due to a permissive constitutional framework and a growth in judicial activism, the courts do in fact adjudicate questions which are essentially political in nature. The evidence further shows that there are no coherent principles or rules to guide the judiciary in its involvement in political questions or to define the governance or development objectives towards which such involvement should aim. Consequently, judgments by the High Court and the Supreme Court of Appeal display a wide range of differences and, in some cases, inconsistencies, in their views on political questions. This is illustrated in the evidence reviewed in this chapter, which shows that Malawian courts both promote and impede informalisation of politics.

The significant impact that informalisation of politics has on inclusive development in Malawi makes it imperative that the role of all institutions should be considered. Given that the evidence indicates that the judiciary does play a significant role in the process, it must be subjected to more rigorous analysis than has hitherto been the case. This requires piercing the veil of political neutrality with which the institution is clothed in liberal legal theory, and subjecting it to the same scrutiny that is faced by other institutions involved in politics and development. Rhetorical appeals to notions of judicial independence and impartiality are outweighed by the imperative of holding to account all institutions that shape the structure and dynamics of politics and development in Malawi.

If judicial power and discourses in Malawi are to have the optimum impact in facilitating inclusive development, there has to be:

- a more explicit recognition of the political role of the judiciary in both scholarly and practitioner analysis;
- a more coherent judicial discourse which addresses the apparent contradiction between rhetorical legal formalism and practical anti-formalism; and
- more scholarly and public debate of the democratic legitimacy of the judiciary's involvement in adjudication of political issues.

Notes

1 Such devices include 'the Political Question doctrine' developed by the United States Supreme Court, which is summarised aptly in the landmark case of *Marbury* v *Madison*, 5 U.S. (1 Cranch) 137, 170 (1803) in the following words: 'Questions, in their nature political, or which are, by the constitution and laws, submitted to the executive, can never be made in this court.' For an illuminating conceptualisation and critique of the doctrine, see Louis Michael Seidman (2004), 'The Secret Life of the Political Question Doctrine', 37 *J. Marshall Law Review* 441–80.
2 *Ajinga* v *United Democratic front*, Civil Cause No. 2466 of 2008.
3 High Court Civil Cause No. 2466 of 2008

4 Civil Cause No. 40 of 2003.

5 Constitutional Case No. 6 of 2006.

6 Also see *Chiume v The Alliance for Democracy*, Civil Cause No. 108 of 2005.

7 Section 10(1).

8 *The Attorney General v Malawi Congress Party*, Civil Appeal No. 22 of 1996.

9 *Chakuamba v Ching'oma*, Civil Cause No. 99 of 1996.

10 *Tembo v Chakuamba*, MSCA Civil Cause No. 230 of 2001.

11 *The State v Electoral Commission, exp. p. Muluzi and Tembo*, Miscellaneous Civil Cause No. 99 of 2007.

12 Civil Appeal No. 25 of 2011. See also *Steven et al v Kasitoni et al.* on Mang'anja customary law of succession to chieftaincy based on testimony of plaintiffs which was not contradicted by defendants because they did not attend court hearing or adduce any evidence.

13 Miscellaneous Civil Cause No. 102 of 2011.

14 Civil Cause No. 1707 of 2005.

15 Civil Appeal No. 109 of 2011.

16 [2000–2001] MLR 140.

17 *Chakuamba v Ching'oma*, Civil Cause No. 99 of 1996.

18 *Mponda Mkandawire v Attorney General*, Civil Cause No. 49 of 1996.

19 In Mponda Mkandawire v Attorney General, Misc. Civil Cause No.49 of 1996.

20 *The State v Electoral Commission, exp. p. Muluzi and Tembo*, Miscellaneous Civil Cause No. 99 of 2007.

21 *Zomba Municipal Assembly v Council of the University of Malawi* (Civil Cause No. 3567 of 2000) [2003] MWHC 90.

22 *Kabango v Kunjawa*, Civil Appeal No. 5 of 2012.

23 *Zomba Municipal Assembly v Council of the University of Malawi* [2003] MWHC 90.

24 *Bandawe [T/A Kaka Motel] v Mzuzu City Assembly* Civil Cause No 63 of 2006.

25 Ibid.

26 *R v Karonga*, African Law Reports (Malawi) Vol. 1, p. 210.

27 On the tension between formalistic definitions of corruption and autochthonous notions of the legitimacy of 'payments' to service social networks of obligation based on kinship ties see Gerhard Anders, 'Like Chameleons: Civil Servants and Corruption in Malawi' in Blundo, Giorgio, and Le Meur, Pierre-Yves, (eds.) (2009) *The governance of daily life in Africa: ethnographic explorations of public and collective services.* Leiden: Brill.

28 *Kamphoni v Kamphoni*, Matrimonial Cause No. 7 of 2012.

29 [1997] 2 MLR 294.

30 Miscellaneous Civil Case No. 1 of 2005.

31 Another instance of judicial overriding of self-regulation by Parliament occurred in the case of *In Re Appeal by the National Assembly et al. against the Ruling of the High Court* [2006] MLR 185 in which the High Court restrained the Speaker of the National Assembly from exercising his powers of declaring vacancies in some seats until the conclusion of related judicial processes. Similarly, in the more recent case of *State v Speaker of the National Assembly, ex.p. Lilian Patel, et al.* Misc. Civil Appeal No. 46 of 2015, the High Court and Supreme Court pre-emptively prohibited the Speaker from exercising similar powers.

32 See note 9 above.

References

Austin, J. and Austin, S. (1861) *The province of jurisprudence determined* (Vol. 2). London: J. Murray.

Banakar, R. and Travers, M. (2014) 'Introduction' in Banakar, R. and Travers, M. (eds.) *Law and social theory.* London: A&C Black.

Barnett, H. (2013) *Introduction to feminist jurisprudence*. London: Routledge.

Bierschenk, T. (2008) 'The everyday functioning of an African public service: informalization, privatization and corruption in Benin's legal system'. *The Journal of Legal Pluralism and Unofficial Law*, 40(57): 101–39.

Cammack, D., Kanyongolo, E. and O'Neil, T. (2009) *'Town Chiefs' in Malawi*. Africa Power and Politics Series. London: ODI Africa Power and Politics Programme.

Chirwa, D. (2007) 'Upholding the sanctity of rights: a principled approach to limitations and derogations under the Malawian Constitution'. *Malawi Law Journal*, 1(1): 3–32.

Dickson, D. (2014) *The People's Government: An Introduction to Democracy*. Cambridge: Cambridge University Press.

Dressel, B. ed. (2012) *The judicialization of politics in Asia*. London: Routledge.

Ellett, R.L. (2008) *Emerging judicial power in transitional democracies: Malawi, Tanzania and Uganda*. Northeastern University, Boston. Available at: https://www.researchgate.net/publication/45062613_Emerging_Judicial_Power_in_Transitional_Democracies_Malawi_Tanzania_and_Uganda (accessed 29 February 2016).

Gauri, V. (2015) 'The Judicialization of Development Policy', in Heller, P. and Rao, V. (eds) *Deliberation and Development: Rethinking the Role of Voice and Collective Action in Unequal Societies*, Washington, DC: World Bank Group Publications, pp. 223–8.

Gaynor, N. (2010) 'Between citizenship and clientship: The politics of participatory governance in Malawi'. *Journal of Southern African Studies*,36(4): 801–16.

Gloppen, S. and Kanyongolo, F.E. (2012) 'Judicial Independence and the Judicialisation of Electoral Politics in Malawi and Uganda', in Chirwa, D.M. and Nijzink, L. (eds.), *Accountable Government in Africa: Perspectives from Public Law and Political Studies*. Cape Town: University of Cape Town Press.

Helmke, G. and Levitsky, S. (2006) *Informal institutions and democracy: Lessons from Latin America*. Baltimore, MD: Johns Hopkins University Press.

Ingram, M.C. (2015) 'Judicial Power in Latin America'. *Latin American Research Review*, 50(1): 250–60.

Kmiec, K.D. (2004) 'The Origin and Current Meanings of "Judicial Activism"'. *California Law Review*, 92(5): 1441–77.

Leiter, B. (2014) 'Marx, Law, Ideology, Legal Positivism'. University of Chicago Public Law Working Paper No. 482, available at http://papers.ssrn.com/sol3/papers.cfm?abstract_id=2465672 (accessed 29 February 2016).

Lindell, I. (2010) 'Informality and collective organising: identities, alliances and transnational activism in Africa'. *Third World Quarterly*, 31(2): 207–22.

Miraftab, F. (2006) 'Feminist praxis, citizenship and informal politics: reflections on South Africa's anti-Eviction Campaign'. *International Feminist Journal Of Politics*, 8(2): 194–218.

Mvula, P., Njaya, F. and Kalindekafe, M. (2014) 'Defragmenting management of the Lake Chilwa basin resources', in Mvula, P., Kalindekafe, M., Kishindo, P. Berge, E. and Njaya, F. (eds.) *Towards Defragmenting The Management System Of Lake Chilwa Basin, Malawi*, Cape Town: University of the Western Cape, pp. 129–31.

Ninsin, K. (2000) 'Informalization And Ghanaian Politics', in Lauer, H. (ed.) *Ghana: Changing Values/Changing Technologies*, Washington, DC: The Council For Research In Values And Philosophy.

Rakner, L., Mukubvu, L., Ngwira, N., Smiddy, K. and Schneider, A. (2004) *The budget as theatre: the formal and informal institutional makings of the budget process in Malawi*. Bergen: Chr. Michelsen Institute. Available at: http://www.cmi.no/publications/

publication/?1928=the-budget-as-theatre-the-formal-and-informal　(accessed　29 February 2016).

Schärf, W., Banda, C., Röntsch, R., Kaunda, D. and Shapiro, R. (2002) *Access to Justice for the Poor of Malawi? An appraisal of access to justice provided to the poor of Malawi by the lower subordinate courts and the customary justice forums.* Available at: http://www.gsdrc. org/document-library/access-to-justice-for-the-poor-of-malawi-an-appraisal-of-access-to-justice-provided-to-the-poor-of-malawi-by-the-lower-courts-and-the-customary-j-ustice-forums/ (accessed 29 February 2016).

Unger, R.M. (2015) *The Critical Legal Studies Movement: Another Time, a Greater Task.* London and New York: Verso Books.

UNDP (U/D) *Inclusive Development*, available at: http://www.undp.org/content/undp/en/ home/ourwork/povertyreduction/focus_areas/focus_inclusive_development.html (accessed 29 February 2016).

Vom Hau, M. (2012) 'State capacity and inclusive development: new challenges and directions'. Effective States and Inclusive Development Research Centre (ESID) Working Paper 2. Available at: http://r4d.dfid.gov.uk/Output/189981/ (accessed 28 February 2016).

Vondoepp, P. (2005) 'The problem of judicial control in Africa's neopatrimonial democracies: Malawi and Zambia.' *Political Science Quarterly*, 120(2): 275–301.

Vondoepp, P. (2009) *Judicial Politics in New Democracies: Cases from Southern Africa.* Boulder, CO: Lynne Rienner Publishers.

Part II

Governance and policy implementation

5 Politics and the public service

Lewis B. Dzimbiri

Introduction

The public service is the main tool governments use to implement various national development policies and deliver services in education, health, community development, transport and maintenance of law and order, among others. It is seen as pivotal for the growth of African economies and the creation of an appropriate and conducive environment in which all sectors of the economy can perform optimally. Governments rely on this machinery to design, formulate and implement its policies, strategies and programmes, and to discharge all routine governmental functions. Human resources play an important and strategic role in the implementation of national development policies. The manner in which civil servants are recruited, selected, appointed, oriented, trained, rewarded and disciplined affect their commitment, motivation and productivity. The overall purpose of this chapter is to analyse the role and impact of politics on public service human resource management systems and service delivery in Malawi.

Using a purposive sampling technique in a cross-sectional study design employing in-depth interviews and questionnaires, this study focuses on ministers, principal secretaries (hereafter PSs) and human resource management directors in key ministries such as Office of the President and Cabinet, Agriculture, Education, Health and the Department of Human Resource Management and Development. The questionnaires solicited responses regarding the broad roles of ministers and PSs in relation to policy formulation, implementation, monitoring and evaluation. Specific questions concentrated on the role of ministers and PSs in public service human resource management, in particular recruitment, promotion, demotion, discipline and transfers. Data collected was analysed through content analysis to derive themes and subthemes based on the responses to questionnaires and in-depth interviews guided by the study objectives. This also applied to secondary data from documents and reports. Central issues examined include the role of elite public servants and politicians in the public administration system in Malawi and the nature and impact of the relationship between these elite public servants and cabinet ministers on a range of issues related to human resource management and service delivery in government departments.

The chapter begins with an overview of the context in which the Malawian public service operates followed by a discussion of the politics and administration interface as a theoretical framework for the ensuing discussion. The aim is to critically examine the role of ministers and principal secretaries in public policy processes and their roles in public service human resource management functions particularly in relation to recruitment, promotion, discipline and transfer.

The public service context in Malawi

Malawi became independent from Britain in 1964. Since then, the country has transitioned from a multiparty democracy to a one-party dictatorship and then returned to multiparty democracy in the 1990s. In the 1960s, and through the 1970s and 1980s, Malawi developed so-called 'Statement of Development Policies', meant to function as development roadmaps providing a list of priorities and strategies that were to function as guidelines for the government. Similarly, in the 1990s, the Ministry of Economic Planning and Development developed the Malawi Poverty Reduction strategy with assistance from the World Bank, and thereafter Vision 2020 in 1998 and the Malawi Growth and Development Strategy (MGDS 1 and MDGS 2) during 2003–12. These documents provided directions for realizing medium and long-term development policies aimed at promoting social and economic development of Malawi.

The documents highlight sustainable economic growth and social development; social support and disaster risk management; infrastructure development; governance and gender and capacity development. They also include agriculture and food security; energy, industrial development, mining and tourism; transport infrastructure and port development. Key priority areas for these national documents are: education science and technology; public health, sanitation, malaria, and management of HIV/AIDS; integrated rural development; green belt irrigation and water development; child development, youth development and empowerment; climate change, natural resources and environmental management (GoM, 2013). The ambitious national plans require an engaged, motivated, trained, disciplined and professional public service.

The public service

A public service is defined as a service that is provided by the government to the people living within its jurisdiction either directly through the public sector or by financing provision of the services to the people. The term 'government' means the authority in which is vested the executive power in a nation according to the constitution. In the context of Malawi, public services include the health service, teaching service, military service, police service; prison service, local government service, parliamentary service, judicial service, anti-corruption service, public enterprises/statutory corporations, office of the ombudsman, human rights commission and the law commission (Kachimera, 2014).

The public service largely consists of educated, well-trained and career-oriented personnel. These include primary and secondary school teachers, field assistants, community development staff, agricultural officers, executive officers, clerical and accounting staff, secretarial staff, human resource officers, administrators, and various professional and technical staff such as engineers, scientists, doctors, health professionals, directors, undersecretaries, lawyers, judges and magistrates. These individuals work in ministries, in government departments and in other branches of government, such as the judiciary, parliament and other public institutions such as city, municipal, town and district councils, parastatal bodies and commissions (Dzimbiri, 2014). The Department of Human Resource Management and Development under the Office of the President and Cabinet is mandated to be responsible for public service administration and management on behalf of the Chief Secretary to the Government. This department provides HRM services and management consultancy services for the public service, conducts policy research, monitoring and evaluation, internal audit services and administrative and general support services

Since Malawi became independent from Great Britain in 1964, it has relied on the public sector as the machinery responsible for the implementation of the national development policies and programmes.

As a former colony (1891–1964), Malawi's public service was influenced by the norms and procedures of the British public service in relation to rules and regulations and governing principles that embrace the principles recommended in the Northcote–Trevelyan Report of 1854, such as political impartiality, objectivity, integrity, accountability, confidentiality, open recruitment, promotion on merit basis. The guidelines of the Public Service Commission created in 1961 by the British colonial administration continue to provide the basis for recruitment, promotion and discipline of public servants in addition to the efficient and effective delivery of public services in the country. Although there was considerable political will by President Hastings Banda's regime to deliver efficient development services, the administrative structures remained highly centralized and the style of management was heavily expatriate-influenced (Kachimera, 2014).

A series of public service reforms were implemented in Malawi following the outcomes of the Skinner Commission of 1964. The Herbercq Commission of 1985 like the Skinner Commission advocated the reorganization of the public service in terms of structure, staffing, governing principles, pay levels, career paths, education, training and conditions of service.

The democratic transition to multiparty politics in 1994 transformed the public service. While the President appointed the Secretary to the Office of the President and Cabinet, principal secretaries were appointed as supervisors of government ministries. Most importantly, however, the openness of the political climate led to the birth of unionism, and representatives of public servants could now negotiate with the government on increased salaries and improved conditions of services. The Malawian Public Service Commission continued to observe and adhere to its fundamental principles of fairness, openness and appointment on merit. A Public

Service Act (1994) was enacted to compliment the new Constitution (1994), which was framed with a view to addressing human rights violations during the period of one-party rule. The immediate challenge for a democratic Malawi was to balance the need for continuity of the public service systems and practices and resolutely exclude the negative practices of the previous dictatorial government. However, the newfound freedom also resulted in lawlessness, and the public service, which was renowned for its discipline during the one-party Banda regime, began to crumble under the pressure to deliver development amidst technical and management skills shortage and weak financial management.

The politics and administration dichotomy

The relationship between ministers and administrative heads of ministries in policy processes need to be understood in the context of the various arguments for or against the separation of politics from administration. The politics–administration dichotomy is the underpinning feature of Max Weber's ideal bureaucracy, where the main role of politicians is policymaking while administrators tackle the task of policy implementation (Rosenbloom, 2008). Weber viewed administrators as instrumental and subordinate to politicians, functioning as technical experts who advise and efficiently execute the decisions of politicians. However, while politicians are in charge of defining the policies to be implemented by bureaucrats, Weber feared that career civil servants might dominate elected politicians (whose tenure of office is a bit shorter) through their superior knowledge, technical expertise and longer experience.

The dichotomy between public administration and politics – which is based on the notion of dividing governmental authority between elected and administrative officials along functional lines – has remained an important question since the emergence of public administration as a field of study in the late 1880s. For example, Wilson (1887) argued for the separation of politics from public administration when he pointed out that public administration lies outside the proper sphere of politics. Public administration scholars have since then proposed numerous explanations and theoretical models in their attempts to understand the role of public administration in the political process. Three schools —have since emerged to explain the politics–administration dichotomy:

- the separation school;
- the political school; and
- the interaction school.

The separation school

The separation school analyses the relationship between politics and administration, arguing that the function of politics is to provide guidance, or, as Wilson (1887) put it, 'setting the task for administration' and public administration functions to provide neutral competence to the policy process. Thus, elected officials provide political guidance through policy leadership and legislative oversight. On the other hand public administrators are responsible for the implementation of policies in conformity with legislative intentions and instructions. Proponents of the separation school argue that good government is usually synonymous with an efficient and effective public service. The effectiveness with which policies are implemented and services are delivered is dependent to a large extent on how these policies are formulated, implemented and evaluated. Under the career service model, a politically neutral public service is recruited on merit, and given tenure to encourage frank and fearless advice and protect it from electoral whims, thus enabling it to serve a government of any political persuasion.

Sossin (2006) outlines six key principles that should govern the politics and administration interface in order to safeguard neutrality of the public service:

- Politics and policy are separated from administration, and politicians make policy decisions and public servants execute these decisions.
- Public servants are appointed and promoted on the basis of merit rather than of party affiliation or contributions.
- Public servants do not engage in partisan political activities.
- Public servants do not express publicly their personal views on government policies or administration.
- Public servants provide forthright and objective advice to their political masters in private and in confidence; in return, political executives protect the anonymity of public servants by publicly accepting responsibility for departmental decisions.
- Public servants execute policy decisions loyally, irrespective of the philosophy and programmes of the party in power and regardless of their personal opinions.

The political school

Scholars belonging to the political school reject the politics–administration distinction as they view public administration to be an inseparable part of the political process (Long, 1954; Bosworth, 1958; Pfiffner, 1985; Miller, 1993). Factors such as vague and ambiguous legislation, lack of technical knowledge and difficulties in monitoring and controlling bureaucratic behaviour are used to justify the critical role of public administrators in the policy process. Indeed, public administrators are viewed as policymakers and policy advocates (Lipsky, 1980). Thus the political approach rejects the subordinate and instrumental role of public administration in relating to elected officials. Such views, however, face challenges of their own, which forced the British public service in the nineteenth century to protest when bureaucrats realized that politicians were handing out public sector jobs to friends and supporters – practices that were exacerbating corruption, favouritism, politicization and inefficiency. As a result, the Northcote–Trevelyan Report (1854) appealed for a meritocratic system that would enhance public administration performance.

The interaction school

The interaction school emphasizes a high degree of collaboration between elected and administrative officials with each maintaining their traditional roles but also adding unique perspectives by crossing traditional boundaries and operating inside each others' terrain. Thus, the interaction school seeks a middle ground between the separation and political schools, and acknowledges the differences between politics and administration in a number of ways, such as logical and psychological differences between politics and administration, and dissimilarities in the perspectives, values, and formal positions of elected and administrative officials (Waldo, 1980; Nalbandian, 1994; Svara, 2001). Yet, what makes the interaction school somewhat different from the separation school is its emphasis on on-going cooperation between elected and administrative officials in the process of policymaking. In the 1960s and 1970s, ministers in Commonwealth Africa were more dependent on the advice of principal secretaries, but since the 1980s the role of ministers has changed to the extent that most ministers are now not only involved in policymaking, but also interested in ensuring that those policies and relevant programmes and projects are effectively implemented (Kathyola, 2010). As better-educated ministers with public sector experience have come into the administration, the tendency for ministers to do much more than their predecessors has increased, with some performing roles that traditionally belonged to the principal secretary. Most ministers at times usurp the roles of a principal secretary (Kathyola, 2010).

Relations between politics and management

The relations between politics and management (administration), as Demir and Nyhan (2008) note, is complex. In reality, a continuum rather than a dichotomy appears relevant in most political systems. The overlap of roles and functions between elected officials and public administrators on policy and administration are diverse, illuminating a more variable version of their day-to-day relations (Demir, 1993). In recent years, the New Public Management (NPM) movement has called for new ways of running governments, as one would run a business, resulting in a reshaping of the relations among politicians, administrators, markets and citizens (Svara, 2001). Existing literature on the interface between politics and administration frequently agrees that in theory there is a division between political and administrative roles but in practice it is impossible to define a marked border between political and administrative actors (Mulgan, 2007).

Role of actors in public policy processes in Malawi: ministers and principal secretaries (PSs)

This section examines the role of ministers and PSs in policy processes in Malawi in order to determine the extent to which Malawi's experience reflect any of the models of politics and administration relationships discussed above.

Ministers in Malawi are 'political heads of government ministries'. Their roles in the public service machinery include, among others, the provision of political leadership and direction of the ministries to which they are appointed. In this regard, they are accountable to the public on the performance of their ministry and as such they articulate policies aimed at enhancing the performance of their ministries. They are answerable to the President for the efficient performance of their ministries/departments and, collectively, for the government. PSs, on the other hand, provide professional leadership in their ministries, and are involved in policy formulation, strategic planning and management, financial management and human resource management. They are the contact points in the public service; their effectiveness in discharging their responsibilities is critical to the ministries' performance. They are also viewed as executive heads of their ministries and departments in which they are responsible for day-to-day operations for all public service matters. As one key informant put it, PSs are essentially 'boundary spanners between the technical and the political structures in the ministry'.

Public policy had been defined by Dye (1995) as 'whatever government chooses to do or not to do' and the public policy process entails a series of related activities in the task of initiating, formulating, legitimizing, implementing, monitoring and evaluating policies in the public sector. In the ensuing sections, we will examine the relationship between politicians and their principal secretaries by focusing on three sets of interrelated processes related to policy formulation, implementation and evaluation/monitoring.

Formulation of public policy

From the above definition of public policy, it is evident that public policy results from the decisions of government to do something. The Government of Malawi faces numerous challenges that affect citizens, including HIV/AIDS, poverty, crime, and drought and food insecurity. Since governments must address such challenges, they are under pressure to formulate a deliberate plan or decision to address public concerns.

Ministers formulate policies through Cabinet committees of which they are members. At ministerial level, their role in policy formulation is to ensure that policies relating to smooth operations of their ministries are articulated and formulated. In this regard, they provide direction to the PSs in order to ensure that proper policies are formulated. Ministers also take the lead in determining policy objectives based on which PSs devise strategies for implementation. Once policies have been developed, ministers approve them before they are submitted to the Cabinet for approval.

In contrast to their ministers, the role of principal secretaries in policy formulation is 'to provide full, honest and impartial advice' (as one informant put it) to the ministers to enable them to articulate proper policy decisions. Another PS argued that they 'provide technical advice in the policy formulation process, as well as advice on how the policies can best be implemented'. At the operational level, PSs allocate financial, material and human resources to supervise the policy formulation process. For example, they may decide to organize workshops and other forums where various stakeholders such as political leaders, civil servants, NGOs and traditional leaders can discuss the issues before developing a draft policy for further refinement.

Policy implementation

According to Hayes (2001), public policy implementation consists of organized activities by governments directed towards the achievement of goals and objectives, articulated in authorized policy statements. The process of policy implementation is affected by various factors such as the nature of the problem, circumstances surrounding them, the administrative machinery in charge of the task and available resources. In Malawi, once policies have been formulated, ministers 'provide political leadership' aimed at their implementation. The role of ministers in policy implementation, as one minister noted, is first 'to lobby for mobilization of resources for the effective implementation' of the policies. At the start of the implementation of a particular policy, Malawian ministers typically preside over a ceremonial opening or placing of a foundation stone. As the implementation process progresses, ministers perform monitoring functions. In this regard, they provide checks and balances to ensure proper implementation of the articulated policies. It is thus not uncommon to hear on radio, television or in the newspapers that a particular minister is touring institutions in his ministry, and inspecting progress being made on projects he or she has officially launched.

Principal secretaries are implementers of the policies formulated by the ministers, and are required to update ministers on the policy implementation process and propose options for overcoming any obstacles in the policy implementation process. They implement the policies through officers below them, such as deputy secretaries, directors, undersecretaries, chief human resource officers and various technical, professional and clerical staff, including artisans. As one informant observed, the PSs implement policies 'to the best of their ability and enable the ministries to achieve their goals' of effective public service delivery. Another respondent claimed that 'PSs are therefore responsible for all the managerial functions of planning, organizing, directing, and coordination budgeting and reporting for the implementation of the policies.'

Policy monitoring and evaluation

Policy monitoring relates to ensuring that a policy is working towards achieving the objectives of an organization. In other words, it entails the routine collection of data on a particular policy in order for management to assess the progress it is making in the implementation process. Administrators produce reports on a daily, monthly and quarterly basis. Policy monitoring examines the schedule (trend) of impact of the policy regardless of whether positive or negative. According to Dunn (1994), policy outcome is an observed consequence of policy action, and such observed consequences may be intended or unintended. The impact of any policy can be positive as well as negative on the target situation or group. It can also impact on the future as well as immediate conditions, or through direct costs in terms of resources devoted to the programme and indirect costs in relations to lost alternatives (Dye, 1995).

In Malawi, ministers are responsible for ensuring that the policies they have formulated with the help of PSs result in the expected impact or results. They are therefore keen to know the political consequences of their policies during and/or after implementation. As they are responsible for the organization of policy reviews and recommendation of improvements where applicable to cabinet and or parliament, a minister's role during the evaluation process is to first assess whether the policy objectives and goals were met and thereafter provide guidance on how to address the gaps, if any.

PSs, on the other hand, are 'responsible for ensuring that they put in place mechanisms for evaluating the policies, and coordinate the process of reviewing these policies'. This can be undertaken through regular management meetings with heads of sections, quarterly reports and mid-term evaluation, as well as end of project evaluation. In some instances, PSs 'use workshops to hear stakeholders' views and perception on successes of the policies' while on other occasions, 'they also use consultants to undertake an independent review and provide a report on achievements and challenges as well as recommendations'. Thus, PSs normally brief their minister on the outcomes of the evaluations and advise on solutions.

From the above discussion, it appears that there is a division of labour between the minister and principal secretaries in policy formulation, implementation and evaluation. Indeed, there is no clear-cut dichotomy to suggest that ministers only formulate policy and principal secretaries only implement it. Each one of them has a role in the entire policy processes. Based on this preliminary discussion, it also appears that the integration school discussed above is more relevant in the context of Malawi in terms of the relationship between politics and administration in policy processes.

Human resource management processes in the Malawian public service

The main roles and responsibilities of top-level civil servants (or 'principal secretaries' (or PSs) as is the case in Malawi) in charge of ministries include managing the human resources of the ministry and to ensure increased productivity and quality of service to the citizenry. It is important to examine the human resource management processes in the Malawi public service in order to determine the nature and impact of the interface between elected politicians and administrative heads of ministries on people management because an efficient and effective public service machinery needs proper systems of appointments, promotion, transfers and discipline handling.

Recruitment, selection and appointment

Recruitment is the process of generating a pool of capable individuals who are stimulated to apply for employment in an organization (Dzimbiri, 2015; Armstrong, 2010). Selection is the process by which managers and others use specific instruments to choose from a pool of applicants a person or persons more likely to succeed in the jobs (Dzimbiri, 2015; Armstrong, 2010). Effective recruitment and selection practices identify job applicants with the appropriate level of knowledge, skills, abilities and other requirements needed for successful performance in a job or an organization. Positive economic outcomes for the organization are highly dependent on hiring people with the right skills or the highest level of these skills.

According to public service procedures in Malawi, the PS plays a very important part in the recruitment and selection processes in a ministry. The PS is required to ensure that the ministry has adequate staff with relevant knowledge, skills and attitudes to adequately support the minister in the implementation of the policies. Recruitment of staff and procurement of resources and other services are based on the activities identified for achieving policy goals. Moreover, where good policies are in place, they will lead to recruitment of suitable and qualified people, making it easy for the principal secretary to manage the implementation process. However, the provision of financial resources (the minister's responsibility) in the policy cycle may positively or negatively affect the motivation of human resources in the ministry.

The PS's role in recruitment is to declare and recommend vacancies to the Malawian Civil Service Commission for advertisement and selection of suitable candidates. Once candidates are selected, the PS is then directed by the commission to make an offer of appointment to the candidates. The first Malawian Public Service Commission – established in 1961 – was modelled on the British system. Over the years, however, the Malawian public service has expanded greatly and more specialized service commissions have been created including the teaching services commission, civil service commission, health service commission, judicial service commission, police service commission and prison service commission. In order to fill vacancies in the ministry, the PS contacts the appropriate commission and provides information on the number of positions available and the qualifications, skills and experience required to fill these. The appropriate commission advertises these positions in newspapers and government circulars, and also receives applications, which it sends back to the PS for shortlisting. Thereafter, the commission conducts interviews either with the PS in attendance or with a representative of the ministry sitting on the interview panel. Once candidates are selected, the commission directs the PS to finalize the appointment.

The above procedure is largely followed for middle- and junior-level appointments in the ministry. Top-level public servants – including the Chief Secretary, PSs, CEOs of parastatals and under-secretaries – are appointed by the President. This trend of politically influenced appointments in the public service is also increasingly the practice in the lower echelons. Indeed, as one PS argued, 'it is an open secret that some ministers influence recruitment by directing top-level civil servants to favour relatives, friends and close contacts of the minister.' Ever since the introduction of democracy and multiparty politics in 1994, successive governments have exercised their influence to appoint, promote, transfer and dismiss senior public servants of their choice without following correct procedures. This has often resulted in frequent allegations of political favouritism in important appointments, which have tended to overlook the qualifications and seniority of relevant candidates. Thus, it has become well accepted that almost all PSs are political appointees of the President. And this trend has resulted in a situation whereby the number of PSs in the public service increased to 96 in 2015, despite far fewer ministries. It is not uncommon, therefore, to find more than one PS in certain ministries (e.g. education, which has three), creating problems of overlap of functions and power struggles. The government has attempted to address this problem in September 2015 by directing that PSs who were not called 'Secretary for . . . ' say education, heath, agriculture, would be demoted to the position of chief director, who is merely a section head. As a result of this strategy, the total number of PSs in Malawi has now been reduced to 21. The issue of political interference in appointment has been highlighted by the Public Service Reform Commission headed by the Vice-President as one of the key perceptions held by various people in Malawi.

Promotion

Promotion is a change of assignment to a job at a higher level in the organization and includes the expansion of benefits and managerial authority over other employees in return for higher pay, benefits and privileges (Armstrong, 2010). Psychologically, promotions help satisfy employees' needs for security, belonging and personal growth. Promotions should receive the same careful attention as any other employment decisions to minimize concerns by those who feel themselves to be more deserving than those promoted.

   In the Malawian public service, the procedures for promotion are similar to those on recruitment, selection and appointment explained above. Thus, the relevant service commission advertises in the newspapers and government circulars, on the recommendation of the principal secretary of a ministry that has vacancies. The commission receives applications from qualified individuals (invariably those already employed in the public service), which it then forwards to the relevant ministry for shortlisting. It conducts interviews of shortlisted candidates, in the presence of a representative of the ministry on the interview panel. The commission then directs the ministry (through the principal secretary) to promote the successful candidates. For other levels above S5, the commission submits a list to the President and recommends that the listed officers be promoted. Once the approval has been granted, the commission effects the promotion. That is, from position of undersecretary (S5) through deputy secretary (S4) and senior deputy secretary (S3), the Civil Service commission simply recommend names to the Chief Secretary to the Government for the President to endorse the recommendations for promotion or even reject the list altogether.

In addition to the above procedure, political interference plays a crucial role in promotions in the public service. Particularly in relation to key appointments, the President has substantial power and influence, which may disregard the public service staff establishment and budgetary considerations. As one key informer lamented, 'It is no wonder that instead of having 40 PSs, we ended up having 96.' Several respondents in the study also cite the case of the Joyce Banda administration, which directed the Ministry of Education to promote all teachers at grade PT4 who had not been promoted since they started working. The consequence of this directive from the President was the promotion of almost 20,000 teachers to PT4 level, which in turn posed enormous burdens on the state exchequer. To make things worse, and given budget constraints, the government was unable to pay these newly promoted teachers their new salaries for over two years. Indeed, this entire scenario could have been avoided had the decision on promotion been placed under the control of the PS in the Ministry of Education. In another instance, a respondent cited the case of 'unqualified officers promoted to district commissioner positions in Neno, Chitipa and Machinga districts, forcing the Minister of Local Government to bring them back to where they belong'. In other words, the minister demoted them to their original grades. This directive was resisted through court injunctions, causing inconveniences and stalemate to service provision in districts affected. As the injunctions still stand, the officers have continued to enjoy the privileges of a higher office to which they were initially promoted.

Demotion

Demotion is the process of reducing an employee's grade because of underperformance or misbehaviour at work. Thus, it is part of disciplining the employee for failure to perform according to a desired standard or for an offence committed while performing duties (Employment Act 2000; Dzimbiri, 2015) The appropriate service commission metes out demotion as a punishment and this applies for the majority of the employees whose appointment or promotion is not handled by the President or the minister. However, demotions can also be effected for senior positions on directives from the political and administrative leadership. The controversial case of district commissioners of Chitipa, Machinga and Chiradzulu (mentioned above) has often been cited by respondents as an example of improper procedures practiced in cases of demotion. There are further controversial cases demonstrating the negative impact of ministers in the public service:

- A directive was issued in 2015 by the Minister of Local Government which aimed at abolishing the position of chiefs in urban areas. This directive was severely contested by the concerned chiefs, who garnered support from fellow chiefs to challenge the decision. The said minister was left out in a cabinet reshuffle of 2015 and the matter died a natural death.

- The appointment, by the President, of a chief secretary to the government to become Malawi's High Commissioner on a foreign posting. This act was viewed as a punishment as the former chief secretary – who was the supervisor of all principal secretaries in government – suddenly had to report to the PS in the Ministry of Foreign Affairs. Such a situation should not have occurred if proper procedures of appointment or transfer were employed, as the officer in question was not at fault. The demotion simply occurred during a change of government, as the officer was perceived to be loyal to the former regime.

Transfer

Transfer is the placement of an employee in another job for which the duties, responsibilities, status pay and benefits are equal to those of the previous job. Others describe a transfer as reassignments to similar positions in other parts of the organization (Dzimbiri, 2015). A transfer requires the employee to change work group, work place, work shift or organizational unit. Transfers make it possible for an organization to place its employees in jobs where there is a greater need for their service and/or where they can acquire new knowledge and skills. Transfers can also be advocated to expose people to a wider range of jobs or to fill open positions with trained employees.

In the Malawian public service, transfer can be between posts or a move to another workstation where there is a vacancy to be filled. Transfer between posts occurs when for instance a secondary school teacher applies and succeeds in an interview for the post of protocol officer in the Ministry of Foreign Affairs. The process also involves the relevant service commission that conducted interviews notifying the relevant ministry of successful candidates. The transfer between posts in this case is the joint responsibility of the two ministries.

However, as with recruitments and promotions, political interference in the transfer of public servants is commonplace in Malawi. There have been numerous such cases over the years – for example, an army commander was transferred to become a general manager of a parastatal body; political leaders without requisite qualifications have been appointed to senior management positions of parastatal bodies; officials from city councils and universities have been transferred to ministries at very high-level positions; junior officers have been transferred to prestigious posts at the direction of a politician. Such arbitrary transfers not only distort the well-established procedures of the public services, but also are a major source of demotivation among public servants.

With the consolidation of democracy in Malawi, political parties are getting accustomed to losing power at regular intervals. When a new government assumes office, it appoints its preferred candidate to the post of Chief Secretary just as it may place its favourite officers in senior management positions and demote, transfer or forcibly retire those it considers loyal to the previous administration. The result of such practices is lack of continuity in experience and a tendency to encourage making hay while the sun shines. Consequently, there are considerable incentives in the public service to extract resources for personal gain while in power, and before a new party is voted into office. Another negative consequence is short-term policies that result from the fear that any long-term commitments will inevitably be reversed by a new leadership. And the PSs feel pressurised to bend rules and generally operate in an unprofessional manner simply to please their political bosses and save their careers.

It was therefore not surprising that most respondents in this study held the view that political interference not only routinely takes place in relation to promotions and transfers, but is often exacerbated when a new government assumes office. The Public Service Review Commission reported the perceived political interference in the Malawi public service, and therefore recommended that certain key positions – Attorney General, Governor of the Reserve Bank, Chief Secretary to Government, Director General of Malawi Broadcasting Corporation, Inspector General of Police, Commander of the Malawi Defence Force, Secretary to the Treasury and Budget Director, amongst others – should follow presidential tenure of office (GoM, 2014: 5). This is a controversial recommendation because of the impact such a system will have on the performance of public servants when they know that their careers terminate after a presidential term. As one informant rightly noted, an important consequence will be 'a lack of continuity in organisational memory, inefficient utilisation of resources and misappropriation of public monies between governments'.

Discipline

Discipline can be defined as actions or behaviour on the part of authorities in an organization aimed at restraining all employees from behaviours that threaten to disrupt the functioning of the organization. It is thus the means by which supervisory personnel correct behavioural deficiencies and ensure adherence to established company rules. The purpose of discipline is to correct behaviour and not just to punish or embarrass an employee. Disciplinary procedures and corrective-action policies establish guidelines for employee performance and behaviour and add an essential component to the overall management system. Disciplinary action initiated by management is a way of counteracting poor work performance and unacceptable behaviour at work. However, proper procedures must be followed in all disciplinary cases.

The Malawi Public Service Regulations stipulate 26 acts of misconduct, including insubordination, absenteeism, theft, corruption, involvement in party politics and financial embarrassment, that can attract disciplinary proceedings. The PSs are keen to oversee the enforcement of discipline in their ministries to ensure that staff are adhering to the public service code of ethics and conduct, Malawi Public Service Regulations, the Public Service Act, Employment Act, administrative circular letters and relevant statutes. Procedures for handling disciplinary matters and the role of controlling officers (PSs) and relevant service commission in the disciplinary process are also stipulated in the Malawi Public Service Regulations. The suspected employee is interdicted from the work place while the alleged misconduct is being investigated. And a hearing must be conducted in a fair and transparent manner, with the participation of the interdicted officer. The decision of the relevant commission – demotion, transfer, withholding of increment or dismissal – is subsequently communicated to the officer, who has the right to appeal.

There are several issues of discipline that the Public Service Commission has noted as prevalent in the Malawi public service. For example, the Commission noted that 'there is a senior government management paralysis with regards to their supervisory roles'. The Commission also noted that junior staff continue to violate set rules and procedures relating to performance and time management, among others, and that PSs and other senior government officials continue to ignore such acts and/or omissions which have put government business in a state of paralysis. This has created what the Commission calls 'camaraderie buddy-buddy relationships between the senior government officials and their juniors'. The Commission further observed that the senior–junior government official relationships are responsible for a state of 'mental siege' on the part of the senior government officials, and paralyses them into inaction (GoM, 2014: 2–5).

It is evident from the Commission's sentiments that 'there is fear by Senior Government officials of their juniors as well as lack of respect by junior staff of their superiors' and 'absenteeism [is] not sanctioned and is contrary to the provisions of the Malawi Public Service Regulations'. The Commission noted that 'such unregulated absenteeism is leading to serious disruption of services and has a negative impact on delivery of services in most ministries, departments and agencies (MDAs)'. Hence, the Commission recommended that senior government officials should exercise their mandates and discipline insubordinate staff without fear or favour, in line with Malawi Public Service Regulations. They also recommended that, 'any absence from the office should be authorised, in line with the provisions and requirements of Malawi Public Service Regulations'. And that 'all Controlling Officers be reminded that they have an obligation to enforce these regulations and ensure that Government services are always provided without disruption'. In addition, the Commission recommended that senior officers be empowered to enforce the rules and regulations of the public service in their MDAs (GoM, 2014: 2–5).

Minister–PS relationship in Malawi

Experiences of most Commonwealth countries in Africa indicate that a tension-filled relationship between a minister and a principal secretary can divide a ministry and turn it into a micro-political battlefield – undermining the overall effectiveness of the organization (CAPAM, 2007). A positive relationship between these two on the other hand can motivate the whole organization to deliver, regardless of the level of technical, managerial and leadership competencies of the minister. Without the support of a competent civil service, political leaders would not be able to effectively translate the aspirations of the people into policies; nor would they be able to ensure that the implementation of these policies have positive impacts on the lives of the people.

In order to avoid friction, the relationship between the minister and principal secretary needs to be founded on 'trust, cultivating values of integrity, professionalism, respect, openness and learning' (CAPAM, 2007: 5). Walter (2007) points out that PSs need to develop their collective self-confidence and are to be responsive to but independent of the minister; they should take care of themselves to avoid burn-out and learn how to work with other PS colleagues instead of undermining each other. What then is the relationship between ministers and administrative heads of the ministries?

According to one of the key informants, 'The relationship between the minister and principal secretary in Malawi varies from one personality to another.' He went on to observe that 'On average it is satisfactory, although in certain cases the professionalism of PSs may sometimes be compromised due to political pressures exerted by ministers especially in resource allocation.' Another respondent noted, 'PSs are political appointees and this sometimes makes it impossible for them to apolitical.' Still others claimed that the relationship is harmonious in some ministries while in others it is 'uneasy and full of suspicion'. Such realities create a number of challenges that PSs face. For example, ministers and their PSs may not have a common understanding and a shared vision of their ministry, and risk ending up making decisions at odds with one another and to the detriment of their ministries. Moreover, they also risk not articulating good policies or recruiting the right calibre of staff, which in the long term may result in the failure to manage the human resources as well as deliver efficient public services.

As a minister noted 'the minister typically wants to deliver results within the shortest possible time in order to win the next election or return to power'. As such he or she may want to take shortcuts in the implementation of the policies. In contrast, the PS may wish to follow correct administrative procedures and this often becomes the source of mistrust and conflict between the two. Another challenge is when ministers make 'ineffectual decisions' for PSs to implement. This adversely affects morale, as professionalism starts to deteriorate. Examples of such decisions include a PS who was asked to open a bank account using a single signature for use by the minister and later, when allegations of misappropriation of funds emerged, the PS was interdicted and charged with misconduct, and eventually dismissed. Another case involved a minister who instructed a PS to procure items outside the procurement procedures. This led to the indictment of the PS on allegation of abuse of public office and subsequent disciplinary hearing and dismissal. Under such instances, a senior official observed that 'PSs are always victims, yet the ministers come out clean.' And a large majority of these incidents are revealed when the minister's term is over or when new ministers have come in. As one PS noted, 'one dilemma is that when the PS stands his ground and says "No" to an instruction from the minister, it is interpreted as insubordination.' A case was cited of a PS who refused to withdraw money from a government account despite the instructions of his minister and was subsequently removed from his position for some time before being posted to another institution outside the civil service.

A good working relationship built on trust and mutual respect between ministers and principal secretaries is paramount for the effective functioning of a ministry. Ministers provide political leadership and the overall direction for their respective ministries while PSs professionally manage and administer day-to-day activities of the ministry. In order for both sets of actors to perform their functions effectively, they need to have a common understanding as well as a shared vision of their ministries, in addition to open communication and a participative style of management. This will help ensure that public servants are encouraged to perform to the best of their abilities; and that good performance is recognized and properly rewarded and the reputation of neither minister nor the PS (or for that matter of the ministry) is not tarnished (Colley, 2005). As one respondent pointed out, 'this requires reasonableness and understanding on both sides.' He further argued that 'properly organised management meetings where staff can appreciate each other's shortcomings and develop mutual trust' should be the proper *modus operandi* in ministries to create a conducive political–administrative interface.

Apart from political interference in appointment and promotion in the public service, the lack of ethics and accountability are another set of challenges. There have been numerous cases reported over the past few years regarding corrupt tendencies in the ministries and government departments, local government and parastatal bodies. In spite of various public sector reforms in procurement, financial management and functioning service commissions, there are enormous public concerns about the prevalence of corrupt tendencies, moral decadence and nepotism in both recruitment and procurement processes. Moreover, a culture of 'allowances' has been institutionalized and there is a tendency among public servants to encourage the organization of unnecessary workshops, seminars and training courses or jump from one holiday resort to another or one country to another (for these workshops, etc.) in order to enhance their incomes by pocketing daily allowances (Dzimbiri, 2014).

There is also growing evidence that the public service machinery has not been very effective in recent years. In addition to a consistent shortage of drugs in hospitals, there are numerous unfilled vacancies in ministries and government departments while an army of unemployed graduates swarm the streets (Dzimbiri, 2014). Moreover, the country witnessed in 2013 a major corruption scandal (termed 'Cashgate') where public funds worth over MKW 20 billion was syphoned from public coffers. It is even feared that, since 2005, Malawi has probably lost close to MK 577 billion with the active involvement of public servants and politicians.

Conclusion

The public service is the main tool governments use to implement various national development policies and deliver services in education, health, community development, transport, maintenance of law and order among others. Governments rely on this machinery to design, formulate and implement their policies, strategies and programmes, and to discharge all routine government functions. However, the relationship between politics and administration has been a controversial subject since the early days of public administration as a field of study. This chapter has analysed the role and impact of politics on human resource management in Malawi.

Central issues examined include the role of ministers and principal secretaries in recruitment, promotion, demotion, transfer and discipline of public servants in order to determine the impact of on human resource management and service delivery in a country struggling to promote development and reduce poverty. The role PSs play in recruiting, promoting, transferring and disciplining public servants affect the delivery of service in that where staff with appropriate skills are recruited or promoted there is effectiveness and efficiency in service delivery. On the other hand, if PSs have not given proper guidance in the process or if they do not enforce discipline, then the service delivery may be adversely affected. Again, where ministers interfere through directives on whom to appoint, promote or transfer, public service morale suffers. There are a growing number of reported cases of laxity and under-performance among public servants who wilfully disregard procedures and regulations. Many do not show up for work on time and/ or leave their offices well before the stipulated time. Malawians have also complained about the arrogance of junior staff, a rise in corruption and deliberate efforts to solicit bribes in lieu of providing a service. And the general deterioration of public services is not only a problem of the immigration and traffic departments, but characterizes the workings of most ministries and departments in the country.

While in theory ministers do not have a prominent role in recruitment, promotion, demotion or transfer of public servants in the ministry, the reality is quite different in practice. Political interference is rampant in the public service. The consequence of this is ineffective service delivery due to frustrations and appointment of inappropriate human resources. Legal suits due to premature termination of contracts, promotion without linking to budgetary provisions and a bloated public service, which becomes inefficient in the proper delivery of public service, are other impacts.

From the perspective of the three theoretical perspectives regarding separation, political and integration schools on the politics–administration relationship, the Malawi experience reveals complexities in the relationships between ministers and top civil servants. While the separation school with its emphasis on separation of politics from administration is relevant to Malawi at the formal level, the reality is very different. A politically neutral public service is recruited on merit, and given tenure to encourage frank and fearless advice and protect it from electoral whims. This enables it to serve a government of any political persuasion. However, the subtle interference of politicians in human resource management and lack of independence of the administrative heads of ministries shown in the discussion reveals the inadequacy of the separation school. The political school, which accepts the separation of politics from administration but rejects the subordinate and instrumental role of public administration relating to elected officials, is also unrealistic in the context of Malawi. It is evident from the above discussion that administrative heads of ministries are subordinate to ministers to the extent of even doing what is professionally or ethically unacceptable. In reality, there is greater integration of the roles of ministers and PSs in policy processes. In public service human resource management, the degree of political interference (which is negative) in areas of appointments, promotion, transfer and discipline is very strong. Thus, the three schools of though discussed in this chapter have partial application in the Malawi context.

Recommendations of the system-wide public sector reforms, published as *Making Malawi Work*, include institutionalizing open competitive interviews for positions that have been reserved for presidential appointment as well as induction for ministers to understand their roles. If these and other recommendations are implemented, there is a greater likelihood that the public service human resource management function will in future experience minimal political interference and its effectiveness will raise the strategic role of the public service in national development.

References.

Armstrong, A. (2010) *A Handbook of Human Resources Management Practice*, 10th edn. London: Kogan Page.

Bosworth, K. A. (1958) 'The Manager is a Politician'. *Public Administration Review*, 18(3): 216–22.

CAPAM (2007) 'Leading for Results: The Critical Role of the Permanent Secretary'. Regional Seminar, January 21–3 Barbados.

Colley, L. (2005) 'Myth, Monolith or normative Model – Evolution of the career service model of employment in the Queensland Public Service 1859–2000', Unpublished PhD Thesis, Brisbane: Griffith University Business School.

Demir, T. (1993) 'Politics and administration: A Review of research and some suggestions', University of Illinois at Springfield; Department of Public Administration. Occasional Paper.

Demir, T. and Nyhan, R. C. (2008) 'The politics–administration dichotomy: An empirical search for correspondence between theory and practice'. *Public Administration Review*. 68: 8–86.

Dunn, N. (1994) *Public Policy Analysis: An Introduction*, Englewood Cliffs, NJ: Prentice Hall.

Dye, Thomas R. (1995) *Understanding Public Policy*, Englewood Cliffs, NJ: Prentice Hall.

Dzimbiri, L. (2014) 'A History of Civil Service in Malawi'. Unpublished draft paper, Lilongwe: Public Sector Reform Management Unit.

Dzimbiri, L. (2015) *Organization and Management Theories: An African Focus integrating structure, people, environment and processes for human happiness*. Zomba: Academic Publishers.

GoM (2013) 'DHRMD', Comprehensive National Human Resource Survey. Lilongwe: Government of Malawi.

GoM (2014) *Public Service Reform Commission: A Look at the Future Making Malawi Work Transforming Malawi's Public Service*. Lilongwe: Government of Malawi.

Hayes, W. (2001) 'The Public Policy Web', available at: http://www.geocities.com/profwork/implement/define.html (accessed 15 September 2015).

Kachimera, P. (2014) 'The History of the Public Service in Malawi'. Unpublished Paper. Lilongwe: Office of the President and Cabinet.

Kathyola, J. (2010) *The Political–Administrative Interface: the key to public sector governance and effectiveness in Commonwealth Africa.* London. Commonwealth Parliamentary Association.

Lipsky, M. (1980) *Street-level bureaucracy: Dilemmas of the individuals in public services.* New York, NY: Russel Sage Foundation.

Long, N. (1954) 'Public policy and administration: The goals of rationality and responsibility'. *Public Administration Review,* 14(1): 22–31.

Miller, H. T. (1993) 'Everyday politics in public administration'. *American Review of Public Administration,* 23(2): 99–116.

Mulgan, G. (2007) *Social Innovation. What it is Why it Matters, How it can be Accelerted.* Basingstoke: The Young Foundation.

Nalbandian, J. (1994) 'Reflections of a "Pracademic" on the logic of politics and administration'. *Public Administration Review,* 54(6): 531–6.

Northcote, S. and Trevelyan, G. (1854) *Report on the Organisation of the Permanent Civil Service.* Submitted to both Houses of Parliament by Command of Her Majesty in February.

Pfiffner, J. P. (1985) 'Political public administration'. *Public Administration Review,* 45(2): 352–6.

Rosenbloom, D. (2008) 'Politics–Administration Dichotomy in US Historical Context'. *Public Administration Review.* 68(1): 57–60.

Sossin, L. (2006) 'Defining Boundaries: the Constitutional Arguments for Bureaucratic Independence and its Implications for the Accountability of the Public Service'. *The Public Service and Transparency,* 2: 25–72.

Svara, J. H. (2001) 'The myth of the dichotomy: complementarity of politics and administration in the past and future of public administration'. *Public Administration Review,* 61(2): 176–83.

Waldo, D. (1980) *The enterprise of public administration: A summary view.* Novato, CA: Chandler & Sharp Publishers.

Walters, S. (2007) 'Working with Ministers: the Political and Administrative Interface. Leading for Results: The Critical Role of the Permanent Secretary'. Regional Seminar, January 21–3 Barbados.

Wilson, W. (1887) 'The study of administration'. *Political Science Quarterly,* 2: 197–222.

6 The political economy of fiscal decentralisation

Implications on local governance and public service delivery

Asiyati Lorraine Chiweza

Introduction

During the past two decades, many developing countries have implemented decentralisation reforms to strengthen local governments and bring the state closer to people and ensure greater accountability of the state in the delivery of services to its citizens. External donors and Malawian policymakers largely viewed the adoption of a democratic decentralisation policy in 1990s as a logical conclusion to the democratisation process and as a way of strengthening local government authorities to improve the delivery of public services. However, since the adoption of the policy in 1998, various studies have shown that the scope for realising the commonly advocated goals of democratic participation, improved service delivery, and poverty reduction have remained largely elusive. Dual administration has persisted and local government functions mainly as an extension of the central government. Studies have further noted that there has been limited participation of the public in local government decision-making processes (Chasukwa et al., 2014). Others claim that there has been a decline in democratic oversight and accountability (Cammack et al., 2007), with horizontal accountability given more emphasis than vertical accountability (Chasukwa and Chinsinga, 2013), which in turn has resulted in the fragmentation of service delivery that is moreover characterised by poor facilities and insufficient equipment (Cammack and O'Neil, 2014). There have been various narratives that have tried to offer plausible explanations to this fragmentation. The first narrative relates the fragmentation to bureaucratic resistance to devolve appropriate sectoral functions and limited institutional integration of the local government system at the district level (Kaunda, 1999; Chiweza, 1998, 2010a; Chinsinga, 2008; Tambulasi, 2010). The second narrative locates the challenges within discourses of inadequate financial, technical, and human capacities (Chinsinga, 2008; Chiweza, 2010b; Kutengule et al., 2014).

There is also a body of literature that relates the locus of these challenges to the logic behind the underlying structure of Malawi's political economy – the nature of political organisation and competition, elite-dominated political settlements, and a broader social contract that puts in place powerful incentives that shape elite behaviour (Chinsinga, 2008; Cammack and O'Neil, 2014). This chapter builds on this discourse and argues that one of the key avenues through which this political logic has become pronounced and has had a crippling effect on local public service delivery is fiscal decentralisation and resource allocation decision-making. This chapter addresses three main questions:

- What is the national pattern of fiscal intergovernmental arrangements that has evolved since democratisation and what are the political economy dynamics underlying this particular pattern?
- Who are the key political and bureaucratic actors in resource allocation decision-making within the District Councils, and how does their behaviour contribute to a weak and fragmented service delivery position for local governments?
- What potential do the 2014 local elections hold towards improvement of local governance and public service delivery for Malawians?

Fiscal decentralisation and political economy

The notion of fiscal decentralisation must be understood within with the context of a broader discussion of decentralisation because the 'level of fiscal decentralisation corresponds to the degree of independent decision making that exercised at the local level' (Bird and François 1998: 3). Fiscal decentralisation refers to the transfer of fiscal powers to sub-national governments. It can also be conceived as a process of reform that involves making choices among four types of policy decisions (Fjelstad, 2001):

- expenditure assignment – a process of defining the responsibilities of central and local government for providing and paying for specific services to citizens;
- revenue assignment, that is, establishing revenue sources as well as tax-raising powers between the central and local governments and giving them authority to decide how to spend their revenue;
- the regulatory policy to monitor and set limits on local government borrowing; and
- inter-governmental policy on revenue sharing enabling a central government to transfer financial resources in the form of grants to local governments.

Fiscal decentralisation is important because the extent to which revenue sources accompany the transfer of administrative responsibilities is crucial to the service delivery success of local government and 'control of revenue sources is the thorniest issue of any decentralization' (León-Alfonso, 2007: 27).

The combination of the different revenue sources is another important factor that influences the degree of autonomy and capability of district councils to meet citizen service demands. Scholars have argued that capacity for service delivery and accountability of local government to local clients is enhanced if local government has access to own-taxes with the right to adjust tax rates (Ahmad *et al.*, 2006). If local expenditures are financed entirely out of grants or transfers from central government and not out of local tax bases, the capacity to implement service delivery programmes will depend on the goodwill of the central actors. Similarly, local voters may have little or no information regarding the resource envelope available to their local government and what those resources are intended to provide. Conditional transfers lead to a more hierarchical system of accountability with the centre holding the local government accountable for proper use of central transfers. Unconditional transfers fall in the category of discretionary resources, for which local government is directly accountable to its local citizens (Bird, 2003). From a theoretical perspective, what are the considerations that determine the selection of a particular form of fiscal decentralisation?

The literature on welfare economics assumes that politicians are driven by public interest concerns, and hence several contributions treat each level of government as a benevolent social planner, maximising the welfare of the residents of its jurisdiction (Lockwood, 2006). Thus the factors that would drive decisions on the optimal assignment of expenditure and tax responsibilities would include economies of scale, spill over benefits, cost of administering taxes, and equity. In practice, there is an emerging consensus in the literature that resource distribution across sub-national governments cannot be explained by efficiency and equity considerations alone, but political variables representing the incentives of central political agents become additional and significant determinants (Ahmad *et al.*, 2006). Bird and François (1998), in their review of fiscal decentralisation in developing countries, have noted that the design of intergovernmental transfers is always and everywhere an exercise not solely in normative economics but also in political economy. Therefore a political economy approach can offer an account of these effects that is plausible because politicians are driven purely by self-interest, for it is individual politicians' preferences in securing and maintaining office by winning elections that shapes the evolution of a fiscal intergovernmental contract (Ordeshook and Shvetsova, 1997).

The preferences of politicians are basically centred on re-election concerns, driven by median-voter demands and competition with other parties. Understanding political elite choices in the shaping of intergovernmental fiscal arrangements in Malawi is particularly pertinent because the logic of national politics since the introduction of multi-party elections has been characterised by patronage and competitive clientelism (Cammack and O'Neil, 2014). In the presence of patronage, and clientelism, decisions are generally taken on other grounds rather than efficiency or equity (Cammack *et al.*, 2007). Thus, instead of acting for the common good, officials tend to follow their self-interest of both political and economic kinds because it is in their self-interest to target policies and public spending towards their respective clienteles in order to secure political support (Ahmad *et al.*, 2006).

The evolution and pattern of fiscal decentralisation in Malawi

Devolution of functions to councils and expenditure assignments

Assigning expenditure responsibilities between levels of governments is the first element of any fiscal decentralisation strategy, as it is believed that finance follows functions. However, the main incentive for ruling party politicians in Malawi is the need to be re-elected and retain power so considerations of decentralisation have not been first and foremost about promoting effective implementation of service delivery functions to the general public, but rather how it might affect the power balance at the local level and enable the party to stay in power. Within the local government arena, Cammack and O'Neil (2014: 67) argue that the most visible effect of competitive clientelism is the incentives it creates for political leaders to be seen to be directly 'delivering development' to their supporters. They argue that the calculated political return of different activities is thus shaped by how visible a good is. As such political leaders will tend to be more inclined towards sector outputs for which they can more obviously claim credit, or that citizens will associate with the particular politician. All successive presidents have fed this dynamic from the top by encouraging citizens to vote for Government MPs as they are the only ones who can 'bring development' to them. These national political discourses create local expectations and have structured the decision-making logics of the political leaders with respect to the implementation of decentralisation.

Driven by these political interests, successive presidents have influenced the pace and extent of devolution of functions in such a way as to retain access and control over allocation decisions of visible development projects in the countryside. Legally, the expenditure powers of local government councils and central government ministries in Malawi are specified in the 1998 Decentralisation Policy and Local Government Act (Malawi Government, 1998b, 1998a). Table 6.1 provides a summary of the functions assigned to Local Government Councils.

The decentralisation policy devolves the service delivery planning, budgeting, expenditure, and management responsibilities of the earmarked services and it makes central government ministries responsible for overall policy coordination, setting and enforcement of sectoral guidelines and standards, quality control, provision of services of a national character, and other functions required to maintain macroeconomic stability.

However, despite the formal articulation of expenditure responsibilities in the policy and legal framework of local government, the actual decentralisation of functions and expenditure responsibilities from the central ministries has been dragging on. There has also not been any overt force by successive presidents to deal with the bureaucratic blockages affecting sector devolution, a feature that demonstrates the reluctance of ruling party leaders to devolve authority, and decision-making power over certain functions. Both President Muluzi and President Mutharika were fearful of opposition party mobilisation via local councils and any formal processes that would have made them lose decision-making control to lower-level officials and the patronage opportunities linked to

Table 6.1 Functions devolved to local government councils

Nature of services	Key functions devolved to local government councils
Education services	Nursery and kindergarten; primary schools; and distance education centres.
Medical and health services	Health centres, dispensaries, maternity clinics and health posts, control of communicable diseases, health education, and environmental sanitation.
Agriculture, livestock and irrigation	Livestock extension, control of livestock diseases, land husbandry, crop husbandry, food and nutrition, and construction, rehabilitation of small dams.
Environmental services	Burial services refuse disposal, sewerage removal and disposal, environmental reclamation, and environmental education.
Roads and street services	District roads, township roads, city roads; estate roads (if done to acceptable standards), street naming, issuing of road permits; and issuing of drivers' licences.
Community development	Women in development, community development, street children and orphans; youth and cultural affairs, district information services.
Public amenities	Sports stadiums, community halls, recreational parks and playgrounds, and public conveniences.
Water services	The provision and maintenance of water supplies including boreholes, piped water projects, protected wells, distribution of water, and gravity fed piped water schemes.
Forestry	Establishment of wood lots and forests, forestry surveys, inventory of forests, Forestry extension, and Forest management.
Fisheries	Licensing and inspection of fishing gear i.e. nets and boats, fisheries extension; and community participation in fish management.

Source: Malawi Government (1998)

these. They therefore played the politics of local governance very deftly by carefully and selectively promoting the transfer of functions at the expense of others even while making rhetorical commitments to decentralisation.

As a result, by 2014, 15 ministries were on record of having devolved some functions to the district councils but very few ministries had actually devolved the whole array of the earmarked functions and resources (Kutengule *et al.*, 2014). Dual administration thus continued to exist in the district councils, with central ministries retaining control over development budget expenditures and capital investments. Only expenditure responsibilities for recurrent budgets over the selected functions have been fully devolved, but, even then, some functions remain under the control of central ministries, for example procurement and distribution of school and teaching materials, recruitment, discipline, and promotion of senior council staff.

Retaining central government control over expenditure responsibility for development and capital investments is an important political strategy of ensuring higher political returns by enabling the ruling president to have access to development resources, which they can use to be visibly seen by the public. These are particularly important as politicians can project themselves as being responsive to local development needs and can allocate the resources they promise at political rallies. Such resources also enable ruling leaders to build their networks and alliances by distributing part of them to government ministers, ruling party MPs and their supporters. The consequence of the selective nature of the implementation of sector devolution is that ministries such as education and health have still maintained their own parallel district implementation plans developed through parallel processes geared towards meeting the sector standards and targets. As a result, there is uncoordinated planning and decision-making over service delivery, with sector and district processes occurring in parallel and overlapping ways (Cammack and O'Neil, 2014). While this may not promote rational planning and integrated delivery of services, there is an explicit political advantage that is gained from these policy implementation incoherencies and the confusion such disjointedness may cause.

Revenue sharing arrangements and an intergovernmental fiscal transfer system

The same trend has been evident with respect to revenue sharing agreements between central and local governments, the design of the intergovernmental fiscal transfers, as well as the rules governing such transfers. Malawi has not had the comprehensive fiscal decentralisation policy and principles that should guide allocation of fiscal resources from central government to local government in such a way as to enhance the capacity of local government to effectively deliver public services in a systematic manner. While some effort towards the development of intergovernmental fiscal transfer formulae was evident during early 2000, this was not allowed to mature into a comprehensive set of policy and principles to regulate central government transfers in an objective manner. Instead, over subsequent years, the executive as well as parliamentarians from both ruling and opposition parties have taken a selected set of decisions that have shaped a compromised pattern of intergovernmental fiscal transfers strategically conceived to shore up their political interests and visibility in delivering local public goods and services.

The main sources of local government finance for the assigned responsibilities are outlined in the Local Government Act (1998) and the Malawi Decentralization Policy (Malawi Government, 1998b, 1998a). Both the Act and the Policy identify three main sources of revenue for Councils which are:

- locally generated revenues, which include property tax, ground rents, fees and licences, commercial undertakings, and service charges;
- ceded revenue (non-tax revenue), which includes toll fees, gambling and casino fees, fuel levy/fee (road maintenance levy), motor vehicle registration fees, and industrial registration fees; and

- central government transfers, which include the General Resource Fund (GRF) and sector transfers.

The principles of assigning revenues to local government require that own source revenues should ideally be sufficient to enable sub-national governments to finance all locally provided services primarily benefitting local residents from their own resources (Bird and François 1998: 11). The experience on the ground has been that locally generated revenues barely sustain the operational and development activities of district councils, who are heavily dependent on central government transfers. On average, locally generated revenues finance only 5 per cent of district council recurrent operational expenditures while central government transfers finance 90 per cent of these expenditures. The root of the problem lies in very limited taxing powers available to the councils. While the central government controls the most buoyant and lucrative sources, the district councils are expected to implement a variety of service delivery functions assigned to them.

Since central government transfers became the mainstay of district council financing, it was deemed important to have clear rules of distribution and allocation between districts. Discussions about the need for such principles started back in 2001 when the Government of Malawi, with the support of external donors, commissioned a study on intergovernmental fiscal transfers. The result was that the National Local Government Finance Committee (NLGFC) proposed a set of formulae to Parliament that emphasised use of population (80 per cent) and poverty (20 per cent) as the basis for the distribution of the General Resource Fund (GRF), the District Development Fund (DDF), and allocation principles for sectors funds across the districts. The formulae were meant to serve as a building block of formal institutions for resource sharing towards equalisation of development and service delivery across the country. Parliament approved the inter-district allocation formulas for the GRF and DDF in October 2002, with a provision for review after three years. The expectation was that the GRF would serve as an unconditional transfer for meeting the development of districts and providing relief on recurrent expenditures of local governments. The National Local Government Finance Committee, donors and other decentralisation policy architects had also anticipated that over time the DDF would evolve into a nationwide discretionary mechanism for development financing that would 'enhance the democratic basis for development across local governments by improving the public's access to the locus of decision making as the fund allows local governments to play a greater role in the policy making process' (Chinsinga, 2009: 9). Indeed, there was an emerging consensus in 2004 among central policy makers, district council officers and development partners that while the DDF was an effective approach of providing discretionary development grants to district councils and consolidating central–local transfers, it needed to be transformed into a harmonised Local Development Fund (Ssewankambo et al., 2004). It was felt that such a mechanism would provide a foundation for a predictable and transparent grant mechanism for local governments.

Until 2014, none of these aspirations was realised and central government was transferring not the required 5 per cent of net revenue but less than 1 per cent. The 2002 formulae approved by Parliament had not been subjected to review after three years as planned and Parliament did not play an active role of monitoring and ensuring that the formulae and the policy requirement of 5 per cent GRF was being adhered to. Neither Parliament nor the executive demonstrated a willingness to support the growth of a set of formal institutions to guide the determination and distribution of central transfers and an integrated fiscal devolution mechanism over the long term. Discussions with key informants revealed that the National Local Government Finance Committee, an institution that is constitutionally mandated to provide guidance on the distribution of resources, submitted formulae review proposals to Cabinet to guide both recurrent and development resource allocation but there was no response.

Similarly, the idea of a single nationwide integrated development financing mechanism did not come to fruition. The initial discussions regarding such a mechanism were spearheaded by the National Local Government Finance Committee and the Ministry of Local Government and Rural Development based on lessons from the implementation of the DDF. Around the same time the Malawi Social Action Fund (MASAF) APL 1 programme was coming to an end and the MASAF Secretariat had started developing a new concept note for World Bank funding under MASAF APL II but one which also focused on the LDF mechanism.

The precise agreements that were made between central government and World Bank are not well known, but what became clear at the inception of the fund was that government adopted a different variant of the LDF. The discretionary element that was a key plank of the design of the fund was lost and central government tightened control over district council development expenditure by earmarking about 90 per cent of the LDF financing to centrally determined projects, mainly building teachers' houses and school blocks. The fund was also set to be managed by an institution outside the regular framework of government called the Local Development Fund Technical Support Team (LDF-TST) but reporting to the Ministry of Finance and Economic Planning instead of being managed by the constitutionally recognised body – the National Local Government Finance Committee. This decision demonstrated policy incoherence and was not consistent with the need for a nationwide discretionary mechanism for development financing that would allow local governments to play a greater role in the district resource allocation making process. It was around the same time that the Mutharika government was preparing for 2009 elections and the issue of school blocks and teachers houses was a key aspect of his election campaign. This reflects the political leaders' incentives to maintain rules that actively undermine collective action but enable them to utilise the systems to shore up their visibility during electoral processes.

Indeed, a pattern of fiscal decentralisation that has evolved over the years has been characterised by increased amounts of sector recurrent conditional grants that are centrally controlled with limited discretionary funding for the councils.

Sector transfers constitute a bulk (90 per cent) of the operational related transactions (ORT) going to district councils, mainly for health, education and agriculture, and these have increased over time. One of the explanatory factors for increased transfers to these sectors is that donor pressure increased at this time, both as a condition for World Bank support and through the design of the health and agriculture sector wide approaches. The use of sectoral grants is limited because such funds are exclusively earmarked for the implementation of sector recurrent programmes and the council as a decision-making body does not have any latitude to vary the use of such funds for service delivery projects identified through the district development planning system. With the withdrawal of donor aid and direct budget support in 2014, funding for most sectors has been drastically reduced and, as a result, service delivery activities in those sectors have been suffering (Kutengule *et al.*, 2014).

The emergence of a Constituency Development Fund

Further policy incoherence was evident when government adopted the Constituency Development Fund in 1996, a programme that involves the use of public funds at local levels that are outside the formal planning, budgeting, and spending framework, and runs counter to the government's professed objective of strengthening local government's capacity to meet local needs (see Table 6.2). Its introduction was negotiated and initiated by the MPs through a private members' motion that was presented by an opposition MP. The narrative justifying its creation was the following:

> The house should consider the creation of the Constituency Development Fund under Ministry of Local Government and to be allocated under the District Assembly vote. The fund while controlled by the District Assembly should be overseen by the Member of Parliament. The purpose of the Fund would be to assist each constituency in maintenance of structures and undertaking minor community based development activities e.g. repairs to boreholes, blown out school roofs, broken bridges etc.[1]

There was unanimous agreement about the above proposal from both ruling and opposition MPs, who felt that this would provide an important alternative that would make elected representatives 'warrant holders and give them a say in resource allocation for their constituencies'.[2] Only two MPs opposed the motion and argued that this was not the right move given the devolution policy. One argued that 'We must accept that we as Members of Parliament we are here to enact Laws … Each part has a duty to perform … We must therefore accept that members of District Assemblies have been given powers to make sure that these funds are directed to beneficiaries.'[3] The few voices against the motion were overruled and the motion was unanimously adopted in Parliament.

Table 6.2 Constituency development fund in relation to gross district council capital expenditures, 2006–14

Year	Own Capital Contribution (MK)	Constituency Development Fund (MK)	Own Capital Contribution as a % of gross capital expenditure	Own Constituency Development Fund as a % of gross capital expenditure
2006/07	30,081,055	386,000,000	7%	93%
2007/08	23,782,202	471,383,013	5%	95%
2008/09	23,589,618	538,486,812	4%	96%
2009/10	47,113,701	537,754,748	16%	84%
2010/11	34,393,202	464,785,935	7%	93%
2011/12	149,665,559	565,488,989	21%	79%
2012/13	131,020,151	1,151,738,886	10%	90%
2013/14	106,512,481	1,151,738,886	8%	92%

Source: Computed from data from National Local Government Finance Committee

The narratives display the MPs' overriding interest to access and control local development resources that would enable them to fulfil their campaign promises, and boost their re-election prospects. The opposition MPs therefore took advantage of their majority in Parliament during this period to use the passing of the budget as a bargaining chip to gain control over local development financing in order to serve their political interests. This case is thus 'a very good example where formal institutions are exploited to sort out informal deals outside the formal governance framework to bolster selfish political goals' (Chinsinga, 2009: 9).

Over time the quest for MPs across the political divide to control local development financing has been increasing and the motivation appears to be shifting from what was initially conceived as maintenance of structures and undertaking minor community-based development activities towards tangible development investments. Initially the amount was MK7 million p.a. for each MP but there have been increased demands from MPs to increase the amount. Later the figure went up to MK9 million pa. During the 2015/16 budget session a push for an increase of the CDF to MK30 million was presented through a private members' motion placed by an MP from the Malawi Congress Party. He argued that in order to guarantee the allocations, 'the CDF should be legislated and be fixed as a percentage of projected government revenue in each year'.[4] This request was supported by the Budget and Finance Committee, although after some negotiations the amount was increased by 58 per cent to MK12 million. By 2014, the Constituency Development Fund had become the largest discretionary central government transfer for development purpose to local government accounting for an average of 90 per cent of district councils gross capital expenditure.

However, the story of the CDF in all the districts is littered with reports of abuse, politicisation of development projects by MPs, and lack of accountability both for the money and for the results that the fund has achieved.[5] Since its introduction various stakeholders including the National Audit Office have raised concerns over the management of the CDF, including the identification, implementation, and monitoring of projects selected, quality of projects, procurement processes, and accounting for project activities (Kutengule *et al.*, 2014). Project identification and resource allocation is largely influenced by the MP with the aid of party functionaries with little or no control by the council as a decision-making body. The CDF does not promote rational planning processes since the projects on which the CDF funds are spent are usually not those identified in district or village development plans but those that will enable them to gain votes and reward loyalists. This constrains the fund's potential to contribute towards effective service delivery or contribute towards the achievement of district development plans.

In a review of the CDF implementation it was noted that project prioritisation and decision-making in an overwhelming majority of cases mainly rested with the MP (Chiweza and Munthali, 2012). Most MPs expressed an understanding that the main criteria which they use to select priority projects is the imperative to try and ensure that at least the projects are spread across the constituency so that they maintain some visibility across the constituency and please voters.

Over the five rounds of elections, one consequence of these expectations and high turnover has been the 'bidding up' of promises made by MPs. Increasingly unrealistic promises of delivering development projects are made to unseat incumbents. Following elections, MPs are often not in a position to deliver on their promises and so they lose their seats because competing candidates are able to 'bid' higher and the process starts again. Victories are contingent on the ability to distribute large numbers of small gifts such as sugar, cloth, and soap to constituents both as an upfront resource transfer and also as a visible sign that the MP can continue to deliver promises after being elected. Competition drives up the investment needed to win and sets the bar higher for subsequent elections. It appears, however, that these issues are at the heart of elections and politics of development in Malawi. Although MPs in Malawi win elections using a variety of means, of primary interest is their ability to 'deliver development' and citizens are encouraged to vote for MPs from the government side, as they are the ones who can 'bring development'.

The main incentive MPs face in the districts is the need to be re-elected. MPs win elections using a variety of means but of primary interest is MPs' ability to 'deliver development'. Afrobarometer data suggests that MPs are seen more as local development officers than in terms of their legislative functions. Some 76 per cent of Malawians expect their MP to deliver goods and services to people in their community in particular.[6] And only 22 per cent would vote for a candidate who would support policies that benefit everyone in the country. This is also seen in terms of how people perceive the role of an MP. Some 40.1 per cent of Malawians see the MPs' primary role as directly delivering jobs and development, while 51.1 per cent believe it is to listen to constituents and represent their needs. Just 4.4 per cent understand that MPs' primary role is to make laws for the good of the country. This leads to MPs having a strong focus on delivering very visible benefits to their constituents in the form of private goods for the benefit of key individuals or 'club' goods, which benefit a small group. MPs also ensure that investment is placed in areas of high support within their constituencies to reward their supporters and guarantee re-election. The need for very visible development results means MPs often emphasise those investments that are most obviously seen, particularly capital expenditure. For example, where solving a service delivery problem involves changes at the centre, MPs typically aim to deliver a new clinic rather than ensuring that there are drugs available in existing clinics.

MPs are in practice not held to account for how they use CDF funds. The design of the CDF oversight system at the local level complicates the relationship between MPs as members of the council seeking accountability of district commissioners and the district commissioners as controlling officers over CDF resources. Formally the district commissioner is the controlling officer for usage of CDF resources. However, MPs bypass formal procurement and accountability procedures and control district commissioners through the use of threats of transfer to unfavorable postings or other informal sanctions. As a result, many district commissioners, and other officers are not able to stand up to the politically strong MPs and they tend to exercise their controlling functions cautiously for fear of repercussions.

District resource allocation and service delivery decision-making in practice

The complex way in which functional and fiscal decentralisation has evolved has had a direct impact on district decision-making and resource allocation. In practice, district consultative forums[7] did not have much decision-making leverage on sector recurrent budgets and the Constituency Development Fund. They also did not carry out the core and legal oversight functions of a council such as approve or enforce by-laws that were out-dated. Further, they could not sanction the council to borrow money because section 15(1) of the Local Government Act prohibits councils (as in elected councils) from delegating its powers to borrow money, make by-laws and standing orders, and levy taxes. Meetings of the district consultative forums served mainly as information sharing forums and decision-making was limited to urgent matters with inadequate attention to examining the performance of the district councils, and over-seeing financial roles (Chiweza, 2010a). While they were approving annual council budgets and work plans, they engaged less in scrutinising district development plans or accounts, monitoring staff, or managing sector committees or resources.

The district consultative forums regularly engaged strongly on questions of resource distribution particularly intra-district allocations of LDF resources. The practice was for the district commissioner and the sector heads to put proposals before the forums, which were then debated and approved by them, making amendments where they deemed necessary. The ability to influence decisions has often been dependent on whether or not the MPs are in government or opposition. For those in government, the seniority of the MP matters quite a lot. Cabinet ministers and senior party officials tend to wield more influence than ordinary MPs. Yet, in all districts, MPs face the same incentives to be re-elected through the delivery of visible investment in their constituencies (Chiweza and Waldock, 2011).

The most contentious debates in the district consultative forums have emerged when officers have presented different allocations to different constituencies, often based on a district-wide approach to assessing local needs. Politicians usually prefer equal distribution of allocated funds along constituency lines rather than the needs-based evidence and technical criteria prioritised by officers. The formal process is that, once the LDF secretariat provides indicative planning figures to the district councils, technical officers are then expected to use relevant sectoral data to make proposals on how the funds received should be distributed within the district. Chiweza (2011) found that in practice, intra-district allocation of LDF resources in many district councils was barely being done according to evidence of need. For example, the guidelines for the teachers' housing project stipulate that, 'it is expected that each Council will use the same criteria in allocating the projects within the district by computation of education zone data on number of schools, number of teachers' houses, and number of teachers.'[8] In practice, MPs prefer to ignore guidelines and push for 'sharing the cake equally among constituencies so that each MP has something to show to his/her constituency for electing him/her' (Chiweza, 2011). As one key informant put it:

> pressure from MPs is less on NGO and donor projects as compared with projects coming through the Councils ... Sometimes you wonder why we have District Development Plans to guide us because most of the things being implemented do not really reflect priority ranking of the plans. Those development programmes put forward by MPs are given highest priority in the District Consultative Forum (Chiweza, 2011).

Thus, formal rules of the game are often suspended to accommodate the interests of powerful political figures and elites. This is often justified on the grounds of serving the 'greater good' of the society where rules are perceived to be limiting e.g. lack of equity in distribution of resources between opposition and government MPs and between ministers and 'ordinary' MPs. These practices impact on the ability of the council sector staff to ensure that resources are targeted towards community needs and deal with existing service delivery inequalities.

There were also some feedback effects. When changes to sector allocations were submitted to the district consultative committee, it had implications for what sector officials presented the next time decisions were to be made. One major tactic adopted in virtually all districts was that sector officials made sure that their proposals for investments were distributed evenly between all constituencies. In many districts this served to neutralise district consultative committee debates on inter-constituency distribution (Chiweza and Waldock, 2011). However, by distributing very limited resources evenly, the districts were not using local knowledge and evidence-based decision-making to tackle areas where poverty was highest – a key justification for decentralisation.

District commissioners and sector heads found the use of this tactic as a way to reduce pressure put on them by MPs. The position of district commissioners is not a politically neutral one and appointments are made directly by the executive – a practice strengthened by the 2010 amendments to the Local Government Act. As a result, district commissioners are vulnerable to political pressure from influential MPs, ministers and chiefs, which can result in their transfer to less attractive posts. This means DCs are often pragmatic, engaging in disputes they think they can win and allying themselves with different interests in the districts to ensure political cover. District commissioners and sector heads are more able and willing to stand up to less-powerful government MPs and opposition party leaders. However, with more senior government MPs, the willingness of the district officials to use their technocratic evidence to positively manage and stand up to such pressures is very much dependent on the officers' calculation of how much informal power the political actors in question hold and the informal reprisals that are likely to be associated with such acts (Chiweza and Waldock, 2011).

Effects on public service delivery

A large number of decisions regarding infrastructural development at district level appear to be reactive and ad hoc (Cammack and O'Neil, 2014). As a result nearly 95 per cent of public expenditure is undertaken by central government and sub-national spending has been relatively low reflecting minimal presence of local government in public service delivery. Table 6.3 illustrates that the share of ocal government spending in total government spending has since 2005 been in the 3–7 per cent range, with an average of 5 per cent. Although comparative data on the importance of local spending is hard to find and interpret, other studies using different samples have found that the degree of fiscal decentralisation in terms of spending tends to be greater in richer countries than poor countries (Bird and François, 1998). For example, Bird (1995) found an average local government share of 22 per cent for developed countries and 9 per cent for developing countries while OECD (1991) found an average share of 26 per cent for developed countries.

Although the data and samples used in the other country surveys may not be directly comparable to Malawi, it is only illustrative of the low level of local government spending in Malawi. This indicates a high degree of centralisation in the responsibility for the provision of public services, despite adoption of a formal devolution policy. This has huge implications on the leverage that local government councils in Malawi can exert over service delivery decisions in their jurisdictions, but also for the services over which they can reasonably be held to account. Local governments have repeatedly been unable to ensure a sufficient supply of infrastructure, essential materials and access to safe drinking water is undermined by the disrepair of many water points in rural areas. This explains why the implementation of decentralisation policy reforms has had little discernible impact on service delivery (Chinsinga, 2008: 93).

Table 6.3 Share of local government spending in total government spending, 2006–14

	Total government expenditure (MK)	Central government expenditure (MK)	Local government expenditure (MK)	Share of local government spending in total expenditure (%)
2005/06*	128,465,369,867	119,654,000,000	8,811,369,867	7%
2006/07	164,047,077,054	154,374,000,000	9,673,077,054	6%
2007/08	191,944,857,700	179,398,000,000	12,546,857,700	7%
2008/09	259,718,618,050	245,840,000,000	13,878,618,050	5%
2009/10	273,491,316,345	257,099,000,000	16,392,316,345	6%
2010/11	311,498,335,655	296,196,000,000	15,302,335,655	5%
2011/12	347,606,234,589	328,103,000,000	19,503,234,589	6%
2012/13	512,129,423,480	488,581,000,000	23,548,423,480	5%
2013/14	675,815,779,299	656,213,000,000	19,602,779,299	3%

Source: Computed from data from National Local Government Finance Committee
* Government started the process of devolving sector budgets to Councils in FY2005/06

Conclusion

The arrival of locally elected councillors is indeed an important milestone in Malawi's local governance system, but the elections alone are not the full answer towards improved local governance and better public service delivery. For councillors to make a difference serious local government reform is essential – and the challenges are immense. A key argument arising out of this analysis is that the impact of the devolution policy on service delivery is largely negated when districts do not control key functions including staff recruitment and when fiscal devolution has not been properly implemented. The current status of district councils is like empty shells that are lacking substantive decision-making powers to drive service delivery effectively. Thus, for councillors to make a difference, functions and funds need to be further devolved. There are huge bureaucratic and political blockages that need to be dealt with. The legal framework and administration need rationalisation and this requires new legislation and policy.

Given a completely new cohort of councillors that was elected in 2014, the majority with little formal education and limited capacity to understand the complex system, the learning curve may take a considerable amount of time. Councillors and MPs from different parties need to cooperate and have a common agenda to improve service delivery in their jurisdictions as both have votes on councils. However, early signs are showing potential for increased conflict and representation battles between the two key locally elected actors: the councillor and the MP, as each vies for control of limited resources as a tool for political recognition among the constituencies as *'mwini chitukuko'* or *'wobweretsa chitukuko'* (someone who brings development). Improved service delivery is unlikely to happen because the elite political settlement in Malawi has not changed. If anything, the 2014 elections and the distribution of votes – with four main parties, none of them polling more than 36 per cent of the vote in the presidential elections, or seats in the National Assembly – may reinforce its competitive clientelist nature.

Notes

1 Excerpts from a UDF MP who presented the private members' motion on CDF. *Hansard*, 39th session of Parliament, Thursday, 27 April 2006, p. 15.
2 Excerpts from a contribution by an MCP MP. *Hansard*, 39th session of Parliament, Thursday 27 April 2006, p. 20.
3 Excerpts from a contribution by a DPP MP. *Hansard*, 39th session, Thursday, 27 April 2006, p. 18.
4 Suzgo Khunga, 'Increase CDF to MK 30 million-MP', *The Nation*, Friday, 26 June 2015.
5 Ephraim Nyondo, 'Who Should Control the CDF Wallet', *The Nation*, Wednesday, 17 November 2014.
6 See http://afrobarometer.org/data/malawi-round-4-data-2008.
7 Up to April 2014, district consultative forums were the main decision-making bodies before the constitution of legally elected councils.
8 Guidelines for the Teacher Housing Project, Malawi Government (2010), p. 2.

References

Ahmad, J., Devarajan, S., Khemani, S. and Shah, S. (2006) 'Decentralisation and Service Delivery', in Ahmad, E. and Brosio, G. (eds) *Fiscal Decentralisation: A Political Economy Perspective*, Cheltenham: Edward Elgar Publishing.
Bird, R. (1993) 'Threading the Fiscal Labyrinth: Some Issues in Fiscal Decentralization', *National Tax Journal*, 46(2): 207–27.
Bird, R. (1995) *Financing Local Services: Patterns, Problems, and Possibilities*. Toronto: Centre for Urban and Community Studies, University of Toronto.
Bird, R. (2003) 'Subnational revenues: realities and prospects', reading for course on Intergovernmental Fiscal Relations and Local Financial Management, Washington, DC: World Bank.
Bird, R. and François, V. (1998) *Fiscal Decentralisation in Developing Countries*, Cambridge: Cambridge University Press.
Cammack, D. and O'Neil, T. (2014) *Fragmented Governance and Local Service Delivery*, London: ODI.
Cammack, D., Golooba-Mutebi, F., Kanyongolo, F. and O-Neil, T. (2007) 'Neopatrimonial Politics, Decentralisation and Local Government: Uganda and Malawi in 2006', ODI Working Paper No. 2, London: Overseas Development Institute.
Chasukwa, M. and Chinsinga, B. (2013) 'Slapping Accountability in the Face: Observance of Accountability in Malawi's Local Governments in the Absence of Councillors', *International Journal of Public Administration*, 36: 354–66.
Chasukwa, M., Chiweza, A. and Chikapa-Jamali, M. (2014) 'Participation in Local Assemblies in Malawi in the Absence of Local Elected Representatives: Political Eliticism or Pluralism?', *Journal of Asian and African Studies*, 49(6): 705–20.
Chinsinga, B. (2007) *The Politics of Poverty Reduction in Malawi*, Johannesburg: EISA.
Chinsinga, B. (2008) 'Poverty Reduction in Malawi: A Critical Appraisal', in Crawford, G. and Hartman, C. (eds) *Decentralisation in Africa: A Pathway out of Poverty and Conflict*, Amsterdam: Amsterdam University Press.

Chinsinga, B. (2009) *The Interface between Local Level Politics, Constitutionalism and State Formation in Malawi through the Lens of the Constituency Development Fund (CDF)*. A Research Report, Chancellor College, University of Malawi. Available at: http://www.eldis.org/go/home&id=58474&type=Document#.VtMO_-b-W5g (accessed 28 February 2016).

Chiweza, A. (1998) 'Is the centre willing to share power? The role of local government in a democracy'. *Bwalo: A Forum for Social Development*, 2(2): 93–107.

Chiweza, A. (2010a) 'Public Sector Reforms and Decentralisation of Public Services: Lessons from Malawi', in Tambulasi, R. (ed.) *Public Sector Reforms*, Dhaka: Codesria.

Chiweza, A. (2010b) *A Review of the Malawi Decentralisation Process: Lessons from selected districts*, Blantyre: Concern Universal and Ministry of Local Government and Rural Development.

Chiweza, A. (2011) *A Baseline Study of the Local Development Fund and its Effect on Water Financing*. Report commissioned by Water Aid, Lilongwe: Water Aid.

Chiweza, A. and Munthali, C. (2012) *Review of the Constituency Development Fund Guidelines*, Lilongwe: National Local Government Finance Committee.

Chiweza, A. and Waldock, S. (2011) 'Political Economy of Local Government in Malawi', Unpublished DFID Working Paper.

Fjelstad, O. (2001) 'Intergovernmental fiscal relations in the developing world: A review of issues', in Levy, N. and Tapcott, C. (eds) *Intergovernmental Relations in South Africa: The challenges of Cooperative Government*, Cape Town: School of Government, University of Western Cape.

Kaunda, M. (1999) 'State Centralisation and the decline of local government in Malawi'. *International Review of Administrative Sciences*, 65(4): 579–95.

Kutengule, M., Kampanje, R., Chiweza, A. and Chunga, D. (2014) *Review of the National Decentralisation Programme II*. Joint Review. Lilongwe: Ministry of Local Government and Ministry of Rural Development.

León-Alfonso, S. (2007) *The Political Economy of Fiscal Decentralisation: Bringing Politics to the Study of Intergovernmental Transfers*, Barcelona: Institut d'Estudis Autonòmics.

Lockwood, B. (2006) 'Fiscal Decentralisation: A Political Economy Perspective', in Ahmad, E. and Brosio, G. (eds) *Handbook of Fiscal Federalism*, Cheltenham: Edward Elgar Publishing.

Malawi Government (1998a) *Local Government Act*, Zomba: Government Printer.

Malawi Government (1998b) *Malawi Decentralisation Policy*, Zomba: Government Printer.

Malawi Government (2010) *Primary School Staff Housing Project: Implementation Guidelines*. Lilongwe: Local Development Fund.

OECD (1991) 'The role of intermediate and local levels of government: the experience of selected OECD countries'. A background document prepared for a seminar on Fiscal Federalism in Economies in Transition, Paris.

O'Neil, T. (2014) 'Will the new government and local councils improve service delivery in Malawi?', available at: http://opendemocracy.net (accessed 1 June 2015).

Ordeshook, P. C. and Shvetsova, O. (1997) 'Federalism and Constitutional Design'. *Journal of Democracy* 8(1): 27–42.

Ssewankambo, E., Chiweza, A. and Nyondo, J. (2004) *Malawi Decentralised Governance Programme: Midterm Review Final Report*, Lilongwe: United Nations Development Programme.

Tambulasi, R. (2010) 'Local Government Without Local Governance: A New Institutional Perspective of Local Governance Policy Paralysis in Malawi', *Public Policy and Administration*, 26(3): 333–52.

7 Searching for a holy grail?

The nexus between agriculture and youth unemployment

Blessings Chinsinga and Michael Chasukwa

Introduction

The question of growing youth unemployment is a pressing policy problem not only in Malawi but also across the African continent. This also rings true in the global context mainly due to the rapidly expanding share of young people as a proportion of the global population. It is estimated that young people (in the 15–24 age bracket) make up as much as 1.2 billion of the global population currently estimated to be 7 billion, which represents a 17 per cent increase since 1995 (de Gobbi and Anang, 2008). The enormity of the problem is borne out of the fact that the youth population boom has been unevenly distributed across the globe with almost 87 per cent of the total global youth population living in developing countries. Existing evidence suggests that the youth population is growing much faster than can actually be accommodated in the labour markets. Sub-Saharan Africa has experienced a disproportionate increase in the number of unemployed young people, rising from 8 million to 10 million between 2007 and 2011. It is against this backdrop that Valle (2012) estimates that youth unemployment is about three times higher than in other age groups in sub-Saharan Africa.

The situation in Malawi is not too far off from Valle's (2012) estimates. While the official unemployment in Malawi is estimated at 9.3 per cent, youth unemployment is projected at about 15.2 per cent, which suggests it is a serious problem, especially since Malawi is a predominantly youthful nation (Chinsinga and Chasukwa, 2012). The main concern is that chronic youth unemployment can be disastrous and entail adverse long-term consequences for the social, economic and political fabric of society unless appropriate measures are taken to deal with it. This chapter focuses on the nexus between agriculture and youth unemployment in Malawi motivated by the fact that, although agriculture is officially described as an engine of economic growth and is the largest employer in the country, efforts to comprehensively address the question of chronic youth unemployment have been few and far between (Chinsinga, 2008; Chirwa, 2008; Chapota, 2009).

The Technical Entrepreneurship and Vocational Education and Training Authority (TEVETA),[1] for example, does not offer its apprentices opportunities in any agricultural-related trades. Similarly, Malawi's latest youth policy does not pay explicit attention to the agricultural sector even though its central theme is the promotion of youth empowerment. We argue that the problem of youth unemployment in Malawi can be successfully dealt with when serious attention is paid to the linkage between youth policies and the agricultural sector, as the agricultural sector is the engine of economic growth and the biggest employer. An agricultural-led industrialization strategy has potential to create decent jobs for young people because it can foster the development of other aspects of the value chain that are currently underdeveloped, such as input supply, processing, storage, marketing and distribution (Kamchacha, 2012).

The main challenge is that politicians have captured nearly all the efforts that have been implemented to address the question of chronic youth unemployment. Youth policies and interventions are primarily designed as a means of capturing young people as a voting bloc and not as a reflection of genuine commitment to bringing about sustainable changes in the livelihoods of young people. Youth policies and interventions are often not well thought out in terms of institutional design, implementation modalities, and the underlying theory of change. This has greatly contributed to the marginalization of the agricultural sector's efforts to combat youth unemployment even though agriculture is officially designated as the leading engine of economic growth and by far the country's biggest employer. Political imperatives often take precedence since these initiatives are often launched either just before or after general elections and their implementation is often marred by excessive political interference. The marginalization of the agricultural sector in combating the problem of youth unemployment is further reinforced by the fact that the current emphasis in Malawi is still very much on primary production which is less attractive to young people compared to other aspects of the agricultural sector value chain such as input supply, processing, storage, marketing, and distribution.

We begin by examining the youth unemployment situation and the potential that agriculture has in terms of addressing the problem. Thereafter we briefly examine how young people have featured in the country's agricultural policy portfolio, as well as the extent to which the agriculture sector is featured in national youth policy as a potential catalyst for the participation of young people in mainstream economic activities and empowerment. We also discuss how agriculture has been neglected in the efforts to combat youth unemployment with particular reference to certain post-1994 initiatives such as the Youth Development Credit Scheme (YDCS), the Youth Enterprise Development Fund (YEDEF), and the Youth Job Creation Initiative (YJCI). We conclude by observing that the agricultural sector has been overlooked as part of a solution for youth unemployment because of the weak patronage platform it offers since the clients themselves have little interest in picking up a career in the agricultural sector.

Youth unemployment in Malawi

According to De Gobbi and Anang (2008), Malawi currently has 6.1 million people in work out of the total population of 15 million. The majority of this workforce plies their trade in the informal sector since only 2.5 per cent are employed by the private sector and a mere 3.6 per cent work in the public sector.

The dominance of the informal sector implies that the majority of Malawians earn their livelihoods as smallholder farmers. Women dominate the informal sector as they make up only 20 per cent of wage employment. Thus, women are more likely to be engaged in informal sector work than men (Durevall and Mussa, 2010). The majority of women work in the agriculture, forestry and fisheries sectors. It is estimated that out of the 6.1 million potential workforce, about 5.7 million are either unemployed or underemployed in subsistence farming or in the formal sector (Durevall and Mussa, 2010).

The National Statistics Office (NSO) paints a grim picture about the status of youth unemployment in Malawi (GoM, 2008). It estimated that 82 per cent of young people (15–29 yrs.) were neither employed nor actively seeking for work. Youth urban poverty is estimated at over 50 per cent. It was further estimated that only 18 per cent of young people were self-employed, which is taken as a proxy indicator for the extent of youth involvement in the informal economy. To put things in perspective, the Methodist Relief and Development Fund (2012) ranked Malawi second in the world in terms of the magnitude of youth unemployment.

The prognosis for future youth unemployment is generally bleak, with young people finding it increasingly difficult to get absorbed into the labour market. In 2008, for instance, 14 per cent of young people had completed tertiary education, but they faced serious challenges in securing formal sector employment. Malawi has also struggled to generate a pool of young people with basic numeracy skills, which is one of the critical requirements for improving employment prospects. And it is estimated that as much as 8.6 per cent of young people (10–29) years drop out of school before the completion of primary education (GoM, 2008, 2010). Youth unemployment is particularly bad in rural areas where so many individuals depend on very small parcels of land for survival (Smith, 1999; Chinsinga, 2008).

Despite numerous challenges, the agricultural sector in Malawi has considerable potential to generate large-scale employment opportunities. Being the single most important sector of the Malawi economy, agriculture contributes 37 per cent of the country's GDP, employs around 80 per cent of the workforce, and contributes over 90 per cent of foreign exchange earnings (Chinsinga, 2008; Chirwa, 2008). Malawi's dualistic agriculture consists of smallholder and estate sectors. Despite being constrained by limited capital and technology, smallholder farmers cultivate as much as 2.4 million hectares, produce about 80 per cent of Malawi's food and contribute 20 per cent of its agricultural exports (Chirwa and Matita, 2012). The dominance of the agricultural sector in the country's economic portfolio has been further reinforced by the progressive decline of the manufacturing sector, from 16 per cent to 11 per cent since the early 1990s.

Chinsinga (2008) argues that, while agro-processing constitutes 26 per cent of manufacturing, it contributes less than 3 per cent to GDP, illustrating how various aspects of the agricultural value chain remain highly underdeveloped.

Thus, although agriculture is the largest sector of the economy, some have argued that it is not as productive as it should have otherwise been (Kamchacha, 2012) and that the sector's full potential is yet to be fully realized. Its limited productivity is mainly due to an overemphasis on primary production, neglecting altogether the complementary aspects of the sector's value chain (Kamchacha, 2012; Chinsinga and Chasukwa, 2013).

A key question concerns the reasons behind the agricultural sector not being prioritized in the efforts to address the problem of chronic youth unemployment in the country. The paradox therefore is that, while agriculture is the largest sector of the economy, it is not the largest employer of the largest demographic group in the country. This raises some serious questions about how the problem of youth unemployment features in the policy processes and in strategic decision making.

Youth and agricultural policy

Malawi witnessed a proliferation of policies for specific sectors following the transition to democracy in May 1994 (Chinsinga, 2007). Following the 1965–69 development plan, the country developed two ten-year statements of development policies (1970–80 and 1987–96). These were basically programmatic outlines of the country's development endeavours in various sectors of the economy. They provided the long-term developmental perspective, which in turn guided the medium-term and annual planning.

Although the statement of development policies did not specifically pay attention to young people, they were well taken care of by the establishment of the Malawi Young Pioneers (MYP) in 1963. The MYP provided for an elaborate strategy for dealing with the question of youth employment and preparing them to take meaningful roles in society. According to Rupiya (2005), the MYP was structured around the Kibbutz model of Israel. The MYP established training bases across the country, which implemented entrepreneurship, technical, agriculture, and leadership programmes among the young people (Kamchacha, 2012). These training bases were established in 21 out of 24 districts across the country and the MYP initiative consequently ensured that Malawian young people were self-employed in agriculture, trade, construction, and carpentry after their training.

The MYP enrolled young people of all backgrounds – from primary school dropouts to university graduates. Regardless of their qualifications, the young people had to undergo three years of rigorous training that emphasized respect, discipline, physical fitness, and dedication to duty (Mandiza, 2009). Those with better educational qualifications were enrolled with various training colleges, whereas the bulk of those with little or no educational attainments returned to their respective communities with a clear mandate to fight three deadly enemies:

ignorance, disease, and poverty. The impact of the MYP recruits returning to their respective communities was reportedly quite significant. One of our informants reported that 'youth training at MYP had significant multiplier effects at the community level because when back to their communities, the MYP recruits were working with everyone to promote modern methods of farming which guaranteed food security'.[2]

While the MYP initiative was viewed positively as an arena that linked young people to agriculture and various vocational training activities, it was condemned by the general public for also functioning as a paramilitary wing of the former ruling party, the Malawi Congress Party (MCP). The MYP was discredited because it progressively became an instrument of political control and social militarization of the Malawi society. Thus, in addition to promoting agricultural production, various vocational skills and entrepreneurship, the MYP acted as the vanguard for the defence of the nation (Rupiya, 2005; Mandiza, 2009).

The love–hate relationship with the MYP was expressed as much in the interviews with various stakeholders. While acknowledging the positive aspects of MYP, they condemned its use as an instrument of political control and terror that led to its abandonment in 1993. For instance, one of the interviewees described the MYP as 'being a very good initiative that allowed youth to become meaningful and useful members of society but it was tainted because some of the youths were used to harass and torture the people that did not agree with government on some of its policies and practices'.[3] The abandonment of the MYP created an institutional vacuum for rural youth, which stakeholders are still struggling to fill.

The transition to democracy in May 1994 was also accompanied by a swift implementation of structural adjustment programmes (SAPs), which have had significant implications on the role of the state in matters of employment. According to Changuta (2002), the apparent vacuum that followed the abandonment of the MYP is not surprising because SAPs recommend a passive role of employment creation to the government. This means that the state should not take deliberate strategic planning and active measures aimed at the generation of employment, especially the creation of youth employment.

The debilitating effects of SAPs invariably popularized what White (2012) calls 'do it yourself employment strategy for the youth'. Instead of encouraging the state to actively drive the employment creation process, international organizations such as the International Labour Organization (ILO), World Bank and the United Nations Industrial Organization are encouraging the state to promote entrepreneurship among young people as a strategy to get them employed. The currency of this philosophy was clearly reflected in the 1996 youth policy, which was designed to take care of the vacuum following the disbandment of the MYP. The major weakness of this policy is that 'it did not foresee the need to link the youth to agriculture as a priority area' (Kamchacha, 2012: 13). This linkage is still absent even in the current (2010) revised youth policy. Although agriculture is widely regarded as an engine of economic growth in Malawi, there is no clear link between the youth policy and the agricultural sector.

The status of current policy

The revised draft youth policy whose mission statement is to create an enabling environment for all young people to develop their full potential in order to significantly contribute to personal and national development, identifies six priority areas although none of these makes explicit linkages to the agricultural sector. These priority areas include:

- education, science, technology and environment;
- sports and culture;
- health and nutrition;
- social services and recreation;
- youth participation and leadership; and
- youth economic empowerment.

This means that the failure of the draft youth policy to close this gap and ensure linkage to agriculture 'will make it fail to achieve the intended goal of youth participation in key development activities' (Kamchacha, 2012: 14).

There has generally been a silence on youth in major policies that have been formulated in Malawi since May 1994. This is evident in the critical reviews of these policies (Chinsinga and Chasukwa, 2012). Young people are not treated and targeted as a distinct category needing attention either in the Poverty Alleviation Programme (1994); Vision 2020 (1998); the Malawi Poverty Reduction Strategy Paper (2001); One Village One Product (OVOP) (2001); the Malawi Growth and Development Strategy (MGDS) (2006); or the Malawi Growth and Development Strategy (MGDS) (GoM, 2012). Young people do not even appear in the sections on crosscutting issues dominated by gender, HIV/AIDS, environment and technology. Similarly, Bennel (2007) argued that young people, as a group, are not a priority for most governments in low-income countries. Consequently, ministries of youth are generally subsumed or combined with other government responsibilities, most commonly culture, sports and education.

Young people are moreover not given attention in the agricultural sector wide approach (ASWAp), which was inspired by the Comprehensive African Agriculture Development Programme (CAADP). Through CAADP, African governments have committed themselves to allocate at least 10 per cent of their annual national budgets to the agricultural sector and aim to achieve a 6 per cent growth target per year (Chinsinga, 2012). The critical review of the ASWAp suggests that young people are not an integral part of the efforts to revive the fledging agricultural sector in the country. According to the National Coordinator of the Civil Society Agriculture Network (CISANET), ASWAp 'has overlooked the importance of youth in agriculture … yet youth make up the biggest proportion of the national population'. He argued that this is not unique to the ASWAp, but rather the trademark of all agricultural-oriented policies. They do not 'actually talk about youth; they simply talk about males and females … and in the minds of the policy makers the distinction between youth and adult farmers does not really matter'.[4]

The neglect of agriculture as a possible source of employment for rural youth is manifested in the country's curricula for vocational training. According to Valle (2012), the curriculum shows a lack of connection between the demand of the labour market and the preparation by the government of the new generation. While 85 per cent of the population live in rural areas – and agriculture accounts for 39 per cent of GDP, over 80 per cent of the labour force, and over 90 per cent of total exports – agriculture is not among the courses offered by the TEVETA. The apparent neglect of agriculture explains why various aspects of its value chain remain hugely undeveloped for it to be fully exploited as a source of viable employment opportunities for young people. Agriculture is viewed by young people mainly in terms of primary production activities that are described as 'unattractive since they make farmers dirty on a daily basis yet these activities are not rewarding at all'.[5]

Young people's perceptions of TEVETA are not encouraging either. They described it as lacking capacity to train as many young people as possible, as was the case with the MYP, but also that its training is perceived as substandard. In a focus group discussion, Likhubula youth club members observed that 'those who have undergone TEVETA programs are not as competitive as those who undergo Trade Tests exams administered by the Ministry of Labour and Manpower Development [sic]'. Moreover, there are concerns that rural youth are marginalized in TEVETA activities because they do not often have adequate information about these opportunities. While these opportunities are meant mainly for rural youth 'they are monopolized by the urban youth since they do not only have ready access to information about these opportunities but they also exploit their networks and connections'.[6]

Explaining the neglect of agriculture

The apparent neglect of agriculture as a potential source of employment for young people is mainly due to the political imperatives associated with a democratic political dispensation in a neo-patrimonial setting. Political elites are often preoccupied with devising strategies that can maintain them in power in the four or five year electoral cycles. According to Poulton (2012), politicians in a democracy need to offer what people want in order to receive their votes, and as such politicians should be inclined to respond to the priorities of the most dominant constituency. However, Joughin and Kjaer (2010) argue that democracies may or may not promote technocratic policymaking that addresses the interests of the median voter. This is often the case because the multiplication of demands on the state resulting from the universal franchise of the citizenry makes democracies more inclined to direct rather than indirect methods of policy implementation, which include subsidies and related hand-outs.

The preference of direct over indirect methods of policy implementation suggests that politicians prefer policies that benefit a large number of people in the short term and are highly visible, such as social policies. They thus prefer to win votes by delivering clientelist privileges rather than the more unattainable development or even public goods (Lindberg, 2003). This implies that elections could be a double-edged sword in the policy processes in a democratic dispensation within a neo-patrimonial context. Competitive elections may reinforce clientelism rather than counteract it because the governing elite would need to have an even tighter grip on material and coercive resources in order to prevent competitive patronage networks from engaging and threatening the state from within the system.

The main question politicians often ask about each policy is how it will help them either to capture power or stay in power. This disposition shapes the kind of policies elites choose and how they are subsequently implemented (Whitfield and Therkildsen, 2011). The bottom line is that ruling elites want to stay in power, and staying in power requires building and maintaining a political organization, which can be achieved through clientelistic or programmatic means. The rest of this section therefore demonstrates how political imperatives have contributed to handling the problem of youth unemployment in Malawi since the transition to democracy in a manner that more or less neglects the agricultural sector in spite of it being a leading sector of the country's economy.

The fertilizer subsidy programme (FISP)

While the implementation of FISP has led to the dramatic expansion of the volume of resources available to the agricultural sector, it has at the same time removed agricultural transformation from the agenda (Chinsinga, 2012). Although the implementation of the FISP since the 2005/06 growing season has greatly raised the profile of the agricultural sector in terms of resources, these are spent almost exclusively on FISP and thereby neglect other potentially transformative activities such as extension, research, irrigation, and infrastructure development. Since the launch of the FISP, the share of the agricultural sector in the national budget has fluctuated between 10.1 and 16.7 per cent. This is in line with the 2003 Maputo Declaration on Agriculture and Food security that underlies the Comprehensive African Agriculture Development Programme (CAADP).

However, Chirwa *et al.* (2013) argue that FISP has degenerated into a political tool – widely viewed by politicians as a quick fix to the problem of food security that often affects the country. FISP is seen as such because it plays a critical role in shoring up a government's legitimacy, as it has become the basis for a social contract between the people and rulers (Sahely *et al.*, 2005). There is thus a political–economic binding of the FISP since the question of food security is firmly at the centre of Malawi's electoral politics. Consequently, it is difficult for politicians to ignore FISP, as it has become the single most important vote winning issue (Chinsinga, 2010). This has greatly affected the way in which FISP is regarded by politicians and how the dynamics of its implementation take shape. Political leaders typically view FISP as primarily a programme to fix the problem of food insecurity rather than a programme that can catalyse fundamental agricultural transformation in the country. FISP is therefore viewed as a standalone programme without any linkages to a wide range of on-going rural development interventions because its main concern, especially from the politicians' perspective, is simply to guarantee food security for the people so that they maintain themselves in power.

It is therefore not surprising that there is little or no effort to ensure strategic and balanced investments in the agricultural sector so as to spearhead fundamental and sustainable structural transformation. It is estimated that up to 75 per cent of the budget for the Ministry of Agriculture and Food Security (MoAFS) is spent on FISP. The amount of resources directed to the provision of extension services, conducting research, and rural infrastructural development is quite negligible, yet these investments are critical to facilitating sustainable development of the sector (Khaila, 2012). We have also previously argued that the young people are overlooked in the implementation of FISP because of the apparent political capture of the programme (Chinsinga and Chasukwa, 2012). The criteria for identifying beneficiaries of FISP exclude young people, the main reason being that 'they do not own land and are energetic enough to work elsewhere to generate income to purchase agricultural inputs on their own from the market'.[7] This means that FISP operates on the premise that young people have adequate skills to make them competitive on the labour market, and that employment opportunities are readily available, yet existing statistics show that it is almost impossible for these young people to get employment in either the formal or informal sectors.

The obsession of politicians with FISP as a vote-spinning machine has made it impossible to shape its implementation dynamics in a way that would make the agricultural sector more productive and attractive to young people. This is because FISP is narrowly focused on principally bolstering production of smallholders growing maize, its availability equating to food security (Smale and Jayne, 2003). This means that even if ung people were to be included in FISP, it would not readily contribute to solving the youth unemployment problem. The young people are not interested in primary production but rather in other value chain aspects of the agricultural sector, such as marketing, processing, storage, and distribution. These are, of course, an integral part of FISP, but they are monopolized by the political elites (World Bank *et al.*, 2011). In one of the FGDs, the participants actually observed that:

> [the] time for us to stick to traditional understanding of farming as in growing maize is long gone. We have seen our grandfathers and fathers growing maize but this has not made any difference in their lives. Farming has ended up being a source of misery. We should aim higher than them and this involves going beyond their way of understanding and practicing farming.[8]

The persistence of the traditional conception of agriculture as exclusively primary production is a cause of concern because it has contributed to the negative perception of agriculture as an occupation of choice among young people. In fact, agriculture does not feature at all as a reliable livelihood strategy for young people. They generally view agriculture as old fashioned, an occupation of the poor, and an inconsequential enterprise. In a focus group discussion (FGD) with a youth club in Ntcheu district, agriculture was characterized as 'an enterprise without a future … if it had a future our parents would have changed their status, yet they have been farming since we were young'.[9] This indicates that the various segments of the value chain in the agricultural sector are not well developed. The point is that activities such as 'input supply, processing, storage and marketing and distribution could provide smart employment with a status equal to white collar employment' (Kamchacha, 2012: 10).

Youth empowerment initiatives after Malawi Young Pioneers (MYP)

The youth initiatives that have been implemented since the abandonment of the MYP initiative have almost entirely ignored the agricultural sector. The main initiatives include the Youth Development Credit Scheme (YDSC) and the Youth Enterprise Development Fund (YEDEF) (Chinsinga and Chasukwa, 2013). The lack of an explicit linkage of these initiatives to the agricultural sector might be attributed to the framing of the youth policy. Neither the initial or revised versions of the youth policy prioritize the agricultural sector as a potential catalyst for sustainable employment opportunities for young people. The main contributing factor to the apparent lack of policy coherence of the youth initiatives seems to be related to the underlying motivations of politicians when they propose and implement these policies. Politicians, without any significant technical input, often conceive these initiatives, which in turn are 'driven primarily by political imperatives rather than a well-thought out vision to transform the livelihoods of the youth'.[10] The political imperatives of these initiatives are underpinned by the timing of these initiatives. They are either launched just before or after elections 'because they either target the youth as a significant voting block or a way of saying thank you to them for voting the politicians into power'.[11]

The Youth Development Credit Scheme (YDCS)

The YDCS was funded to the tune of MK70 million when it was launched in August 1996 with financial support from the Commonwealth Credit Initiative. It was conceived as a revolving credit facility, and it was managed by the now defunct Small Enterprises Development Organization of Malawi (SEDOM), a quasi-governmental body. The YDCS targeted young men and women aged between 15 and 30 who had developed viable business plans and were ready to get started. It was a credit facility with concessionary interest rates pegged at 15 per cent against the prevailing market interest rates in the range of 20–25 per cent (Chinsinga, 2002).

The Youth Enterprise Development Fund (YEDEF)

The YEDEF was launched in 2010 with an initial capital of MK3 billion. The main objective of YEDEF is to provide easily accessible loans to young entrepreneurs in the form of capital equipment and working capital enabling them to venture into various areas including the agro-food sector (Chinsinga and Chasukwa, 2013). The loans are provided groups of at least ten young people or in some rare cases to individuals who have gone through a self-selection process duly appraised by the YEDEF district committee. When it was introduced, YEDEF targeted young people aged between 18 and 30 but the eligibility age bracket has since been extended to 35. According to its guidelines, the fund caters for school leavers, both skilled and unskilled, who are expected to engage in various trades such as agricultural production, construction, carpentry and joinery, panel beating, welding, and metal fabrication. The vision of YEDEF is to support groups of young people who have proven technical business skills as a means for them to earn independent livelihoods and even create employment for their fellows, particularly in rural areas.

Performance review of YDCS and YEDEF

A critical analysis of both YDCS and YEDEF shows that they have not been very successful. The dismal performance of these initiatives is attributed mainly to the fact that they were characterized by excessive political interference. Even though they were championed as youth initiatives, 'the primary targets were youths that were aligned to the parties in power at a particular moment'.[12] Both initiatives have failed to pass the sustainability test because they have been heavily politicized (Chinsinga, 2002; Whitby, 2012). The administrators of these initiatives are often forced by politicians to skip the laid-down procedures. The argument is that 'politicians put pressures on us to disburse loans to groups or individuals of their choice regardless of the laid out procedures. All they want is to gain political mileage.'[13] With particular reference to YEDEF, this became more or less the official policy when President Mutharika publicly declared that 'priority in disbursing YEDEF loans should be given to DPP youth cadets'.[14]

It is therefore not surprising that both YDCS and YEDEF have had dismal track records. YDCS could not be sustained as a revolving fund because the repayment rate was less than 10 per cent (Chinsinga, 2002). A recent assessment shows that the repayment rate for YEDEF is as low as 23 per cent (Chinsinga and Chasukwa, 2013). The prominence of politicians in deciding who should benefit or not from these initiatives has 'created the impression that the money given out is free money'.[15] Consequently, the popular perception about YEDEF is that 'the loan was meant to be a thank you to all those youth that contributed to the landslide victory of the party in the 2009 presidential and parliamentary elections'.[16] The decision to extend the age bracket to 35 for YEDEF's beneficiaries was therefore meant to 'expand the catchment of patronage as a strategy to mortgage the youth in readiness for the 2014 elections'.[17]

While in its design YEDEF is also expected to serve as a source of readily accessible credit to graduates from various vocal education training institutions, the review revealed that this linkage does not exist in practice. No graduates from vocational training institutions have benefited from YEDEF (Whitby, 2012). Priority consideration is given to young people who are politically connected. Even if the graduates were to benefit from YEDEF, this could not have had a positive impact on the agricultural sector. As noted earlier, the TEVETA curriculum does not include any modules on agriculture (Valle, 2012). Nevertheless, under the auspices of its Skills Development Initiative, TEVETA (2009) offers short-term training in agriculture but only upon request from communities. The demand for such training is essentially non-existent because communities are expected to shoulder the costs of delivery, which they cannot afford. The failure of this initiative to take off further reinforces the marginalization of the agricultural sector in the efforts to combat youth unemployment especially since the majority of new agriculturalists are reluctant to work in rural areas because 'they cannot fulfil their dreams as a network generation'.[18] They can't imagine themselves living in areas without electricity and Internet connectivity. This is greatly contributing to the emergence of an orphaned generation of farmers who are hardly supported by a coherent system of provision of extension services, which is quite critical to spearheading potential agrarian transformation.

Bringing back agriculture into youth development?

The Youth Job Creation Initiative (YJCI) launched by President Banda on 15 March 2013 appeared poised to bring back agriculture to the fore of youth development. The YJCI was launched in pursuance of the aspirations of the national youth policy and the Malawi Growth and Development Strategy (MGDS II) (GoM, 2012). It was further justified as a strategy for dealing with the problem of chronic youth unemployment by exporting unskilled, skilled, and semi-skilled labour to countries where they could acquire skills and knowledge that would in turn be put to productive use here at home upon return. The target countries for youth labour export included South Korea, Kuwait, and the United Arab Emirates.

The YJCI targets young people aged between 19 and 25 with aspirations to work in the services, tourism, and agricultural sectors. It was announced at the launch of the YJCI that the government had secured a youth labour export contract with South Korea under which up to 100,000 young people would be engaged.[19] The Ministry of Labour floated two adverts for employment opportunities in South Korea, one of them generic in nature while the other had a particular emphasis on the agricultural sector. The generic advert stipulated the following attributes of the prospective applicants:

- must be Malawian aged between 19 and 25;
- should have a minimum of the Malawi School Certificate of Education (MSCE);

- should be able to communicate in English;
- must be willing to undergo medical test at a designated hospital;
- should have a valid passport or be able to acquire one;
- should be able to raise money to pay for visa; and
- should have no criminal record.[20]

The advert with a bias towards the agricultural sector jobs asked for applicants with a degree in agriculture specializing in livestock management. This was touted as a programme that would:

> build capacity for the youth by engaging them in productive agricultural activities throughout the period of the contract and, at the end of the contract, the youth would put into practice the knowledge and skills gained as part of youth participation and empowerment.[21]

The YJCU was further described as an opportunity to make most young people productive since 'most of our youth are just sitting idle in villages and towns, they are not working, they are not in school, this is an opportunity for them to be productive'.[22]

The YJCI has more or less fallen through. It hit a dead end when the government of South Korea denied having sealed a youth labour export deal with the Malawi government. The rebuttal came through the African Division of South Korea's Foreign Affairs Ministry observing 'our government has not received any official request from Malawi that they want to send their workers to our country.'[23] Meanwhile the future of the initiative hangs in the balance. The first batch of 336 successful recruits who were ready to take up their posts in South Korea have been told to wait for fresh communication as to when exactly they will leave for South Korea.

Had the YJCI succeeded, it could have made important contributions to the development and subsequent transformation of the agricultural sector. Agriculture in Malawi remains grossly undeveloped and the exposure of a good number of young people to the South Korean advanced agricultural system could have helped to modernize Malawi's agricultural sector because the youth – often referred to as the 'Cheetah generation' – are not only receptive to new ideas, but also willing to adopt new practices quickly.

However, a critical review of the YJCI raises some serious doubts as to whether it would have facilitated the achievement of the desired transformation of the agricultural sector. The review shows that the institutional design of the YJCI would have made it extremely difficult for it to contribute meaningfully to the utilization of the skills and expertise that the beneficiaries would have acquired at the end of their contracts in South Korea. This is the case because the recruitment of young people for the South Korea job opportunities was done entirely by the district labour offices without the involvement of their counterparts from the agricultural sector. Moreover, no programme document was produced that 'stipulated how upon returning to the country, the youth would be taken on board so that they fully contribute to the country's socio-economic endeavours particularly in the agricultural sector'.[24] This shows that YJCI's linkage to the agricultural sector was very much a political rhetoric rather than a well-thought-out linkage at the technical level within the broader scheme of national development efforts.

It is therefore not surprising that the YJCI has been both praised and condemned as a strategic ploy to woo the youth vote ahead of the May 2014 general elections. Just like with YDCS and YEDEF, the popular perception is that YJCI is motivated more by political imperatives of winning an election than the genuine commitment to bringing about sustainable changes in the livelihoods of the young people who constitute about 60 per cent of the total population and are thus the biggest single voting bloc. This perception was rendered more credible when the Minister of Labour said that 'for the initiative to be fairly implemented there is need for the involvement of MPs who will help us identify youths from their respective constituencies'.[25]

Structural and funding constraints

There is an acknowledgement that the promotion of youth visibility in a coherent fashion in policy circles is undermined by structural constraints and limited funding for the sector (GoM, 2012). In terms of structural constraints, there is destructive competition between the Ministry of Youth Development and Sports (MoYDS) and the National Youth Council of Malawi (NYCoM) because there is a lack of clarity regarding their mandates. This has resulted in fierce contests between the two bordering on which is best positioned to champion the youth agenda. The persistent conflictual relationship between them has made it difficult for the two institutions to work together in championing the youth cause with a sense of purpose and unity of direction. This has made collaboration with other stakeholders difficult, to the detriment of young people, especially in view of the fact that youth issues are crosscutting in nature. The failure to collaborate with other sectors, particularly agriculture, is underlined by the absence of any reference to it in the revised draft policy, which makes it difficult to ensure that young people participate in key development activities (Kamchacha, 2012).

The youth sector is not prioritized in terms of funding and expenditure. Though young people constitute the largest proportion of the population funding for the youth sector has been quite negligible as a matter of routine. In the 2010/11 financial year, for instance, only MK826.69 million was allocated, which is hardly adequate to empower the MoYDS and NYCoM to implement their activities on notable scale and in a transformational manner. Funding projections in MGDS II to the youth sector are not encouraging either (GoM, 2012). It is projected that by the 2015/16 financial year, the government will have increased budgetary support for child development and youth empowerment from 1.6 per cent out of the 39.1 per cent of resources allocated to social development.[26]

Conclusion

There is no doubt that Malawi grapples with the question of chronic youth unemployment. This is, of course, not unique to Malawi. It is a serious problem across the developing world. It is a particular cause of concern in Malawi because some 60 per cent of its total population falls into the youth category. The future socio-economic prosperity depends on young people getting adequately prepared, and finding opportunities, to put their skills and expertise to proper use. The problem of chronic youth unemployment threatens to put to waste the potential demographic dividend that comes with predominantly youthful populations.

There have, of course, been concerted efforts on the part of the government to address this problem. Apart from the MYP, however, none of the initiatives developed to combat youth unemployment has paid particular attention to the agricultural sector in spite of its being Malawi's leading employer. This has further been reinforced by the fact that neither the initial nor the revised versions of the youth policy have made an explicit linkage between having a vibrant agricultural sector and empowerment of its young people. The preoccupation of politicians with agriculture as primary production focused principally on growing maize for purposes of ensuring food security has made it difficult to develop other aspects of the value chain of the sector that would have made it more attractive to young people (Anderson, 2011). Moreover, the support programmes to the agricultural sector do not include the young people, which makes it impossible to fully exploit its potential as the biggest employer in order to combat the problem of chronic youth unemployment.

The efforts to deal with youth unemployment such as YDCS and YEDEF are often not well thought through for them to achieve the desired strategic impact regardless of the fact they do not explicitly put particular emphasis on agriculture. Indeed, these programmes have received unfavourable reviews. This is mainly because the programmes are principally conceived and implemented to satisfy political goals rather than being a useful tool for improving the livelihoods of the young people. Both in terms of their timing and modalities of implementation, these programmes are designed to either capture or appease young people as a vocal political constituency. It is clear that policies or programmes directed at youth empowerment are driven by short-termism, motivated by the selfish desires of politicians to maintain themselves in power. This has greatly contributed to the marginalization of the agricultural sector in dealing with youth unemployment.

Notes

1 TEVETA is a semi-autonomous governmental organization mandated to facilitate the provision of technical, entrepreneurial and vocational education and training in Malawi. It is the operationalizing body of the 1998 National Policy on Technical, Entrepreneurial and Vocational Education and Training.
2 Interview with a project officer for YONECO, Ntcheu, 27 January 2013.
3 Interview with a principal officer at the Ministry of Sports and Youth, Lilongwe, 23 January 2013.
4 Ibid.

5 Focus group discussion (FGD) with members of Likhubula Youth Club, Zomba, 2 February 2013.
6 FGD with members of Tithanidzane, Tigonjetse and Tipewe Youth Clubs, Ntcheu, 28 January 2013.
7 Interview with the district agricultural development officer (DADO), Ntcheu, 4 February 2013.
8 FGD participants with Likhubula Youth Club, Zomba, 2 February 2013.
9 FGD participants with Bwalo la Ana Youth Active Community Organization (BLAYACO), Ntcheu, 27 January 2013.
10 Interview with an official in the Ministry of Youth Development and Sports, Lilongwe, 28 January 2013.
11 Interview with an NGO official, Lilongwe, 31 January 2013.
12 Interview with an NGO official in Zomba district, 6 February 2013.
13 See "YEDEF for DPP Youth", *The Nation*, 6 March 2010.
14 Ibid.
15 Interview with the district youth officer, Zomba, 3 February 2013.
16 Interview with one of the senior officials of Ntcheu District Council, 24 February 2013.
17 Interview with an NGO official, Lilongwe, 23 January 2013.
18 Interview with the Chief Economist in the Ministry of Agriculture and Food Security (MoAFS), Lilongwe, 18 January 2013.
19 See "The Widening Gyre of Korea Saga: A Chronology", *Sunday Times*, 9 June 2013.
20 See *The Nation*, 22 March 2013.
21 See *The Nation*, 28 May 2013
22 Ibid.
23 See "Youth Export Palaver", *Africa–Asia Confidential*, 6(8) June 2013.
24 Interview with an agriculturalist at Bunda College of Agriculture, Lilongwe, 10 April 2013.
25 See "Malawi to Export Youth Labour to South Korea: President Banda Launches Initiative", *Malawi News Agency*, 15 March 2013.
26 The MGDS II identifies child development, youth development and empowerment as key priority areas under the theme of social development.

References

Anderson, A. (2011) 'Maize Remittances, Smallholder Livelihoods and Maize Consumption in Malawi', *Journal of Modern African Studies*, 49(1): 1–25.
Bennel, P. (2007) *Promoting Livelihood Opportunities for Rural Youth: Knowledge and Development*, Rome: International Fund for Agricultural Development (IFAD).
Changuta, F. (2002) 'The Socio-Economic Situation of Youth in Africa: Problems, Prospects and Options'. Available at: www.yesweb.org/gkr/res/bg.africa.doc (accessed 28 February 2013).
Chapota, R. (2009) 'National Policy Dialogue Synthesis Report: True Contribution of Agriculture to Economic Growth and Development in Malawi and its Policy Implications on Extension and Radio Programming'. Pretoria: Food, Agriculture and Natural Resources Policy Network (FANRPAN).
Chinsinga, B. (2002) 'The Politics of Poverty Alleviation in Malawi: A Critical Appraisal', in Englund, H. (Ed.) *A Democracy of Chameleons: Politics and Culture in New Malawi*, Stockholm: Elanders Golab and Nordiska Afrika Institutet.
Chinsinga, B. (2007) 'Reclaiming Policy Space: Lessons from Malawi's Fertilizer Subsidy Programme', A Paper Presented at the World Bank Development Report Workshop, 21–24 January, Institute of Development Studies (IDS), Brighton.

Chinsinga, B. (2008) 'Exploring the Politics of Land Reforms in Malawi: A Case Study of the Community Based Rural Land Development Project (CBDRLDP)', IPPG Discussion Paper Series No. 20. Manchester: University of Manchester.

Chinsinga, B. (2010) 'Seeds and Subsidies: The Political Economy of Input Programmes in Malawi', Future Agricultures Working Paper No. 13, Institute of Development Studies (IDS), Brighton.

Chinsinga, B. (2012) 'The Political Economy of Agricultural Policy Processes in Malawi: A Case Study of the Fertilizer Subsidy Programme', Future Agricultures Working Paper No. 39, Institute of Development Studies (IDS), Brighton.

Chinsinga, B., and Chasukwa, M. (2012) 'Youth Agriculture and Land Grabs in Malawi', *IDS Bulletin*, 43(6): 67–77.

Chinsinga, B., and Chasukwa, M. (2013) 'Agricultural Policy, Employment Opportunities and Social Mobility in Rural Malawi', Institute of Development Studies (IDS), Brighton.

Chirwa, E. (2008) 'Land Tenure, Farm Investments and Food Production in Malawi', IPPG Discussion Paper Series, No. 18, Manchester: University of Manchester.

Chirwa, E., and Matita, M. (2012) 'From Subsistence to Smallholder Commercial Agriculture Farming in Malawi: A Case of NASFAM Commercialization Initiative', Future Agricultures Working Paper No. 37, Institute of Development Studies (IDS), Brighton.

Chirwa, E., Matita, M., Mvula, P., and Dorward, A. (2013) 'Repeated Access and Impacts of the Farm Input Subsidy Programme in Malawi: Any Prospects of Graduation?' Future Agricultures Working Paper No. 65, Brighton: Institute of Development Studies (IDS).

De Gobbi, M., and Anang, R. (2008) 'The Enabling Environment for Sustainable Enterprises in Malawi', Small Enterprise Programme, Job Creation and Enterprise Development Department. Geneva: International Labour Organization (ILO).

Durevall, D., and Mussa, R. (2010) 'Employment Diagnostics: Analysis on Malawi', Geneva: International Labour Organization (ILO).

GoM (2008) *Population and Housing Census: NSO*, Government of Malawi,. Zomba: Government Printer.

GoM (2010) *Malawi Demographic Health Survey*, National Statistics Office (NSO), Government of Malawi, Zomba: Government Printer.

GoM (2012) *Malawi Growth and Development Strategy (MGDS) II*, Government of Malawi, Lilongwe: Ministry of Economic Planning and Development.

Joughin, J., and Kjaer, A. (2010) 'The Politics of Agricultural Policy Reform: The Case of Uganda', *Forum for Development Studies*, 37(1): 61–78.

Kamchacha, C. (2012) 'Current and Emerging Youth Policies and Initiatives and the Links to Agriculture: Malawi Case Study Report', Pretoria: Food, Agriculture and Natural Resources Policy Analysis Network (FANRPAN).

Khaila, S. (2012) 'Rethinking Agricultural extension in Malawi', Civil Society Net on Agriculture (CISANET) Discussion Policy Paper. Lilongwe: CISANET.

Lindberg, S. (2003) '"It's Our Time to Chop": Do Elections in Africa Feed Neo-Patrimonialism Rather than Counteract it?' *Democratization*, 10(2): 121–40.

Mandiza, E. (2009) 'Civil–Military Relations in Malawi: An Historical Perspective', in Williams, R., Cawthra, G. and Abrahams, D. (Eds) *Ourselves to Know: Civil–Military Relations and Defense Transformation in Southern Africa*, Pretoria: Institute for Security Studies.

Methodist Relief and Development Fund (2012) 'Tackling Youth Unemployment in Malawi', Available at: www.mrdf.org.uk/images/tackling-youth-unemployment-in-malawi (accessed 22 March 2013).

Poulton, C. (2012) 'Democratization and the Political Economy of Agricultural Policy in Africa', Future Agricultures Working Paper No. 43, Institute of Development Studies (IDS), Brighton.

Rupiya, M. (2005) 'The Odd Man Out: A History of the Malawi Army since July 1964', in Rupia, M. (Ed.) *Evolutions and Revolutions*, Pretoria: Institute for Security Studies.

Sahely, C., Groelsema, B., Marchione, T., and Nelson, D. (2005) 'The Governance Dimension of Food Security in Malawi', Lilongwe: USAID.

Smale, M., and Jayne, T. (2003) 'Maize in Eastern and Southern Africa: Seeds of Success in Retrospect', EPTD Discussion Paper No. 97: International Food Policy Research Institute (IFPRI).

Smith, W. (1999) *Safety Nets in Malawi: How Much? For How Many?* Lilongwe: World Bank.

TEVETA (2009) 'Malawi Labour Market Survey', Lilongwe: Technical Entrepreneurship and Vocational Education and Training Authority.

Valle, F. (2012) *Exploring Opportunities and Constraints for Young Agro-Entrepreneurs in Africa*, Rome: FAO.

Whitby, G. (2012) 'The Development Situation in Malawi: How can the UK best help to improve opportunities for economic growth, job creation and meeting the millennium development goals (MDGs)?' A Report submitted to the Commons Select Committee: London.

White, B. (2012) 'Agriculture and the Generation Problem: Rural Youth, Employment and the Future of Farming', *IDS Bulletin*, 43(6): 9–19.

Whitfield, L. and Therkildsen, O. (2011) 'What Drives States to Support the Development of Productive Sectors? Strategies Ruling Elites Pursue for Political Survival and the Policy Implications', DIIS Working Paper 15. Copenhagen: Danish Institute for International Studies.

World Bank *et al.* (2011) *Malawi: Poverty Reduction Support Credit, Fertilizer Procurement Review of the 2010/11 Farm Input Subsidy Program (FISP)*, World Bank, Ministry of Finance, Ministry of Agriculture and Food Security and Office of the Director of Public Procurement and Central Internal Audit, December 2010–February 2011.

Part III
Activism, aid and accountability

8 Against all odds

Parliamentary oversight over a dominant executive

Nandini Patel

Introduction

After almost two decades of embracing multiparty democracy, most legislatures in Africa continue to face the crisis of a dominant executive – a hangover of the military or civilian one-party state of the 1960s to the early 1990s where they rubber stamped the laws and legislations made by the executive. Indeed, the dividing line between party and state in Africa remain blurred. The persistence of a one-party culture is almost pervasive across the continent irrespective of regime change, making an over powerful executive endemic and destructive to democratic progression. Two interrelated factors are responsible for this:

- weak institutionalisation of democratic pillars, such as the rule of law, participation, representation and accountability; and
- the tendency to follow informal practices and norms, thereby setting aside formal rules and procedures.

The critical question is whether the democratic institutional reforms of the 1990s have been in line with an evolving culture of democracy with respect to adherence to the rule of law. Is there adequate space for representation of citizens' interest and welfare?

The adoption of democratic order with embedded principles of checks and balances requires the legislature to be a vital democratic institution serving as a bridge between state and society by carrying out its legislative, oversight and representative functions in ways that strengthen the good governance values of accountability, transparency and participation (Parliamentary Centre Canada, *et al.*, 2005). In this setting, legislatures typically perform three vital functions – legislation, representation and oversight – and parliamentarians owe their allegiance to the party, the electorate from their constituencies and to the nation at large. While the effectiveness of democratic legislatures is based on a plethora of factors – constitutional framework, political system, political culture, level of independence of constitutional bodies – much also depends on the effective utilisation of the tools for oversight that are at the disposal of the legislature irrespective of whether it is a presidential or parliamentary type of government.

The tools mainly refer to the parliamentary oversight committees and ministerial questions and the role these play as scrutiny mechanisms. In nascent democracies, the effective utilisation of these tools is often impeded by constraints of resources, capacity and political commitment.

The focus of this chapter is on a strong three-party scenario that emerged in Malawi in 1994, with the establishment of multiparty democratic order where the opposition (with a majority in parliament) could participate fairly effectively in exercising their accountability role through the parliamentary committee system. During this period, however, several bills that were subsequently deemed to violate the provisions of the Constitution were pushed through by the ruling party. The bills included an attempt to abolish the upper house of parliament and an attempt to extend the presidential term limit to a third term. The ensuing bitter disputes and deliberations in Parliament contributed to an overall weakening of the checks and balance system and generally weakened the role of the opposition.

The stable three-party composition of parliament collapsed with the 2004 elections. The party system witnessed fragmentation, mainly due to the contentious presidential third term issue, and there was a dramatic increase in the number of independent MPs (40) who were elected to parliament without party affiliation. The period between 2005 and 2008 was characterised by a tug of war between the executive and the legislature. The major cause of this was the formation of the Democratic Peoples' Party (DPP) – a new political entity within a year after President Bingu wa Mutharika took office and defected from the political party (UDF) that helped him get elected. Elected MPs were lured by the president to defect from their parties and swear allegiance to the newly formed DPP, and thereby provide support to the presidency. Thus, Mutharika survived an entire term with the support of MPs who had crossed the floor in violation of constitutional provisions. During this period, parliamentary sittings were shortened and once prorogued. Despite such hostile relations between the legislature and the executive, the Malawian parliament made a concerted effort to perform its oversight role amidst numerous challenges.

The landslide victory of the DPP in the 2009 elections not only vindicated the president's decisions to form a new party, but also provided hope for democratic consolidation, economic development, and normalcy and stability in the executive–legislature relationship. Unfortunately, subsequent years witnessed the legislation for draconian laws that curbed freedoms and stifled dissent as the DPP enjoyed an overwhelming majority in parliament. When Vice-President Joyce Banda assumed office following the death of President Mutharika in 2012, the executive–legislature tensions were once again revived. Despite being elected on a DPP ticket, Banda went on to form the People's Party (PP) by encouraging MPs to once more cross the floor, and like Mutharika survived for the rest of her term despite heated debates in parliament on the unconstitutional manner in which the PP was created. In the run up to 2014 elections, the Cashgate scandal – labelled the biggest corruption scandal in Malawi's history – brought renewed focus on the oversight role of parliament.

In the ensuing sections, I analyse the Malawian Parliament's oversight role during these critical junctures and draw conclusions on the prospects for it to play this role more effectively.

Theoretical perspectives on the legislature–executive relationship

In both long-established and new democracies, the legislature is given the power to check the power of the executive through a number of tools and mechanisms. Oversight is one of the tools of accountability to guarantee that government initiatives meet their stated objectives and respond to the needs of the community. Pelizzo *et al.* (2006) distinguish between 'oversight potential' and 'effective oversight'. Effective oversight entails legislatures actually overseeing the actions and activities of the executive and the extent to which such oversight function has an impact on the political system and, more specifically, on governmental behaviour. In contrast, oversight potential denotes the set of formal powers and instruments that legislatures have to oversee government activities regardless of whether these powers and instruments are actually used. A legislature's oversight potential is measured by the number of oversight tools available in a given country and how it affects the level of democracy. In most of the fledgling democracies, there is a gap between the formal powers that exist on paper and the actual powers that are available.

Another dimension of oversight relates to 'enforcement' or 'answerability'. Answerability refers to the obligation of the government, its agencies and public officials to provide information about their decisions and actions and to justify them to the public and those institutions of accountability tasked with providing oversight. Enforcement entails that the public or the institution responsible for accountability can sanction the offending party or remedy the contravening behaviour (O'Donnell, 1998) Even in mature democracies like the United Kingdom, the enforcement function of parliamentary committees is limited. There are very few explicit provisions for Parliament to enforce its will, or in which sanctions could be brought to bear on the non-compliant party (Gorden and Street, 2012). In the United States, the Congressional Committee has investigative powers, which it used quite extensively in, for example, the Watergate and Iran–Contra cases. Moreover, officials are compelled to testify at the hearings (except in matters of national security) and a refusal to testify can be cited for contempt of court – a criminal offence. However, in African democracies of the 1990s – which have largely adopted the American style of presidentialism – legislatures have not yet assumed the oversight role of the US Congress. We will, in subsequent sections of this chapter, discuss the legal frameworks available in Malawi for securing 'answerability' and 'enforcement'.

The legislature's role in approving the national budget is key, and it is often claimed that its 'power of the purse' is a fundamental feature of democracy. The vast majority of democratic constitutions require appropriations and taxation measures to be approved by the legislature in order to become effective (IEA, 2009). This is a challenging role for many legislatures given their resource constraints and limited capacity to undertake a delicate balancing act. However, it is now increasingly recognised that legislatures can play an important role in promoting economic governance, improving financial transparency and holding the executive to account. Enhancing legislative scrutiny of the budget and oversight of its execution is thus considered as a means of strengthening government accountability and controlling corruption.

The committee system is crucial for legislatures to play the above roles. Some scholars have argued that viable (albeit undeveloped) committees are now emerging in African legislatures, and bills introduced by the executive for passage in the legislature are no longer 'rubber stamped', but increasingly scrutinised and often amended before being passed into law. The involvement of civil society organisations in the legislative process is increasing, and the extensive oversight of the executive by the legislature is bearing positive outcomes (Bolarinwa, 2015).

Whilst it is true that committees contribute significantly to the vibrancy of the legislature, they are not decision-making bodies, except with respect to their own internal proceedings. They have no standing independent of the legislature. The committees report to the legislature, often with recommendations for decision for legislation and oversight. Generally, committees have a multiparty composition with members possessing expertise and experience in a specific field. Therefore, a committee represents political diversity and yet strives to arrive at unanimous recommendations for action. Their key role makes them important and visible. Individuals from within the legislature and outside often seek to engage with committees in order to influence outcomes.

A myriad of factors impede the objectivity and efficiency of parliamentary committees in countries like Malawi, including lack of technical expertise, inadequate resources and various types of pressure from administrative officials and party leaders. Indeed, the system of executive domination is often perpetrated by denying financial autonomy to Parliament. Although Parliament should in principle be funded directly as an organ of state or statutory expenditure, it is in Malawi funded via the Treasury, making access to funds unpredictable. And, although the parliamentary reform programme undertaken with foreign donor support in 2006 strongly recommended the securing of adequate and predictable budget and adherence to a fixed calendar for parliamentary sittings, these recommendations are yet to be implemented in the country (PRC, 2006).

The legislature alone cannot, of course, guarantee accountability across the entire range of governmental activity. There are other forms of scrutiny performed by extra-parliamentary bodies, and legislatures must work closely with these bodies. As Griffith (2005) argues, 'Parliament's role is in disentangling the key political issues from technical scrutiny, interpreting their significance and using this as the basis on which to challenge Government.' As it forms the apex of a hierarchical structure of scrutiny, legislatures must maintain a strong and relationship with extra-parliamentary accountability bodies such as the Human Rights Commission and the Ombudsman in addition to maintaining regular and close contact with civil society organisations.

Executive accountability to Parliament in Malawi

'Cashgate' – where large sums of public funds were stolen by a group of politicians and civil servants, causing major difficulties for the Malawian state in providing basic services – created large-scale public anger and mounted considerable pressure on the parliament to perform its designated oversight role. And, since the 2014 elections, demands on the President to appear before Parliament to respond to questions on the budget have been mounting. Thus the Legal Affairs Committee has claimed that the President would be violating the Constitution if he did not appear before the House during the debates on the 2015/16 expenditure plan. The committee went on to draw attention to two distinct provisions in Section 89 of Malawi's Constitution dealing with the requirement of the President to appear before Parliament (Constitution of Malawi 1994). Section 96(1)(e) of the Constitution requires ministers to be present in parliament and answer questions pertaining to their ministries when called upon to do so. This happens rather frequently in Malawi, although some ministers are summoned more often than others. Parliamentary records in the period 2005–2008 show that cabinet ministers have on average been asked around 200 questions during each sitting of parliament. For instance, in one session of 15 days, 200 questions were addressed by MPs to various ministers, largely on education, transport, health, irrigation and water (Institute for Policy Interaction, 2010). Indeed, as constituency infrastructure development was the focus of this particular sitting, MPs were asked to document visible changes in their constituencies after their elections. During this period, ministers in charge of statutory corporations or parastatals were similarly required to present annual reports to Parliament.

Section 97 of the Constitution, however, makes ministers responsible to the President for the administration of their own ministries/departments. Some argue that this has resulted in a skewed understanding of accountability for most public functionaries, who seem to offer their loyalty to their political and bureaucratic superiors and not to the citizenry. Therefore, accountability to rights holders remains weak, neglected and a missing link in Malawi's democracy. While the Constitution highlights accountability of ministers to the President, it does not make any mention of their accountability to citizens (Kamchedzera and Banda, 2012). Recent measures of public opinion in Malawi indicate that Malawians value their Parliament's legislative and oversight roles, but are highly critical of the performance of parliamentarians (Afrobarometer, 2014). In a number of studies on political attitudes, Malawians have expressed their dissatisfaction on the performance of their elected representatives. There also appears to be an emerging consensus on the need for effective oversight role of Parliament in holding the government to account in general and to ensure that the executive appears before the legislature routinely on matters of public finance and financial integrity.

Malawi has adopted a system whereby cabinet ministers are recruited from the ranks of the legislators, although it is not an absolute requirement; non-elected technocrats can serve as ministers. The wearing of two hats by some MPs has arguably diluted the accountability role of the Parliament. The practice also contravenes the separation of powers principle, though it has become entrenched in the country's political system with successive presidents inflating their cabinets whenever they wished to garner support in Parliament for controversial bills (Patel and Tostensen, 2006). Thus, President Bakili Muluzi's cabinet swelled to 46 when he was trying to secure a third term in office. Similarly, President Bingu wa Mutharika's cabinet size rose to 42 during the period when Parliament debated Section 65 of the Constitution, dealing with floor-crossing MPs. During both these junctures, all the 40+ cabinet ministers were drawn from the national assembly.

Parliamentary oversight via committees

The strained executive–legislature relations impeded the functioning of the legislature in many ways like curtailed sittings of Parliament, and less frequent meetings of parliamentary committees. A negative public perception evolved especially during 2005–8 on the role of Parliament in that it was viewed as wasting time on political bickering, especially in relation to the controversial Section 65 (crossing of floor by MPs), rather than discussing matters of public importance. While it is true that the committees often became the stage for a tug-of-war between the executive and the legislature, they also performed some notable work. The report of the Public Accounts Committee on the investigation into the operations and management of the credit scheme can be a case in point. The credit scheme account was purportedly opened as an operating account for Malawi Rural Development Fund (MARDEF). The Secretary to the Treasury had allegedly diverted MK20 million from the scheme, to an account with the Finance Bank of Malawi. The Finance Minister ordered an audit on the account by the National Audit Office and the report was subsequently investigated by the Public Accounts Committee. The committee report accused the government of diverting the fund for clandestine political activities such as 'buying' members of the opposition to support the government. The government on its part dismissed the report as flawed as it did not comply with provision SO 181 of the Standing Orders of Parliament, which gives an opportunity to the accused (and in this case some of the accused were cabinet ministers) to make submissions to the committee. The matter, commonly known as the 'Kutengule case', brought to light the role of the Public Accounts Committee and instilled hope in parliamentary oversight.

Similarly, the Budget and Finance Committee (BFC) made important contributions to parliamentary oversight by way of detailed and constructive responses to the budget; and many of its suggestions were actually accepted by the government. The budget session of 2008 was particularly heated as the ongoing wrangle over the constitutional section on the crossing of the floor by MPs reached its climax with the political climate warming up for the upcoming 2009 elections. But what had gone rather unnoticed during these years of executive–legislature tensions related to the Budget versus Section 65 saga was the commendable contributions of the BFC on the budget.[1] The committee also made many other pertinent recommendations on the allocations for specific items in the three key ministries – agriculture, health and education. For example, on the implementation of the farm inputs subsidy programme (FISP), the committee observed that the government paid excessive attention to the Ministry on Agriculture and Food Security and relegated other key ministries such as Natural Resources and Environment to the background. Concerns were particularly raised on rampant corruption emanating from the fertilizer subsidy, as it was the supporters of those in government who largely tended to benefit from the programme.

The birth of the integrated financial management information system (IFMIS) took place during this term of Parliament when, in 2006, the government announced that it would roll out IFMIS across all ministries with the aim of improving and strengthening public finance management. In the budget session of August 2008, the opposition expressed concern over the generally poor financial management of ministries and departments, and urged the government to tighten up loose ends in the financial management system in order to safeguard donor confidence. This was perhaps indicative of an emerging problem, which exploded beyond anyone's imagination a few years later in the scandal referred to as 'Cashgate'.

The relationship between the Public Appointments Committee of Parliament and the President was adversarial and tense during the tenure of Bingu wa Mutharika. When the President submitted the names for executive appointments to Parliament, the committee rejected them. These included the candidatures for the Inspector General of Police and the Director of Public Prosecution. The committee and several civil society organisations demanded the recall of Malawi's high commissioner to South Africa, whose credentials were apparently not adequate for the appointment. There was also agitation to the abrupt suspension of the Director of the Anti-Corruption Bureau. This acrimony between the executive and the legislature left many important offices vacant for long periods of time. One institution most affected by this was the Malawi Electoral Commission (MEC). When the tenure of four election commissioners expired in 2006, the President appointed new commissioners without consulting the opposition. Thus several opposition political parties blocked these appointments through court injunctions. Throughout 2007 such executive appointments were challenged through the courts. The Electoral Commission finally became operational barely 14 months before the 2009 elections.

The Legal Affairs Committee played its oversight role perhaps by going to the extreme of initiating impeachment proceedings against President Bingu wa Mutharika on seven grounds. The main charges related to the President forming his party after winning elections on the ticket of another party, misusing public funds in poaching MPs to join his newly formed party (DPP), and the subsequent defections of MPs violating the constitutional provision on floor crossing (Section 65). There were also charges of arbitrarily hiring and firing public officials. The impeachment petition was challenged by the President in court on the ground that Section 65 on crossing of floor contradicted the constitutional section on freedom of association. The Supreme Court in 2007 ruled on this matter, upholding Section 65 to be an integral part of the Constitution, which could not be repealed. Despite the Supreme Court ruling, the Mutharika government completed a full term of office with total impunity.

The Parliament then realised that impeachment procedures were not laid down in the Standing Orders of the House. Nonetheless, the Legal Affairs Committee drafted the impeachment procedure and presented it to Parliament, while the President decided to refer the procedures to the Supreme Court to determine their constitutional validity. The issue dragged on until 2013, when Parliament finally approved the new Standing Orders, which also included the impeachment procedure.

The new Standing Orders are a positive step towards enhancing oversight. They give opposition parties the chairmanship of crucial oversight committees and a stricter enforcement of the requirement for the President to be present in Parliament during the budget session. In the forthcoming sittings of Parliament, many of these features will be put to test. The revised Standing Orders also clarify the position of the leader of opposition, which at one time was a controversial issue as ruling parties have historically tried to interfere in the appointment process. The rule now clarifies the leader of opposition must be a parliamentary leader elected by the party not in government and having the greatest numerical strength in Parliament at any point in time and officially announced as such by the Speaker.

Despite the tense executive–legislature relations, the Malawian Parliament has always been visible for one reason or another. Indeed, Parliament has been able to assert itself as an independent institution, particularly in the period 2005–9, when each of the thirteen parliamentary committees conducted regular meetings for the first time since 1994 (Freedom House, 2012). This signalled positive efforts to develop institutional capacity and greater legislative policy expertise. Given that the post-2004 election period was one of the most confrontational and tension-filled in terms of the relations between the executive and the legislature, it seems ironical that it was during this very period that the Parliament reforms strategy was passed. The reform strategy aims at giving Parliament the autonomy to set its own calendar, and control over its own budget to fully conduct all its activities without delay, including, among other things, a fully staffed and well-equipped secretariat.

Controlling corruption

In a political system where patronage and clientelist practices are deeply imbedded, there are an abundance of opportunities for corruption in the bureaucracy and in wider political circles. Moreover, the body that is primarily entrusted to curb corruption (i.e. Parliament) often turns out to be the main culprit. A number of cases demonstrate the existence of systemic corruption in the Malawian political system. For example, during the campaign for extending presidential term limit in 2003, four cabinet ministers led the campaign 'Moving with a Bag of Money' to buy off opposition MPs; 22 MPs were 'abducted' and more that 40 MPs were allegedly bribed by the regime to support the Third Term Bill. One MP, however, refused the MK100,000 bribe and exposed the scam (Hussein, 2005). Similarly, when President Mutharika formed the Democratic Progressive Party (DPP) in 2005 – abandoning the United Democratic Front on whose mandate he won the elections – over 70 MPs defected from their parties in violation of the Constitution to join the DPP. This mass defection perceivably was not free of charge. The MPs were allegedly 'bought' to give the Mutharika government the support in legislature. And when the UDF made an impeachment attempt to oust Mutharika, there were rumours of the former president Mulizi arranging large sums of money to buy parliamentary support in that mission.

The death of the sitting President in April 2012 and the subsequent revelation of his wealth, which was way beyond what he had declared at the time of taking over office in 2009, gave momentum to the debate on declaration of assets by public office holders.[2] When Vice-President Joyce Banda assumed office following a failed coup attempt by President Mutharika's inner circle, it paved the way for some corrective measures to improve governance. In particular, legislative oversight was strengthened during this executive transition. Parliament passed the much-awaited Assets Declaration Bill, which mounted pressure on public officials to publicly declare their assets. The legislation also applied to the President herself, who was placed under public scrutiny. The Public Appointments Committee was reconstituted to include declaration of assets and empowered to monitor disclosure of assets under section 88(3) of the Constitution. There was considerable demand for the President to declare her assets after assuming office in order to provide moral leadership in the fight against corruption. However, the President refused to comply with this requirement until the very end of the term. While Joyce Banda had declared her assets at the time of taking oath for the Vice-Presidency, the demand now was for her to declare her assets upon taking oath of the office of the President. Her non-compliance was construed as disregard for Parliament and also disrespect for the demands of civil society, whose support she enjoyed in defeating the coup of Mutharika's inner circle which attempted to prevent her from assuming the presidency following the death of Bingu wa Mutharika. The broader conclusion of this saga is the tendency of the executive to disregard formal legal requirements in particular and the rule of law in general.

The Assets Declaration Bill contained stringent punitive measures for failure to declare assets, including removal of officers guilty of non-compliance with the law and procedures to impeach the president. The legislation came in the wake of 'Cashgate' – the biggest corruption scandal ever witnessed in the country, which involved misappropriation and theft of an estimated US $20–$100 million (Smith, 2015). The scandal became public when Malawi's budget director was shot under mysterious circumstances, and huge sums of cash in both local and foreign currency were found in the vehicles and homes of some civil servants, most of them low-ranking junior accountants. A British audit firm, commissioned by DFID, conducted a forensic audit of this scandal. However, when the report was submitted to the Public Accounts Committee, it was rejected on the grounds that the report was incomplete, as it did not reveal the names of those involved.

Indeed, the report did not provide details of transactions and names in order to 'limit the risk of prejudicing any current or future legal action'. The report went on to state that 'Where we believe fraud, theft or unethical actions have taken place the details have been referred to the relevant Law Enforcement Office of the Police and Anti-Corruption Bureau through the Office of the Auditor General' (Baker Tilly Ltd, 2014). The Auditor General's office subsequently provided a similar explanation explained to the parliamentary committee that the decision not to disclose intricate details on the case was reached to avoid prejudicing any criminal proceedings against those whose deeds were uncovered by the forensic audit. The failure to disclose such details, however, did not go down well with an increasingly agitated civil society in the country. The umbrella organisation of faith bodies, the Public Affairs Committee (PAC), held a stakeholders conference, where it demanded that Parliament examine the full forensic report together with other controversial issues such as reported loss of maize in the country's grain reserves and the proceeds from the sale of the presidential jet. Similarly, a civil society organisation forum demanded an emergency sitting of Parliament to take stock of the dire economic situation created by the Cashgate scandal.

Challenges facing the legislature

Since the advent of multiparty democracy in Malawi, there has been a visible executive dominance over the legislature emanating largely from the presidential nature of Malawi's political regime, which assigns Parliament a secondary role. The general framework of executive–parliamentary relations laid down in the Constitution provides opportunities for accentuating this subordinate position through iterative practices. The persistence of personalised patronage in Malawian politics has further entrenched the culture of parliamentary subservience. The numerical strength of opposition parties in the legislature since 1994 created a situation of adversarial relations between the executive and the legislature, whereby the executive felt threatened owing to its relatively small number in the legislative body. Consequently, the executive resorted to retaining political control by wresting the needed majority through overt and covert means without strengthening Parliament as an institution. Most importantly, the strategy included denying Parliament the resources necessary to operate, thereby transferring control to the executive. The executive further undermined the institution by convening parliamentary sessions only when it needed parliamentary approval to sanction its operations (e.g. budget approval). Parliamentary committees including the meetings of the Standing Committees were held subject to availability of funding, and government funds were released only when committees were expected to focus and cooperate on an executive-driven agenda.

The continuation of the asymmetry in access to various types of resources between the executive and legislative branches is detrimental to Parliament's ability to perform its function. The current situation is one of a well-staffed executive with access to expertise and informed by its ministries, while the national assembly relies on an overworked and under-resourced support structure, lacking adequate capacity to render much-needed support for legislative functions. The executive moreover uses popular items in the budget – creation of a constituency fund or an increase in sitting allowances – as instruments to garner support from MPs (Patel, 2008).

Since 2005, there has been much focus on giving Parliament the mandate to set its own calendar, prepare its own budget and develop institutional capacity that is needed to deliver its basic roles and responsibilities. However, a decade down the line, the situation is not very different except for the physical structure of a Parliament building that was built with aid from the Chinese government. Contrary to the provisions of the law, Parliament still does not determine its own budget. Each year, it prepares estimates against a credit ceiling predetermined by the Ministry of Finance and submits the same to the Treasury. The estimates are then included in the national budget, which is presented to Parliament by the finance minister before the commencement of the next financial year. A recent report on strengths and weaknesses of the Malawian Parliament highlights a series of weaknesses, including:

- lack of autonomy from the government;
- readiness to set aside established rules and procedures;
- failure to implement operational guidelines;
- nonadherence to the budget;
- individual needs of MPs often override parliamentary service needs in relation to available finances;
- unclear distinction between political and administrative functions;
- lack of a communication strategy;
- failure to manage suppliers;
- low adoption of technology;
- inadequate office space for MPs and staff; and
- lack of implementation of outreach programmes.

Moreover, the report notes that most MPs lack a clear understanding of what parliamentary oversight entails in practice (Gilfillan, 2015).

Frequent changes of membership moreover pose a major challenge to the continuity and functioning of the committee structure (Manzi, 2013). The power to appoint and remove committee members rests with the party whips. There is no rule that guarantees membership tenure and hence committees witness frequent changes in their composition. And, according to the Secretariat, the survival of the committees continues to rely largely on the whims of the executive. For example, the erratic and inadequate availability of funds from the Treasury hinders committees from carrying out their desired activities. As a result, the committees almost invariably have a large backlog of reports from the Auditor General and fail to implement capacity building programmes for its members and the parliamentary secretariat. Although Parliament, through its Parliamentary Service Commission (PSC) is mandated to recruit its own staff, the PSC is required to seek authority from the Department of Human Resource Management (DHRMD) to fill vacant posts.

DHRMD frequently declines to grant the authority to Parliament to fill vacant posts, resulting in a shortage of staff (Manzi, 2013). Thus, it is often not a matter of lack of competence or willingness on the part of MPs to exercise their oversight functions, but rather the lack of tangible and operational support (Rotberg and Salahub, 2013). For example, the Public Accounts Committee in 2013 was wrestling with audit issues from previous years, and was thus best prepared to examine and investigate the workings of Malawi's government and its executive branch. Likewise, the Budget Committee was meeting very infrequently and was hardly an equal partner with the Minister of Finance and his staff.

Notwithstanding the functionality of the committees, it should be noted that, even in cases where the committees have scrutinised cases in the past and found proof of misconduct and/or irregularities, no further visible action has been forthcoming. Indeed, ministers stepping down on grounds of moral turpitude have not been heard of in the Malawian context. In other words, Parliament has been able to extract answerability to be some extent from the executive through the use of oversight tools but has largely failed to undertake the twin function of enforceability in terms of stringent punishment. But securing answerability has been in itself useful in raising public awareness and reaction to important and sensitive issues.

Conclusion

In its two-decade-long democratic journey, Malawi has faced some serious threats to democratic survival but has come out safely and successfully. However, there is no guarantee that there will not be future threats of democratic reversals. The tendency of elected politicians and leaders to blithely ignore the rule of law and get away with impunity persists regardless of party allegiance or educational and professional background. On a positive note, however, the strengthened position of the independent media offers a glimmer of hope in the same manner as the rise of a young and ambitious new middle class. These developments have raised demands on formal governmental institutions to deliver development and improve public services. It is against this background that the Malawian Parliament has demonstrated that it has the potential, and can be an effective mechanism, for ensuring accountable governance despite facing numerous practical weaknesses. Combatting these weaknesses requires concerted efforts, and the emerging positive public attitude towards Parliament in general and oversight in particular is an encouraging sign. It is therefore crucial that parliamentarians maintain professionalism by focusing on technical scrutiny while being detached as much as possible from political wrangles. This will require regular and rigorous training on understanding the oversight role of MPs. Moreover, MPs who also serve as ministers need to be guided on their accountability as ministers not only to the President but also to Parliament. A sense of collective responsibility to Parliament as a cabinet should be demonstrated to gain pubic confidence and trust in government.

Weaknesses in the political party system greatly hinder the functioning of democracy at large and of Parliament in particular. Factional politics largely emanating from lack of internal party democracy has plagued the Malawian Parliament as illustrated with reference to the presidential term limit case. Party transformation is a prerequisite for parliamentary transformation. Many scholars (e.g. Barkan *et al.*, 2010) argue that legislatures in Africa are undergoing a noticeable change in terms of amending rules and procedures to be make themselves more robust, build stronger committees, expand professional staff, improve communication system so that greater influence can be exercised over government policies and their oversight responsibilities can be carried out more effectively. Thus legislatures in the continent including Malawi are evolving in order to enhance their power and function in the overall processes of democratic governance.

Notes

1 The BFC pointed out a number of assumptions of the government which were unrealistic and therefore untenable such as: the growth of money supply by 12.2 per cent in 2008/9. In 2007 money supply grew by 36 per cent due to increased economic activity by the private sector. In 2008 with the bank rate declining from 15 per cent to 12.5 per cent private sector demand for liquidity was likely and price stability was unlikely to be maintained. The lack of correlation in 2007 between money supply and prices was striking when inflation remained at 8 per cent while the money supply grew by 36 per cent. The committee queried the reliability of inflation statistics as it did not seem to be reflecting the reality on ground. Extracted from the Malawi Parliamentary Observation Reports 2005–8, Institute for Policy Interaction. 5th Meeting 38th Session, 11–31 October 2005.

2 Unofficial sources say he had MK150 million. The Speaker of the House refused to make it public. At the time of his death unofficial sources say it was MK61 billion.

References

Afrobarometer (2014) 'Malawi Round 6 questionnaire'. Available at: http://www.afrobarometer.org/countries/malawi/malawi-round-6-questionnaire (accessed 19 February 2016).

Baker Tilly Ltd (2014) 'Cashgate: A summary report on the findings arising from work carried out into Fraud and mismanagement of Malawi Government's Finances'. National Audit Office of Malawi, 1 April–30 September 2013.

Barkan, J.D., Mattes, R., Mozzafar, S. and Smiddy, K. (2010) 'The African Legislatures Project', 1st findings, Center for Social Research, University of Cape Town.

Bolarinwa, Joshua Olusegun (2015) 'Emerging Legislatures in Africa: Challenges & Opportunities', *Developing County Studies*, 5(5).

Freedom House (2012) 'Countries at the Crossroads, 2012 report'. Available at: https://freedomhouse.org/report/countries-crossroads/2012/malawi (accessed 19 February 2016).

Gilfillan, Stewart (2015) 'Report on visit to the Malawi National Assembly', Assistant Chief Executive to Scottish Parliament, 19–27 March. Available at http://www.scottish.parliament.uk/abouttheparliament/53448.aspx (accessed 19 February 2016).

Gorden, Richard and Street, Amy (2012) *Select Committees and Coercive Powers: Clarity or Confusion?* London: The Constitution Society.

Griffith, Gareth (2005) 'Parliament and Accountability: The role of Parliamentary Oversight Committees', Briefing paper No 12/05, ASPG Conference on Parliament and Accountability in the 21st Century: The Role of Parliament Oversight Committees, Sydney 6–8 Oct 2005.

Hussein, M. (2005) 'Combating Corruption in Malawi: An assessment of the enforcing mechanisms'. African Security Review, 14(4). Available at: https://www.issafrica.org/pubs/ASR/14No4/Contents.htm (accessed 19 February 2016).

IEA (2009) *The Parliamentary Budget Oversight in Kenya: Analysis of the Framework and Practices since 1963*, Research Report Series No.19. Nairobi: Institute of Economic Affairs.

Institute for Policy Interaction (2010) *Malawi Parliamentary Observation Reports 2005–2008*, Institute for Policy Interaction in collaboration with the International Research & Consulting Center (IRCC) Switzerland.

Kamchedzera, G. and Banda, C.U. (2002) 'Research on the Right to Development, the Quality of Rural Life, Legislation and the Performance of State Duties', Research Dissemination Seminar Number Law/2001–2002/001, Zomba, Faculty of Law, University of Malawi.

Manzi, J.J. (2013) 'Improving Financial Oversight: Role of the Public Accounts Committee Clerk: Malawi's Experience', presentation at the 3rd Westminster Workshop for Public Accounts Committees, held in London, 24–27 June. Available at: http://slideplayer.com/slide/4532204/ (accessed 19 February 2016).

O'Donnell, G. (1998) 'Horizontal Accountability in New Democracies', *Journal of Democracy* 9(3): 112–26.

Parliamentary Centre Canada and World Bank, (2005) *Controlling Corruption: A Parliamentarian's Handbook*, 3rd edn. Available at: http://www.parlcent.org/en/resources/handbooks-and-guides/ (accessed 28 February 2016).

Patel, N. (2008) 'The Representational Challenge in Malawi', in *Towards the Consolidation of Malawi's Democracy*, Konrad Adenauer Stiftung, Occasional Paper No.11, Malawi.

Patel, N. and Tostensen, A. (2006) 'Parliamentary–Executive Relations in Malawi 1994–2004', CMI working Paper 2006: 10. Available at: http://www.cmi.no/publications/publication/?2336=parliamentary-executive-relations-in-malawi-1994 (accessed 19 February 2016).

PRC (2006) 'Terms of Reference, Minutes of the meeting of the Reforms Committee', Parliamentary Reforms Committee, 23 May.

Rotberg, Robert I. and Salahub, Jennifer Erin (2013) 'African Legislative Effectiveness, Research Report', North–South Institute. Available at: http://www.nsi-ins.ca/publications/african-legislative-effectiveness/ (accessed 19 February 2016).

Smith, D. (2015) 'Money from Malawi's Cashgate Scandal allegedly funded electoral campaign', *Guardian*, 13 February. Available at: http://www.theguardian.com/global-development/2015/feb/13/malawi-cashgate-scandal-money-funded-electoral-campaigns (accessed 26 February 2016).

9 The impact of emerging donors on development and poverty reduction

Dan Banik and Michael Chasukwa

Introduction

The traditional foundations of foreign aid have been numerous. In addition to political ideology, foreign policy, commercial interests and national security, there are large elements of altruism and a desire to reduce global poverty. The world of foreign aid is complex and includes Official Development Assistance (ODA, which are concessional flows with a grant element of at least 25 per cent) and development, humanitarian and emergency aid provided by non-governmental organizations, civil society organizations, bilateral donors and multilateral agencies. Ever since the end of the Second World War, and the provision of capital by the United States to Europe, there has been considerable interest on the extent to which foreign aid promotes economic development. And many contributions, including feminist theory, participatory and human rights-based approaches, have challenged the assumption that economic growth and market liberalization alone will help to reduce poverty. Indeed, the entire concept of assisting poor countries to achieve economic development and social welfare has been much debated in recent decades. And the international discourse is currently focused on the rapidly changing objectives of aid, the instruments used to deliver aid, the effectiveness of aid measured in terms of concrete results, the players involved in the aid business, and the institutions governing the relationship between developed and developing countries.

In recent years, many of the so-called emerging economies are increasingly influencing social and economic policies around the world. In particular China, but also India, Brazil and South Africa, are interacting in numerous ways with poorer countries, including so-called South–South dialogues. These give access to natural resources and new and growing markets, and also reduce the dependence of African countries on traditional forms of aid from the Global North. These emerging countries and their policies represent a counterweight to the policies and development aid models that have for long been promoted directly or indirectly (e.g. through multilateral institutions) in poor countries by the Global North.

Malawi's economy is heavily dependent on (Western) foreign aid, which funds almost 40 per cent of the national budget. However, China is increasingly supporting a wide range of projects (from infrastructure and health to education and agricultural technology) that appear to complement Western efforts to promote development and reduce poverty. The purpose of this chapter is to critically analyse and highlight the impact of ideas, values and tangible benefits resulting from China's engagement in Malawi. Rather than providing budget support to governments, and conditioning aid on support for democracy and gender equality, the Chinese model has consistently emphasized the principles of 'win–win', 'mutual respect', 'friendship' and 'non-interference'. China has further projected the idea that state-to-state relations ought to be beneficial for itself and the aid recipient country, and conducive to each other's national development. Hence, it has introduced in public discourse of Malawi terms such as 'complementarity', 'potential' and 'opportunity'.

The aim of this chapter is to provide a more nuanced understanding of the nature of foreign aid policies implemented by new donors such as China in Malawi. The study is based on fieldwork carried out in several phases over a period of five years during which we interviewed key informants from various ministries (e.g. Ministry of Foreign Affairs, Ministry of Trade and Industry), business communities in rural areas, civil society organizations, judges in the Malawian Supreme and High Courts, journalists and editors, Malawian employees involved in Chinese projects and Chinese project staff. We have also examined articles appearing in the print media (e.g. *The Nation, Weekend Nation, Daily Times* and *Malawi News*) as well as online media sources.

Starting with a brief overview of the history of foreign aid in Malawi, we examine how and to what extent Chinese aid to Malawi has had a positive impact on development and poverty reduction. We argue that Chinese foreign aid and investments have contributed significantly to addressing macro-level national and community problems. Indeed, Chinese aid is remarkable because it focuses on the neglected and 'orphan' sectors such as infrastructure and energy. The spillover effects of macro-oriented projects have been the generation of new employment opportunities and the growth of small and medium-scale business enterprises run by Chinese nationals in urban and semi-urban areas where local communities have access to a large range of Chinese products at affordable prices. The controversies surrounding China's activities in Malawi primarily relate to the inability of local businesses to compete with the Chinese, the quality and durability of infrastructure projects and disagreements between the Malawian and Chinese governments regarding who should cover the high costs of maintaining the Chinese-built infrastructure projects.

Development aid to Malawi: A brief overview

Malawi's development indicators are not very impressive, and the International Monetary Fund ranked the country the second worst performing economy in the world in 2013. And in 2015, the World Bank placed Malawi among the poorest in the world based on the GDP per capita. Almost 54 per cent of the population lives on less than US$1.25 a day, and the country faces an acute shortage of foreign exchange, which makes important essential goods, including medicines, extremely difficult to access. Moreover, the Malawian economy is highly vulnerable to various types of shocks as it is highly dependent on the agriculture sector, which generates over 90 per cent of foreign exchange earnings and employs around 85 per cent of the population (Chinsinga, 2008).

Tobacco accounts for 60 per cent of the country's foreign exchange earnings, but the weak exporting base in general has put considerable pressure on an economy that is otherwise among the fastest growing consumer markets in the world (Euromonitor Research, 2014). Indeed, consumer spending grew 18.2 per cent in 2014 and total consumer expenditure was expected to reach US$5.6 billion by the end of 2014, reflecting spending of on average US$335 per capita. The precarious nature of the economy frequently results in budget deficits, which in turn have highlighted the country's dependence on foreign aid. Thus, aid as a share of GNI has averaged around 24 per cent over the past two decades. And van der Meer *et al.* (2008: 17) find that foreign aid as a proportion of the national budget averaged 38 per cent over the period 1994–2006, the bulk of which were grants which constituted 72 per cent of all foreign aid received. Malawi regularly falls short of financial resources to fund government activities, which in turns results in greater reliance on support from foreign donor agencies. Much of the aid from western countries is directed at supporting the national budget. For example, Norway provided NOK50 million in 2013 as budget support to Malawi while an additional NOK250 million was provided to the country through other actors, including government agencies as well as civil society organizations.[1]

The interaction between the government and various international organizations and donor countries has been consistently fraught with growing tension. While the government has complained of erratic disbursement patterns that have an adverse impact on its ability to deliver effective public service, donors have often frozen or cancelled aid allocations following allegations of mismanagement and large-scale corruption in the public services. Budget support was first suspended in 2002 and then in 2003, 2011 and 2013 due to concerns about abuse of resources. For example, between 2002 and 2005, the Danish Government froze all its aid to Malawi because of allegations of widespread corruption and financial mismanagement. A group of donors – the Common Budgetary Support Group (CABS) – suspended aid in 2003 when president Bakili Muluzi was trying his utmost to amend the Constitution that would allow him to extend the constitutionally provided two-term office to a third term. CABS once again suspended aid during president Bingu wa Mutharika's second term in office (2009 to mid-2012) on the grounds of worsening economic and political governance, which included several controversial pieces of legislation and executive decisions such as the amendment of the penal code (Injunctions Bill), amendment of the Media Bill and postponement of local government elections. Similarly, Germany froze its general budget support in 2011 because of Malawi's reluctance to improve local governance and be financially prudent (Resnick, 2012).

Following the now infamous 'Cashgate' scandal in 2013 – where public officials were accused of siphoning off more than US$30 million – several donors suspended budget support as well as reduced their aid allocations to Malawi. Thus, the CABS and other key donors suspended their budget support in 2013–14, and are currently non-committal of supporting the national budget in the immediate future until Cashgate as well as other previous scandals (e.g. undocumented use of US$200 million by the Democratic People's Party government in 2005) are resolved. The aid regime in Malawi has thus been characterized by withdrawals and suspensions. Indeed, every political leader in charge of the country since the onset of democracy in 1994 has faced numerous challenges in dealing with the donor community. And, in all cases of suspension and withdrawal of aid, donors have cited mismanagement of resources, poor political and economic governance and violation of human rights.

Aid volatility is also high because of the sheer number of donors implementing various projects in Malawi. According to some estimates, there are over 31 donors providing official development assistance in Malawi with nearly 800 aid projects covering 2,900 activities (Weaver *et al.*, 2014). Another source, the Malawi Government Aid Atlas (Malawi Government,, 2014b), puts the figure of development partners at 38 'including 10 United Nations funds, programmes and agencies; 16 bi-lateral donor agencies and a collection of 12 multilateral and other bodies' (Taylor, 2014). The negative effects of aid withdrawal and suspension by the traditional donors have been partially offset by financial support from the emerging donors. A quick glance of the budget atlas shows that China committed approximately US$96 million in the 2010/11 financial year, and half of this amount was disbursed as loans. Similarly, India disbursed another US$73 million and Arab donors contributed US$19 million in the same period (Malawi Government, 2014b).

The arrival of the new donors

The architecture of development aid has changed dramatically in the past decade, and there are numerous new entrants in the aid industry. These new donors include many so-called 'emerging countries' such as China, India, South Korea, Thailand, Turkey, Brazil, Russia, South Africa, the United Arab Emirates, Kuwait and Venezuela (Woods, 2008; Callan *et al.*, 2013). The Busan Partnership for Effective Development Cooperation (2011) emphasized the need to recognize emerging country donors because of the substantial amounts of aid that they are willing to provide to developing countries and the resulting change of the rules of the game in terms of aid modalities. Thus, Callan *et al.* (2013) find that the contribution of emerging donors to aid aimed at developing countries is currently 7–10 per cent of all aid provided. Chinese aid alone is estimated to be in the range of US$2–3 billion annually (Lengauer, 2011: 5) whereas Saudi Arabia provided US$5 billion in 2011 (Callan *et al.*, 2013).

China has been one of the most dominant actors in relation to providing aid and undertaking investments in Africa. However, China is not a new actor in Africa, having been active on the continent for several decades. Nonetheless, its activities – and the volume of aid and related activity – have dramatically increased, and China is now Africa's largest trading partner with a substantial aid and investment portfolio in virtually every country on the continent. China's development aid and investment activity has, over the years, been the subject of much scholarly attention. Most western analyses of China in Africa have, however, been overwhelmingly negative, focusing on the controversies around the blurred boundaries between aid and investments, the lack of transparency on aid practices, and the lack of focus on democracy, human rights and gender equality. The Chinese government insists that the assistance it provides to African countries is not based on charity, but rather on the principles of 'win–win', 'non-interference', 'mutual respect' and 'friendship', underscored by China fulfilling its obligations of international solidarity with developing countries (Banik, 2013: 7). The general framework of how development aid should be delivered from China to African countries is discussed and stipulated in proceedings of the Forum on China–Africa Cooperation (FOCAC) established in 2000. The actual details guiding bilateral agreement are discussed by Chinese and African government officials; more specifically by officials from the political leadership in the recipient country and, in Beijing, the Ministry of Commerce, Ministry of Finance and Ministry of Foreign Affairs.

The recipient country usually submits to the Chinese embassy a list of development projects that it wishes China to fund. The list is sent to Beijing, and the Ministry of Commerce (MOFCOM) makes a decision regarding the number and type of projects it will fund. The list is then sent back to the recipient country government upon which both parties agree on the exact nature of Chinese assistance that will be provided – the volume of grants, the exact terms of concessional loans and the extent of investment activities by Chinese state-owned enterprises. By funding projects at the request of the recipient country, China believes that, unlike western donors, it operates within the national development policy of the recipient country and thereby does not impose any restrictions or conditionalities. In trying to practice a 'win–win' relationship, China exercises 'soft power;' which embraces elements of grants, soft loans and cultural diplomacy (Ramo, 2004; Breslin, 2011; Li et al., 2014) without the typical requirements of democratic accountability and financial transparency that characterizes western aid disbursements (Halper, 2010).

China's development aid practices have often been praised by African leaders for its flexibility and friendliness when compared to the practices of western donors. For example, former Senegalese President Abdoulaye Wade noted that China 'offers the same things Europe has been offering at a better price with excellent conditions and with absence of intrusive conditionalities' (cited in Opoku-Mensah, 2009: 13). Other politicians and civil servants have similarly been grateful for much-needed capital that the Chinese have injected into local African economies in addition to improving infrastructural capacity through construction of roads, schools, hotels, universities, bridges, parliament buildings and presidential palaces. The rhetoric in most western countries has, however, been one of suspicion, questioning the true motives of China, and the western media has been quick to label Chinese aid practices as an important component of China's imperialist strategy with the aim of satisfying its hunger for natural resources and establishing itself as a global superpower. Accordingly, many traditional donors have lamented the lack of emphasis by the Chinese on good governance and respect for human rights, including respect for the rights of women and homosexuals – typically matters on which the West and Africa continue to disagree. Thus, China has from time to time been variously labelled a 'rogue donor' for providing aid that promotes authoritarianism, deepens patronage and encourages non-transparency (Naim, 2007; Lengauer, 2011). Others have argued that Chinese aid modalities in Africa have weakened local institutions (Moss *et al.*, 2006), and that while the Paris Declaration of 2005 stresses mutual accountability and transparency of parties, Chinese policies have sometimes used soft power to block western aid to African countries. For example, China is accused of blocking ODA from the World Bank to Nigeria in 2007 when the two parties, after prolonged negotiations, had agreed to a US$5 million project to upgrade the national railway system. Apparently, just before the agreement could be signed, China offered the Nigerian government US$9 billion to radically improve the entire national railway network: an agreement based on 'no bids, no conditions, and no need to reform' (Naim, cited in Lengauer, 2011: 28). Some have therefore argued that emerging donors such as China are reluctant to participate in pooled funds, which require transparency and accountability.

China in Malawi

After decades of receiving development aid from Taiwan, Malawi switched its diplomatic ties to China in December 2005. By aligning itself with China, Malawi was able, like the rest of Africa, to access substantial grants, concessional loans, private sector investments and technical assistance on a scale much larger than what Taiwan was willing to offer. While government officials and even certain local communities have praised China for being 'a friend in need, and a friend indeed', some quarters of Malawian society have been critical of the so-called 'new colonist' and 'new imperialist' motives behind China's generosity (Makwerere and Chipaike, 2012; Ayodele and Sotola, 2014).

With traditional donors withdrawing or holding back vital budget support on the grounds of financial mismanagement and lack of confidence in domestic public financial management systems, China's importance in Malawi has risen considerably. The withdrawal (albeit temporary) of traditional aid has pushed Malawi to further cement diplomatic ties with China – a move signalled by current president Peter Mutharika, who in his 2014 inaugural speech stated, 'We will continue with traditional relationships, but we are now looking for new friends in emerging economies such as Brazil, China, India, South Africa and Russia.'[2] The current political discourse in the country gives the impression that the 'Look East' policy will continue to preoccupy the minds of the Malawian political leadership as several ministers are worried that traditional donors will not resume their aid practices anytime soon. The finance minister made the following observation in October 2015:

I would like to emphasize this very strongly. We should not proceed on the premise that the donors will come back soon with their budgetary support purses ... I would have difficulty in proceeding on the basis of expecting bilateral donors to come back.[3]

The statement of the finance minister followed a state visit to China by the president of Malawi in September 2015, and the president's subsequent meetings with a high-powered delegation from China at the African Union Summit in Ethiopia as well as interactions with visiting government and business delegations from China to Malawi. Moreover, several ministers have in the recent past visited China at regular intervals to cement the ties between Lilongwe and Beijing.

Accessing information about the scale and magnitude of Chinese development assistance is extremely difficult, as China does not publish aid data for specific countries and sectors. As such, we have had to rely on news reports and official speeches of Chinese officials, which highlight four overarching 'pillars' of assistance to Malawi:

- infrastructure development;
- agriculture and food security;
- health and medical care; and
- education and human resources.

On paper at least, these correspond relatively well to the six priority areas of Malawi's Growth and Development Strategy (MGDS):

- agriculture and food security;
- irrigation and water development;
- transport and infrastructure development; energy generation and supply;
- integrated rural development; and
- prevention and management of nutrition disorders, HIV and AIDS (Government of Malawi, 2006).

Based on available information, it appears that China has stuck closely to the clearly defined set of activities categorized under the four pillars mentioned above. Successive Chinese ambassadors and visiting delegations have conveyed the message that 'business is business' and that Malawi should strive for social and political stability in order to achieve economic development (Banik, 2013). And, while we believe China indeed does not impose aid conditionalities in the manner in which western donors do, it is apparent that adherence to the One China principle is key to the China–Malawi relationship. Banik (2013) examined a large number of speeches, media reports and policy documents relating to China in Malawi and concludes that six broad sets of features characterize China's relationship with Malawi:

- predictable aid from a 'sincere friend' and a 'reliable partner', despite financial crises and global challenges;
- assistance based on 'visible and tangible results', with priority given to so-called 'landmark' infrastructure projects that instil a sense of national pride and progress;
- Malawi is considered to be a special case of assistance, as China has seldom made such a large commitment to a country within such a short span of time;
- expectations on the volume of aid is kept at a realistic level with Chinese officials typically insisting that China is the world's largest developing country, and must continue to address poverty reduction within its own borders;
- the leadership of Malawi (irrespective of ruling party) is effusively praised for its vision to promote better ties with China and promote economic development;
- China portrays its assistance to Malawi as a result of its international responsibility or show of solidarity with the world's poor.

In the ensuing sections of this chapter, we will examine the impact of Chinese assistance on economic development in Malawi, structured around the following categories:

- addressing the finance and technical gap;
- promoting infrastructure development; and
- interrogating non-interventionist policy and development aid modalities.

Although China is active in numerous sectors, our focus in this chapter is on the infrastructure development component, which has been the most significant and visible part of Chinese aid practices in Malawi.

Addressing the development finance and technical cooperation gap

Malawi's switch of diplomatic relations from Taiwan to China was motivated by a number of reasons including casting the net wider for development finances. Malawi did not participate in the third Forum on China–Africa Cooperation (FOCAC) held in November 2006, where 48 African countries (out of the then 53 countries) that had diplomatic relations with China took part with most of the countries represented by heads of states themselves. This was a big blow to Malawi because the implication was that Malawi would not benefit from the new type of strategic partnership that China pledged. Indeed, the FOCAC meeting declared that not only would China double its aid to Africa by 2009, but that it would establish a range of instruments to further African development:

- establish a China–Africa Development Fund to promote investments by Chinese companies in Africa;
- provide preferential loans and preferential buyer's credits;

- cancel all debt incurred from Chinese interest-free government loans that had matured by 2005;
- open Chinese markets for exports from 31 highly indebted and least developed countries in Africa;
- radically increase the number of Chinese government scholarships earmarked for African students; and
- increase the number of senior agricultural experts and youth volunteers sent on deputation to Africa; and build rural schools and hospitals.[4]

The diplomatic ties between China and Malawi, which commenced a year after the third FOCAC, opened the taps of development financing and technical cooperation opportunities. The first round of China–Malawi negotiations resulted in agreement on an assistance portfolio consisting of grants, concessional loans and contractor-investor package amounting to more than US$1.056 billion for the period 2008–12 (Banik, 2013: 11). With such a massive resource inflow, pressure on the Malawian government was somewhat released given that budget support from western donors became increasingly unpredictable. In addition to filling the financial gap, Chinese development assistance during 2008–12 was directly or indirectly crucial in alleviating the macroeconomic problems that Malawi was facing manifested in the shortage of foreign exchange and fuel.

China has also been flexible in assisting Malawi to implement its development projects and responding to emerging issues. Thus, Malawi has benefited from extra grants and soft loans outside the first round negotiation framework as determined by circumstances on the ground. For instance, China approved a US$500,000 grant in December 2014 for the China–Malawi–UNDP Disaster Management and Risk Reduction project to help support poor and vulnerable communities located within Malawi's 15 identified disaster-prone districts. Malawi also subsequently received several grants (US$25 million and US$16 million) and an interest-free loan (US$8 million) in January 2015.[5]

In October 2015, a second round of negotiations between the two countries was concluded during President Mutharika's official visit to China with Malawi being promised a development assistance package worth US$2 billion. This latest round of negotiations on finance and technical cooperation has come at a critical juncture, when traditional donors have withdrawn their budget support and the Malawian government is facing enormous challenges in providing essential public services. The development package covers different sectors and ministries, and encompass infrastructure development, education, capacity building, defence and security, and agriculture. Following this new package of benefits, the president of Malawi has repeatedly praised China for being a 'true and trusted friend'.[6]

Infrastructure development

The Chinese have registered their presence in Malawi much more in the infrastructure sector than in any other sector. However, it is the Malawian government that has in reality emphasised this focus on infrastructure. On their part, the Chinese have lived up to their promise of negotiating and funding projects at the request of the recipient country, guided by the principle of non-interference. Interviews with key government officials, professionals and politicians indicate that China's involvement in infrastructure development in Malawi is not a one-sided affair. For the Chinese, infrastructure projects are commercially viable because they open up markets for the supply of goods. Such projects also encourage the Chinese private sector to diversify its geographical scope, investment outlay and business opportunities. Moreover, China has demonstrated throughout the world that they have sophisticated organizational capacity to undertake large and complex projects. In Africa alone, the so-called 'stadium diplomacy' strategy of the Chinese has reaped rich dividends in the form of grateful local populations who are thrilled by the sight of soccer stadiums recently constructed in Cameroon, Mozambique, Tanzania, Ghana, Angola, Equatorial Guinea, Gabon, Ivory Coast, and Zambia.[7] Similarly, agricultural technology demonstration centres (ATDCs) – which provide training and exposure to high-yielding varieties of seeds and effective agricultural practices – have been constructed in Mozambique, Liberia, Mali, Cameroon, Senegal, Sudan, Uganda, Togo, Sierra Leone, Mauritania, Democratic Republic of Congo and Guinea.[8] In other parts of Africa – including Malawi, Egypt, Ethiopia and Tanzania – hotels and international conference centres have been constructed in order to boost tourism.

Tables 9.1 and 9.2 provide an overview of the major projects undertaken in Malawi with assistance from China, including a newly constructed ATDC in Salima (Malawi) and a conference centre and stadium in Lilongwe. The Chinese package to Malawi has also involved projects financed by private and quasi-state institutions such as the Anhui Foreign Economic Construction Company, which built the SAGECOA Golden Peacock hotel in Lilongwe. Other projects involving the Chinese include the Balaka Cotton Plantation and Processing project funded by China–Africa Development Fund, expansion of Chileka international airport in Blantyre and the construction of the Kam'mwamba coal-fired plant, both financed by Export–Import Bank of China but implemented by Gezhouba Group Corporation.

Most Malawians, who see visible and tangible results of the cooperation with China, have celebrated the spate of infrastructure projects implemented in the country. Such projects are also a boon for national and local politicians, who believe the construction of much-needed infrastructure helps them gain political mileage with their constituents. A cabinet minister we interviewed indicated that 'visibility is important in politics and the Chinese understand this element … The Chinese are wonderful because they are helping us with tangible projects that people can see for themselves.'[9] President Mutharika has also recently observed that 'Malawi is most grateful for tangible and visible projects financed by China … These are transforming our country for the better.'[10] Similar sentiments have been expressed in the past by different political figures, including former president Bakili Muluzi, who was extremely sceptical of invisible projects

Table 9.1 Major examples of Chinese assistance to Malawi in first phase, 2008–12

Project	Location	Cost US$	Source	Status
Parliament building	Lilongwe	41 million	Grant	Completed, May 2010
Karonga–Chitipa road, 101 km	Karonga–Chitipa	70 million	Grant	On-going
Furniture to Ministry of Foreign Affairs	Lilongwe	300,000	Grant	Completed
Bingu international conference center, presidential villas and luxury hotel	Lilongwe	90 million	Concessional loan	Completed ahead of schedule in April 2012
Bingu national stadium	Lilongwe	65–70 million	Concessional loan to be repaid in 20 years	Completed, November 2015.
Malawi University of Science and Technology	Thyolo	70–80 million	Concessional loan	Completed 2013
SAGECOA Golden Peacock Hotel	Lilongwe	15 million	Investment by Anhui Foreign Economic Construction Company (contractor and investor)	Completed, August 2011
Balaka cotton plantation and processing project	Balaka	25–30 million	Investment funded by the China–Africa Development Fund	On-going
Chipoka agricultural demonstration center (maize, cotton and horticulture)	Salima	8 million	Concessional loan	Completed 2015

Source: Banik (2013), media reports, press releases from the Malawi State House and China's ambassador to Malawi

Table 9.2 Major examples of Chinese assistance to Malawi in second phase, 2013 to date

Project	Location	Cost US$	Source	Status
300 Megawatt Kam'mwamba Coal Fired Power Plant	Covering some districts in the southern region	667.2 million	Concessional loan (Exim Bank of China to be implemented by Gezhouba Group Corporation Limited of China)	Starting 2016
E-Government (National Identity) Project	National and government ministries	50 million	Concessional loan	Starting 2016
The Chileka International Airport	Blantyre	285.4 million	Concessional loan (Exim Bank of China)	Starting 2016
Tsangano-Neno-Mwanza Road, 140 km	Ntcheu, Neno and Mwanza	169.4 million	Concessional loan	Starting 2016 (subjected to further technical review)
Mangochi-Makachira Road, 129.5 km	Mangochi	151.7 million	Concessional loan	Staring 2016 (subjected to further technical review)
Upgrading Phombeya-Makanjira–Nkhotakota-Chatoloma 220 KV power line	Balaka, Mangochi, Nkhotakota, Kasungu	189.3 million	Concessional loan	Starting 2016 (subjected to further technical review)
Lilongwe dual carriage way (Kanengo-Mchinji roundabout)	Lilongwe	45 million	Concessional loan	Starting 2016 (subjected to further technical review)
a) Construction of the Blantyre District Hospital and Cancer Centre (US$23 million)	Blantyre	25 million	Grant	Starting 2016

Project	Location	Cost US$	Source	Status
b) Procurement of police vehicles for the Malawi Police Service (US$2 million)	Malawi police			Completed, 2015
a) Construction of a technical teacher training college (US$5 million)	---	25 million	Grant	Starting 2016
Construction of community technical colleges (US$6 million)	---			
Promotion of value addition activities in the Ministry of Industry and Trade (US$5 million)	---			
Procurement of Equipment and Exchanges Programmes for Professors/Lecturers at the Malawi University of Science and Technology (US$2 million)	Malawi University of Science and Technology			Unknown
Procurement of Office Equipment and Furniture for the Ministry of Trade and Industry (US$1 million)	Ministry of Trade and Industry			Unknown
Support for Technical Services for the Bingu National Stadium (US$1 million)	Lilongwe (Bingu National Stadium)			Unknown
Construction of a New Ministry of Foreign Affairs Building (US$3 million)	Lilongwe			Unknown

Source: Banik (2013), media reports, press releases from the Malawi State House and China's ambassador to Malawi

when he famously argued that 'Democracy alone is not enough … Malawians don't eat democracy'.[11] It is thus becoming evident that the political leadership of Malawi increasingly prefers Chinese development assistance rather than western aid. China is viewed to provide much-needed 'hardware' development projects as opposed to 'software' development interventions that traditional donors fund.

Chinese assistance for infrastructure development has also received support from professional bodies. For example, the Economics Association of Malawi recently argued in favour of Chinese aid when it came out with the following statement:

> If we don't borrow, will we be able to construct an airport? It is a fact we cannot raise our own resources and the loans will be for good intentions such as Blantyre District Hospital. Only if we were borrowing for consumption, then we would be in trouble.[12]

A recent project that has been widely praised within the country is the Malawi University of Science and Technology (MUST), constructed on a private stretch of land donated by former president Bingu wa Mutharika. Built with a concessional loan of US$80 million from China, MUST opened its doors to students in October 2014 with the aim of improving access to higher education. For many years, the country's three public universities – University of Malawi, Mzuzu University and Lilongwe University of Science and Technology – were struggling with capacity constraints, and large groups of qualified students were excluded from enrolment. With an enrolment capacity of 5,000 students (only 452 students had been admitted as of October 2015),[13] MUST offers relatively new academic programmes in Malawi that are closely aligned with the Malawi Growth Development Strategy (MGDS II) and aimed at transforming Malawi from an importing to an exporting nation by exploring and expanding the manufacturing, processing and mineral sectors. Thus, a long term goal for MUST is to offer undergraduate and postgraduate degrees in technology and business-related fields, chemical engineering, medical bioengineering, metallurgy and mineral processing engineering, earth sciences, meteorology and climate science, innovation and entrepreneurship.[14]

Controversies about MUST being constructed on private land and perceived as a 'patronage' project for people in Thyolo district (home of both former and incumbent presidents) have been mitigated by national strategic reasons. The government has realized that fuelling the manufacturing and export agendas require well-trained personnel – a scarce resource in Malawi. MUST was thus commissioned to develop a highly skilled workforce which could adapt available technology to local situations. Furthermore, as Malawi is diversifying revenue resources, the minerals sector has become a priority although the country faces a major shortage of skilled workers.

Overall, borrowing from the Chinese for infrastructure development projects has the acceptance of a large number of Malawians primarily because of the resulting employment opportunities such projects create. These projects, apart from providing increased possibilities for job seekers, also make important contributions towards improving access to public services. They also additionally have important spill-over effects by stimulating economic growth in local communities where the investments are located. It comes therefore as no surprise that Malawi has continued to heavily support infrastructure development projects also in the second phase of its development assistance cooperation with China.

Domestic antagonism: A recipe for invoking 'non-interference' policy?

China's aid and investments has been largely applauded by African leaders, who value the focus on infrastructure development as well as the Chinese policy of non-interference in the politics of their countries. The 'non-interference' policy has, unsurprisingly, attracted criticism from the traditional donors who argue that China is returning African countries to the age of dictatorship and bad governance (Collier, 2007; Wilkin, 2011). Similar concerns have also been raised in Malawi.

Trade between Malawi and China has increased following commencement of the diplomatic relations in 2008. Indeed, the volume of trade jumped from US$42.8 million in 2008 to US$250 million in 2013.[15] However, by accounting for 18 per cent of all imports, there is a trade imbalance as China is currently ranked second in terms of countries from which Malawi imports various goods and services. China's percentage share of trade with Malawi has been consistently high – 93 per cent in 2009, 86 per cent in 2011 and 82 per cent in 2012.[16] The main benefits of the considerable increase of imports from China to the Malawian market have primarily been access to cheap goods for large groups of the urban and rural groups. The Chinese have also changed the market landscape for the better with an element of competition, which they have introduced in the local economy. Except for the construction projects that typically tend to bring senior managers and skilled workers from China, Chinese development projects have attracted numerous Chinese companies to invest in Malawi, thereby promoting employment generation. As of 2012, there were 196 companies from China registered in Malawi in the following sectors: manufacturing (132), tourism (15), services (37), agriculture/farming (8), import and distribution (1), building and borehole drilling (2) and mining (1).[17]

The rapid increase of trade relations between China and Malawi has not been without friction and antagonism. The influx of Chinese workers and small-time traders in the country has resulted in a small but growing amount of resentment among the local population, often amplified by sensational stories appearing in the media highlighting abuse of privileges as well as economic crimes committed. For example, some Chinese nationals have been caught breaking the law – trying to externalize foreign exchange,[18] copying trademarked Malawian products[19] and violating workers' rights.[20] Local business owners have complained of having to face stiff competition from Chinese colleagues who not only have well-stocked shops, but also offer products at extremely affordable prices. A retailer in Karonga district – where the business community staged demonstrations against the Chinese in August 2015 – had the following to say: 'This place is a hive of activity since it is a border area. Business used to be good until the Chinese invaded us, bringing cheap goods and taking away our customers.'[21]

Protests by the business community forced the government to enact a law banning foreigners trading in rural areas. The Business Licensing Act (2012) aimed at protecting local businesses by allowing foreign traders to do business only in the cities of Lilongwe, Blantyre, Mzuzu and Zomba. The new legislation also required foreign traders to apply for a business permit that stipulates the nature and type of businesses they are allowed to conduct. Such applications are to be scrutinized by the Chief Business Licensing Officer and approved by the Investment Approval Committee, requiring that the applicants deposit a minimum of US$250,000 with Malawi's central bank as initial capital.[22]

The Chinese government supported the Malawian government's decision to ban foreign traders from operating in the rural areas on grounds that it was within the legal mandate of Malawi government to do what was best for its citizens. In the interest of keeping their non-interference policy intact, the Chinese ambassador to Malawi observed:

> It is up to the Malawi government to thoroughly screen the Chinese nationals willing to invest in the country. These are small vendors and why should the Malawi government allow them to do business? They are capitalising on government's failure to screen foreign traders.[23]

China has also been cautious about the damage that small-time Chinese vendors can unleash on its public image. However, to what extent China will keep avoiding interference in Malawian domestic affairs is unclear. For example, the Chinese embassy issued a warning in December 2014 stating that Chinese investors would relocate to neighbouring countries following growing insecurity of Chinese nationals in Malawi. For a poor country like Malawi that is struggling to bring traditional donors back, the above threats may be understood in some quarters as an indirect way of 'interfering' with local affairs.

Implications for aid modalities

Malawi is a signatory to the Paris Declaration on Aid Effectiveness that calls for ownership, harmonization, alignment, managing for results and mutual accountability in relation to foreign aid (Owa, 2011). It is also a party to other aid agreements (e.g. the Accra Agenda for Action, the Busan Partnership for Effective Development Cooperation) that are aimed at curbing aid proliferation and fragmentation as well as extracting commitments from donors and recipients to use aid for intended purposes. The aid effectiveness declarations have been domesticated through different policy frameworks including the Malawi Development Cooperation Strategy (2014–16), which outlines the preferred means of delivery resources from the Global North to include:

- general budget support;
- sector budget support and programme-based support;
- basket funds/trust funds;
- project support to government;
- project support channelled through NGOs or directly administered funds; and
- technical assistance and commodity aid (Malawi Government, 2014: 38–9).

Budget support remains the preferred aid modality for most African governments as the funds go direct into the public financial management system, over which the government exercises substantial control. China, however, does not provide its development assistance to Malawi through such channels. Moreover, China is not a member of any group of donors such as the CABS discussed earlier. Neither does it contribute to basket funds where donors pool their resources to fund a project/programme using government or NGO structures. And, although it is currently involved in an FAO trust fund with activities in Malawi, Chinese development assistance is primarily delivered through concrete projects. The Chinese government as well as contracted companies and investors use their own bank accounts and financial management systems, which are very different from those of the Malawian government. Moreover, the concessional loans provided by the Exim Bank of China are extremely risk averse, and, in striving to meet targets on time and ensure quality and cost effectiveness, the Chinese are wary of using the apparatus of the Malawian government. The Chinese model in reality has a very explicit business component, as borne out in the institution entrusted to lead the aid process in Beijing – the Ministry of Foreign Trade and Commerce (Li *et al.*, 2014). Interestingly, despite its obvious preference for budget support, the Malawian Government is not pushing for budget support from China, perhaps realizing that the Chinese will never consider the budget support option.

Although project-based aid by the Chinese has resulted in considerable benefits for Malawi primarily in terms of employment generation, it is not without problems as it has revived some of the failed aid modalities of the 1960s. For example, the World Bank admitted in the 1980s that 75 per cent of its agricultural projects in Africa had failed (Hancock, 1989). The dismal performance of project aid was a result of lack of ownership (well-designed technical projects that missed local input) and a lack of participation by the local constituents. The Chinese version of project aid has been relatively more successful primarily because it has been closely tied to commercial activity, which also ensures that projects are completed on time. For example, the Bingu International Conference Centre and an adjoining five-star hotel and presidential villas were completed 10 months ahead of schedule (Banik, 2013). For the few projects that missed the schedule, the problems have been internal: shortage of regular electricity,[24] theft of materials at the construction site[25] and shortage of fuel.

Our interactions with civil society organizations, media persons and government officials have provided many valid arguments in support of China bypassing governmental structures on grounds. As one respondent argued:

> The Chinese make use of every second available. You agree on timelines and they deliver. If their projects were forced to go through our public structures, they would have been stuck with procurement procedures and would have been severely delayed.[26]

The Cashgate scandal and subsequent withdrawal of budget support by CABS and other donors have strengthened the case for increased project aid from

China. Ironically, traditional donors have now begun channeling their aid through specific civil society-run projects, not very unlike the Chinese model, having lost faith in the public administration of Malawi to deliver aid-supported services effectively. Thus on a visit to Malawi in June 2015, the UK minister of development announced a major increase in DfID Malawi's bilateral programmes in 2015 including a 'broad portfolio of investments'.[27] This aid, the minister observed, was aimed at NGOs, multilateral institutions and civil society organizations; and not intended for the Malawian government as the UK government could not risk channelling such large funds through government financial systems.[28]

The Chinese model, however, is not without its limitations. For example, the simplified and short-term oriented Chinese model of undertaking all activities on its own (mainly through tenders granted to Chinese private sector actors) is proving difficult to manage. The government of Malawi, like many other African nations, is demanding longer-term commitments from China, including support for the maintenance of recently completed infrastructure projects. At the same time, China is facing growing pressure to align its activities with other donors, including those from the west as well as emerging economies. There are also several initiatives afoot where China is collaborating with multilateral organizations (e.g. though financing of strategic trust funds) and others in so-called trilateral initiatives implemented in Africa. All of these trends appear to be moving the Chinese model closer to western aid modalities. However, without a dedicated aid agency – such as the UK's DfID, Norway's Norad or Sweden's SIDA – China will find it difficult to undertake increasingly complex tasks associated with its aid and investments around the world. There is also growing worry within Africa that with the global economic slowdown and lower projected growth rates of the Chinese economy, development financing from China will be sharply reduced in the near future.

Conclusion

China's development assistance strategy in Malawi is based on very different practices and procedures from that provided for in the Paris Declaration. Indeed, unlike most western donors, China does not abide by the principles of harmonization, alignment and managing results. The Chinese aid and investment strategies primarily function in isolation to the strategies of other activities in the field (i.e. are not harmonized) and China does not participate in providing basket funds. Similarly, China avoids involving the Malawian administrative service in the implementation of its projects, preferring to continue with a strategy of involving Chinese contractors, some of whom go on to make substantial investments of their own in the country upon completion of their contracts.

Despite the rhetoric often found in western media outlets, we do not find substantial evidence to indicate that western donors and the Chinese are competing in Africa. Rather, the picture that emerges from our study is that western donors accept that they and China are involved in very different sectors and very different types of activities. Although China also provides aid directed at the agricultural and medical sectors, in addition to stipends and grants for travel to China, this chapter has mainly highlighted Chinese activities related to infrastructural projects implemented in the country. The Chinese neither support the Malawian government through budget support nor explicitly promote democratic consolidation or gender equality. Therefore, western donors believe that their activities usefully complement those of China in Malawi. However, the Chinese believe their aid practices are much more in tune with what Malawi requires, rather than western practices that seek to impose western values and conditionalities on the recipient country.

What does cause concern and results in suspicion among both western actors as well as sections of Malawian society is the secrecy that exists in the Chinese aid management system. Without transparency in relation to disbursement patterns and volume of aid earmarked for certain activities, it is often difficult to understand Chinese strategies and practices. It also becomes difficult to evaluate the impact of Chinese activities in the absence of a dedicated aid agency and an evaluation department that can undertake impact evaluations. Moreover, without the active involvement of Chinese civil society organizations, the decisions by the Chinese government are not scrutinized with the aim of making aid policies even more effective. The secrecy in aid practices creates other problems, most importantly the lack of predictability in the recipient country administrative apparatus. For example, after the Malawian president had recently briefed the media regarding a new development assistance package from China worth US$1.3 billion, the finance ministry was unable to provide specific details of the arrangement including the repayment period of the concessional loan and the interest rates applicable.[29]

We have argued that, to a large extent, Chinese aid is working in Malawi and is making substantial contributions to development and employment generation in tune with local needs. As the foreign minister of Malawi recently observed, 'Today, we have no doubt that the decision (to switch diplomatic ties) was made for a good cause, especially looking at what China has done to this country'.[30] The availability of alternatives to western aid has been a blessing for Malawi, which now can approach several donors simultaneously. Despite the overall positive picture, the volume of Chinese aid to Malawi remains low, and most of the large projects are funded through concessional loans. As Chinese firms gain a stronger footing in Malawi, it will be interesting to follow the extent to which their business practices are in tune with national development priorities.

Chinese aid can indeed be a window of opportunity for Malawi as it seeks to reduce its aid dependency as well as demand different types of support from those traditional donors that choose to continue their presence in the country. As Whitfield and Frazer (2010) and Woods (2008) argue, developing countries can often exercise 'reverse conditionality' and enhance negotiation power by carefully making use of evolving domestic factors in their relations with external donors and multilateral institutions. The constant threat of the withdrawal of western aid may well provide the Malawian government with an incentive to exercise stronger control over its development trajectory.

Notes

1 For further information, see https://www.regjeringen.no/en/aktuelt/budget-support-malawi/id738930/ (accessed 10 November 2015).
2 A.P. Mutharika, 'Malawi President Peter Mutharika Inaugural Speech,' *Nyasa Times*, 2 June 2014. Available at: http://www.nyasatimes.com/2014/06/02/malawi-president-peter-mutharika-inaugural-speech/ (accessed 21 January 2015).
3 'Donors unlikely to resume aid in Malawi-Goodall', *Nyasa Times*, 19 October 2014. Available at: http://www.nyasatimes.com/2015/10/19/donors-unlikely-to-resume-aid-in-malawi-goodall/ (accessed 24 October 2015).
4 Y. Bangura, 'Big Leap in China-Africa Ties', January 2007. Available at: http://www.un.org/africarenewal/magazine/january-2007/big-leap-china-africa-ties (accessed on 22 August 2015).
5 A.P. Mutharika, Brief on the People's Republic of China, January 2015, Ministry of Foreign Affairs and International Cooperation, Lilongwe .
6 Ibid.
7 Y. Kazeem, 'China's "Stadium Diplomacy" in Africa and Its Top Beneficiaries', 29 March 2013. Available at: http://venturesafrica.com/chinas-stadium-diplomacy-in-africa-and-its-top-beneficiaries/ (accessed 20 October 2015).
8 H.L. Sun, 'Understanding China's Agricultural Investments in Africa', Johannesburg, South African Institute of International Affairs, 2011.
9 Interview with a Minister, Lilongwe, 15 September 2015.
10 A.P. Mutharika, Brief on the People's Republic of China, January 2015.
11 P. Clottey, 'Africa must first tackle poverty, says Ex-Malawi President', 19 June 2013. Available at: http://www.voanews.com/content/africa-must-first-tackle-poverty-says-ex-malawi-president/1685354.html (accessed on 2 July 2015).
12 'Chinese Loans Necessary for Malawi Development: Economists back Mutharika,' *Nyasa Times*, 29 October 2015. Available at: http://www.nyasatimes.com/2015/10/29/chinese-loans-necessary-for-malawidevelopment-economists-back-mutharika/ (accessed 29 October 2015).
13 Y. Simutowe, 'Low Female Students intake at Malawi University of Science and Technology: We don't want to become Boys only University', *Nyasa Times*, 28 October 2015. Available at: http://www.nyasatimes.com/2015/10/28/low-female-students-intake-at-malawi-university-of-science-and-technology-we-dont-want-to-become-boys-only-university/ (accessed 29 October 2015).
14 Malawi University of Science and Technology. Available at: http://www.must.ac.mw/ (accessed 19 October 2015)
15 K. Jassi, 'Bank for Increased Malawi, China Trade', *Daily Times of Malawi*, 26 June 2015. Available at: http://www.times.mw/bank-for-increased-malawi-china-trade/ (accessed 23 July 2015).
16 T.C. Thindwa, 'China–Malawi Relations: An Analysis of Trade Patterns and Development Implications', *African East-Asian Affairs: The China Monitor*, 4: December 2014, Centre for Chinese Studies, Cape Town, South Africa.
17 'Origins of Investors, Sectors, Investment and employment'. Malawi Investment and Trade Centre (MITC), 2012.
18 E. Njoloma, 'Measuring the Unconditionality of China's Support to Malawi', 28 May 2012. Available at: http://www.montfortmedia.org/2012/05/measuring-the-unconditionality-of-chinas-support-to-malawi/ (accessed 13 December 2013)
19 'Expat Chinese Guilty of Copying Malawi Football Team Jersey', *Want China Times*, 15 January 2012. Available at: http://www.wantchinatimes.com/news-subclass-cnt.aspx?id=20130115000024&cid=1103 (accessed 19 February 2014).
20 H. Osman, 'Who is Monitoring Plight of Malawian Workers under Foreign Traders', *Nyasa Times*, 10 January 2014. Available at: http://www.nyasatimes.com/2014/01/10/

who-is-monitoring-plight-of-malawian-workers-under-foreign-investors/ (accessed 18 November 2015).
21 C. Ngozo, 'Malawi Checks China's Africa Advance', *IPS News*, 4 August 2015. Available at: http://www.ipsnews.net/2012/08/malawi-checks-chinas-african-advance/ (accessed on 22 February 2015).
22 'Malawi bans foreigners to trade in rural areas: Chinese affected with new law', *Nyasa Times*, 11 May 2015. Available at: http://www.nyasatimes.com/2015/05/11/malawi-bans-foreigners-to-trade-in-rural-areas-chinese-affected-with-new-law-2/ (accessed 2 June 2015).
23 C. Ngozo, 'Malawi Checks China's Africa Advance', *IPS News*, 4 August 2015. Available at: http://www.ipsnews.net/2012/08/malawi-checks-chinas-african-advance/ (accessed 22 February 2015).
24 'Malawi National Stadium Project 80 % complete: China-Funded', *Nyasa Times*, 18 April 2015. Available at: http://www.nyasatimes.com/2015/04/18/malawi-national-stadium-project-80-complete-china-funded/ (accessed 28 May 2015).
25 E. Phimbi, 'Bingu Stadium ready by Nov 30 despite theft setbacks', *Nyasa Times*, 29 October 2015. Available at: http://www.nyasatimes.com/2015/10/29/bingu-stadium-ready-by-nov-30-despite-theft-setbacks/ (accessed 30 October 2015).
26 Interview with public official, Lilongwe, 22 June 2015
27 Z. Chilunga, 'UK to Support Malawi not through govt financial systems', *Nyasa Times*, 24 June 2015. Available at http://www.nyasatimes.com/2015/06/24/uk-to-support-malawi-not-through-govt-financial-systems/ (accessed 18 October 2015).
28 Z. Chilunga, 'UK to Support Malawi not through govt financial systems', *Nyasa Times*, 24 June 2015. Available at http://www.nyasatimes.com/2015/06/24/uk-to-support-malawi-not-through-govt-financial-systems/ (accessed 18 October 2015).
29 'Chinese Loans Necessary for Malawi Development: Economists back Mutharika', *Nyasa Times*, 29 October 2015. Available at: http://www.nyasatimes.com/2015/10/29/chinese-loans-necessary-for-malawidevelopment-economists-back-mutharika/ (accessed 29 October 2015).
30 G. Chaponda, 'China and Malawi: Friends with Benefits', *Nyasa Times*, 18 December 2014. Available at: http://www.nyasatimes.com/2014/12/18/china-and-malawi-friends-with-benefits/ (accessed 25 July 2015).

References

Ayodele, T. and Sotola, O. (2014) 'China in Africa: An Evaluation of Chinese Investment', Lagos: Initiative for Public Policy Analysis.
Banik, D. (2013) 'China's Aid and Poverty Reduction in Africa', in G. Yu (ed.), *Rethinking Law and Development: The Chinese Experience*, London: Routledge.
Breslin, S. (2011) 'The Soft Notion of China's "Soft Power"', Asia Programme Paper: ASP PP 2011/03, London: Chatham House.
Callan, P., Blak, J. and Thomas, A. (2013) 'Emerging Voices: Callan, Blak and Thomas on the Landscape of Emerging Aid Donors'. Available at: http://blogs.cfr.org/development-channel/2013/04/02/emerging-voices-callan-blak-and-thomas-on-the-landscape-of-emerging-aid-donors/ (accessed on 23 May 2015).
Chinsinga, B. (2008) 'The Malawi Fertiliser Subsidy Programme: Politics and Pragmatism', Future Agricultures Consortium Policy Brief 22, Brighton: Institute for Development Studies.
Collier, P. (2007) *The Bottom Billion: Why the Poorest Countries are Failing and What can be done about it*, Oxford: Oxford University Press.

Euromonitor Research (2014) 'Top 5 Fastest Growing Consumer Markets in 2014', Available at: http://blog.euromonitor.com/2014/10/top-5-fastest-growing-consumer-markets-in-2014.html (accessed 6 March 2015).

Government of Malawi (2006) 'The Malawi Growth and Development Strategy', Lilongwe, Government of Malawi.

Halper, S. (2010) *The Beijing Consensus*. New York: Basic Books.

Hancock, G. (1989) *The Lords of Poverty*, New York: Atlantic Monthly Press.

Knack, S. (2001) 'Aid dependence and the quality of governance: Cross-country empirical tests', *Southern Economic Journal*, 68(2): 310–29.

Lengauer, S. (2011) 'China's Foreign Aid Policy: Motive and Method', Center for East West Cultural and Economic Studies, Robina, QLD: Bond University.

Li, X., Banik, D., Tang, L. and Wu, J. (2014) 'Difference or Indifference: China's Development Assistance Unpacked', *IDS Bulletin*, 45(4): 23–35.

Makwerere, D. and Chipaike, R. (2012) 'China and the United States of America in Africa: A New Scramble or a New Cold War?' *International Journal of Human and Social Science*, 2(17): 311–19.

Malawi Government (2014a) 'Malawi Development Cooperation Strategy', Lilongwe: Ministry of Finance, Economic Planning and Development.

Malawi Government (2014b) *Malawi Aid Atlas*, Lilongwe: Ministry of Finance, Economic Planning and Development.

Moss, T., Pettersson, G. and van De Walle, N. (2006) 'An Aid-Institutions Paradox? A Review Essay on Aid Dependency and State Building in Sub-Saharan Africa', Working Paper 74, Washington, DC: Centre for Global Development.

Naim, M. (2007) 'Rogue Aid', *Foreign Policy*, 159: 95–6.

Opoku-Mensah, P. (2009) 'China and the International Aid System: Challenges and Opportunities', Working Paper No.141, Aalborg: DIR & Department of History, International and Social Studies, Aalborg University.

Owa, M. (2011) 'Revisiting the Paris Declaration Agenda: An Inclusive, Realistic Orientation for Aid Effectiveness', *Development in Practice*, 21(7): 987–98.

Ramo, J.C. (2004) 'The Beijing Consensus', London: The Foreign Policy Centre.

Resnick, D. (2012) 'Two Steps Forward, One Step Back: The Limits of Foreign Aid on Malawi's Democratic Consolidation', Working Paper No. 2012/28, Helsinki: United Nations University Press.

Taylor, A.J. (2014) 'Review of the Functionality of Sector Working Groups in Malawi', Lilongwe: Ministry of Finance, Economic Planning and Development.

van der Meer, E., Tostensen, A., Slob, A. and Jerve, A.M. (2008) 'Managing Aid Exit and Transformation Malawi Country Case Study', Swedish International Development Agency.

Weaver, C., Davenport, S., Baker, J., Findley, M., Peratsakis, C. and Powell, J.C. (2014) *Malawi's Open Aid Map*, Washington, DC: IBRD/World Bank.

Whitfield, L. and Frazer, A. (2010) 'Negotiating Aid: The Structural Conditions Shaping the Negotiating Strategies of African Governments', *International Negotiation*, 15: 341–66.

Wilkin, S. (2011) 'Can Bad Governance be Good for Development?', *Survival: Global Politics and Strategy*, 53(1): 61–76.

Woods, N. (2008) 'Whose Aid? Whose Influence? China, Emerging Donors and the Silent Revolution in Development Assistance', *International Affairs*, 84(6): 1205–21.

10 Women, media and culture in democratic Malawi

Happy Mickson Kayuni

Introduction

When Malawi gained independence in 1964, with Kamuzu Banda as its first president, the country quickly reverted to a one-party state. Banda's administration limited the rights and freedoms of Malawians while concentrating enormous power in the hands of the president. Although the president frequently referred to himself as a staunch defender of women rights, very little in terms of improving the welfare of women was achieved in the three decades during which he ruled the country. Indeed, there was a complete absence of legislation introduced in parliament aimed at promoting the interests of women in the social-political arena. Ironically, it was during Banda's rule that Malawi signed the Convention on the Elimination of all Forms of Discrimination Against Women (CEDAW) in 1979. Civil society organisations and related networks were virtually non-existent, except for a few affiliated with the ruling Malawi Congress Party (MCP). Apart from the MCP's own Women's League, women were also encouraged to join and be active in the Chitukuko Cha Amayi muMalawi (CCAM) – an organisation run by one of Banda's closest confidants, Mama Tamanda Kadzamira. CCAM was established as a charity in 1985 and started off as a sub-organisation of MCP's League of Malawi Women (Tengatenga, 2006). The literal translation of its name is 'Women's development in Malawi'. It therefore mainly focused on the women's developmental issues. In this regard, it disbursed small business loans and provided vocational training to women for income generation activities (Green and Baden, 1994). In the long run, its identity became blurred as it was partially incorporated in the mainstream government structure with a Principal Secretary of the organisation being represented in the Office of the President and Cabinet. Since the organisation was deemed to be too close to the MCP, it didn't survive after the 1994 multiparty elections.

The absence of a vibrant civil society was a major obstacle towards promoting the idea of gender equality in the country until 1994, when Malawi embraced democracy and a multiparty system. The current Constitution of Malawi highlights several provisions that relate to promotion of gender equality and women's rights. Specifically, the Constitution prohibits discrimination in any form on grounds of race, colour, sex, language, religion, political or other opinion, nationality, ethnic or social origin, disability, property, birth or other status. Although Malawi has over the years passed several important pieces of legislation supporting the rights of women, translating these into practice in order to secure social, political and economic benefits has remained a major challenge. However the presence and acknowledgement of several networks, coalitions and alliance of actors – that regularly fight for gender equality in the country – has brought renewed hope (White, 2007; Kanyongolo and Wadonda-Chirwa, 2009).

This chapter focuses on the 2009 and 2014 parliamentary elections in Malawi, with a particular focus on the interplay between gender, media and culture. A gender equality campaign (also known as the 50:50 campaign) – which was launched by the Ministry of Women and Child Development (MoWCD) in collaboration with NGO Gender Coordination Network (NGOGCN) – was aimed at increasing the number of women representatives in parliament. In the spirit of the 1995 Beijing conference, the campaign recognised the media as a major player towards achieving the goal of gender equality. This is evident in the fact that a special media task force was established to facilitate and coordinate activities. It is generally agreed that media plays a critical role in shaping political views and social behaviour and that the media has the potential of dramatising and legitimatising the forces of political power. It is this perceived notion, that media creates the culture of how to behave and what to think, feel, believe and desire, that the Malawi gender campaign tried to take advantage of.

This chapter argues that, although the media enhanced the debate on women representation in parliament, the whole programme and process was based on an unsustainable political premise. To what extent was the overarching patrimonial culture challenged in the 50:50 campaign? What role did the media play in the 50:50 campaign, and to what extent can its role be attributed to the success or failure of the campaign itself? I argue that political socialisation is more comprehensive but the approach that the media in Malawi has taken in relation to gender issues has been excessively narrow, over-simplistic and oriented towards the short term. Rather, the creation of a successful political culture requires a more inclusive approach with an emphasis on the development of new societal identities. These identities are typically built over time and hence the process aimed at promoting gender equality should not necessarily be limited to electoral periods. I will examine the 50:50 campaign within a cultural homogenisation narrative. Cultural homogenisation is a process whereby the international perceptive (in this case, gender equality) subdues the local perspective and ultimately dominates the local understanding and interpretation of the social phenomenon. The gender equality campaign in Malawi is an example of an international perspective that has not successfully been localised. The media in Malawi has been caught up in the pressure to domesticate the international cultural homogeneity against a strong patriarchal system. Using Afrobarometer[1] survey research results from 2002 to 2014, I argue that despite over a decade of efforts to encourage and promote the participation of women in politics, fewer women than men today are interested in political engagement. This implies that the core social fabric that defines social relations in the country – patriarchy

– and the conditions that allow it to thrive are yet to be thoroughly addressed. In this regard, the 2009 and 2014 electoral campaigns can be regarded as the failure cultural homogeneity in the area of gender relations.

Democracy and the gender equality goal

Several studies have examined the link between gender rights and quality of democracy. Rizzo *et al.* (2007) conducted a survey in Arab and non-Arab Muslim societies and found that respondents who subscribed to gender equality notions were also strong supporters of democracy. In another study – and based on their analysis of 65 societies that represent 80 per cent of the world's population – Inglehart *et al.* (2004) argue that 'countries that rank high on civil rights and political liberties, have much higher proportions of women in parliament than countries with low levels of freedom'. They nonetheless highlight the fact that there are some notable exceptions. For example, although China is not democratic, it has a large number of women parliamentarians. In contrast, several democratic countries such as the United States, Japan and France have low percentages of female representation in their legislatures. The overall trend, however, is that there is a strong and positive correlation between levels of democracy and increased female representation in legislative bodies. Consequently, Inglehart *et al.* conclude that 'if the majority doesn't have full political rights, the society is not democratic'.

To buttress the above-mentioned linkages, Yambo-Odotte (1994) examines the case of Kenya in 1992, when the country reintroduced a multiparty system of governance. She argues that the media played a critical role in enhancing a positive image of women candidates and, more importantly, she explains how the introduction of women as candidates enhanced the democratic discourse. When a growing number of women decided to compete for elected office in 1992 (through support from international bodies), Yambo-Odotte (1994: 21) observes that 'one consequence of this was that the print and electronic media approach to women's issues changed, literally overnight', and the media now began claiming 'that the democratization process was incomplete if women did not actively participate in the quest for political leadership'. Yambo-Odotte further explains that male candidates did not focus on substantive issues while their female counterparts 'focused attention on issues which, for over thirty years of independence, had not been adequately addressed'. These included 'the lack of clean water for all, inadequate health facilities, the lowering education standard, and the deteriorating agricultural sector' (Yambo-Odotte (1994: 22).

The media provided a major boost for the women candidates, and a video entitled *If Women Counted* apparently transformed the mind-set of most Kenyans at that time. This video – produced by women activists – followed the campaign of 19 female parliamentary candidates and other local government contenders. The video inspired many future women candidates and with the contributions of other gender-sensitive media prompted many people to rethink their values to the extent that 'it is now becoming commonplace to meet Kenyans of either gender who are very proud to be associated with issues of gender sensitivity' (Yambo-Odotte, 1994: 23). Although Kenya is not a model nation as far as gender representation in parliament is concerned, it has nonetheless made significant progress since multiparty politics in 1992. This is precisely why information and communication rights, which are essentially the hallmark of the media 'are essential preconditions for women to fully exercise their civil and political rights – to organise, network, make their knowledge and ideas visible and advocate for gender justice' (United Nations, 2013: 24).

Similarly, Gallagher (2002) observes that the commercialisation of media in most Asian countries has significantly transformed the way people perceive women. In this regard, commercial cable and satellite channels as well as privatisation of formerly state-run media have introduced market-oriented content in the media, and, in relation to gender equality, this type of content arguably projects a positive image of women. The market-oriented image contrasts greatly from the previously established perception that women's role is limited to being a housewife and a mother. Thus, one of the most important challenges to gender equality is culture (United Nations, 2013) and an important instrument to combat negative perceptions of women is the media.

It is beyond the scope of this chapter to link democracy, gender equality *and* development, but I will try to summarise some of the important strands in this debate. Inglehart and Welzel (2009) argue that, apart from the need for the establishment of supportive social structures and inculcation of relevant cultural values, there is a strong correlation between democracy and development. Democratic ideals of inclusiveness, accountability, participation and transparency are essentially the building blocks of a realistic and holistic social-economic development of any society. At the global level, the linkage between gender and development has largely been championed by the UNDP through the wider human rights versus development nexus debate (Sano, 2000). Since the introduction of the first annual Human Development Report by the UNDP in 2000, the link between development and gender has taken a wider and more comprehensive appeal. A development agenda that ignores social and political rights of women is unlikely to be sustained. A quest for women's rights is thus ultimately also a quest for development of society.

When the international women's movement was gaining momentum in the 1970s and 1980s, it placed considerable emphasis on issues of poverty, health and education for women. However, the movement did not pay much attention to media-related strategies in achieving the above-mentioned goals (Gallagher, 2002). By the early 1990s, however, attention gradually shifted to appreciating the role of media in enhancing gender equality. Thus, although the media was seldom mentioned in the documents resulting from the first three United Nations conferences on women (1975–85), the situation changed when the Beijing Platform for Action was adopted at the Fourth World Conference on Women in 1995 (Gallagher, 2002; Hassim, 2003). At this conference, the role of the media took centre stage and 'media' was subsequently included in one of twelve 'Critical Areas of Concern'.

At the centre of gender equality, which has a direct implication for democratic principles, are the basic issues of power, values, access and exclusion; and media is generally regarded as one of the main actors in addressing these issues. As Chimba (2006: 6) points out, the media can be 'a major source of definitions and images of social reality, including the representation of women and definitions of femininity'. Thus in relation to politics, the media has the capability to strengthen the 'status quo in power arrangements in society' or even establish new suitable arrangements (Chimba, 2006: 6). This is why information and communication rights, which form the hallmark of the media, 'are essential preconditions for women to fully exercise their civil and political rights – to organise, network, make their knowledge and ideas visible and advocate for gender justice' (United Nations, 2013: 23). The way media operates and articulates issues is profoundly entrenched in political and economic contexts. The move towards gender equality involves *inter alia* the wider process of cultural change and democratisation (Inglehart *et al.*, 2004).

The media and cultural homogenisation

Culture is broadly defined as the cumulative acquisition and internalisation of knowledge, experience, beliefs, values, attitudes, meanings, hierarchies and relations by a group of people, which is passed on from one generation to another (Castells, 2004; Ong, 2006). This definition of culture incorporates elements of language, ideas, customs, taboos, institutions and ceremonies. Cultural homogenisation as a concept implies that a perceived superior (wider or international) culture invades a local culture, and in the process the superior culture becomes the dominant culture (Fotopoulos, 1999; Strelitz, 2001; Neyazi, 2010). Ultimately every member in the locality accepts this wider culture and society gradually becomes more homogenous.

According to Ogburn and Nimkoff (1964), there are two types of culture. Material culture refers to mode of dress, types of food consumed, use of technology and other related issues. The non-material aspects refer to values, customs, beliefs, norms and all other aspects, which facilitate the acceptance or rejection of the aforementioned material culture. Cultural homogenisation may take both of these forms, and although the material aspect is more visible the non-material has more long-lasting impact (Beynon and Dunkerley, 2000; Neyazi, 2010). In the ensuing sections, we will therefore focus on the non-material culture in gender relations.

Cultural homogenisation is not a completely top-down process. To the recipient community, the dominant culture has to be contextualised and this involves a process whereby new meaning is attached to the integrated foreign cultural elements (Beynon and Dunkerley, 2000; Lewellen, 2002). And Fotopoulos (1999: 5) argues that every community has a particular prevailing culture, which can be explained in relation to the social dominant paradigm: 'the system of beliefs, ideas and the corresponding values which are dominant in a particular society at a particular moment of its history'. In other words, the underlying argument is that, for any society to reproduce itself, it must ensure that its dominant beliefs, ideas and values are in tandem with the existing institutional framework. Thus, for a democratic society to flourish, the dominant social beliefs, ideas and values within it have to be consistent with the corresponding democratic institutions and practices. In exceptional circumstances, individuals may move from a minority position to challenge the social dominant paradigm and set in motion a process of irreversible social change. In such cases, societies may be looked upon not merely as *collections of individuals* but *social individuals* who have the capacity to create a new society according to their preferences while at the same time they are a creation of the society they belong to. Cultural homogenisation entails that the social dominant paradigm is increasingly taking a regional and international perspective. Accordingly, culture is becoming less complex and highly predictable in every society, and, in the political arena, the pressure for gender equality has been an important component of the international cultural homogenisation process.

From a gender perspective, the patriarchal notion may be regarded as a dominant social paradigm that needs to be interrogated if gender equality has to be achieved in most African countries, including Malawi (Allanana, 2013). The assumption in the patriarchal narrative is that the underlying inequalities between men and women can be explained by male-dominated social and cultural attitudes and institutions, which systematically subjugate women (Kramarae, 1992; Stacey, 1993).

The 50:50 campaign as a form of cultural homogenisation

The past few decades have witnessed a substantial expansion of women's political representation around the world. Despite such overall positive trends, women remained underrepresented in all national parliaments in 2012, except in Rwanda and Andorra (IPU, 2012). The increase in women's presence in the political sphere has sparked a theoretical debate since the early 1990s regarding the appropriate thresholds for women's representation (Hughes and Paxton, 2007; Krook, 2009; Krook, 2010; Muriaas and Kayuni, 2013). The debate has been highly influenced by Phillips's (1995) critique of liberal democracy and her 'politics of presence' argument. According to Phillips, the liberal framework places excessive emphasis on the importance of representing variation in ideas, and does not sufficiently value representation of people for who they are. She thus promotes an understanding of representation that resembles what Pitkin (1967: 60) termed 'descriptive representation': the notion that the demographic composition of a legislature should accurately reflect that of the whole nation. In other words, the legislative assembly should 'mirror' the various identities found in the society.

The idea of mirror representation paved the way for a discussion of specific thresholds for women's representation, using terms such as 'critical mass', 'gender balance', and the more recent phrases '50:50 balance' or '50–50 parity' (Meintjes, 1996; Ahikire, 2009). In the 1990s, the women's movement adopted the idea of a critical mass. In other words, for women to have an impact in key political institutions such as legislatures and influence public policies, their representation should be increased to constitute 30 per cent of total membership. The term 'critical mass' was adopted from nuclear physics, where a certain quantity is required to initiate an irreversible chain reaction (Dahlerup, 2006). At the turn of the millennium, the demands of women's movements around the world grew stronger. They adopted a more explicit interpretation of mirror representation, arguing that since women make up about 50 per cent of the citizens in any given country, they should hold an equal share of seats in decision-making bodies. Consequently, the aim of many women's activists was to reach 50:50 gender balance or parity in political decision making.

According to Melanie *et al.* (2007), the current discourse on gender quota may be regarded as the third wave in the international women movements' goals and discourse. The first wave focused on the right to vote, the second wave focused on increasing women's representation and the current wave, which started in the 1990s, focuses on settling specific thresholds for women's representation. This current trend of debating threshold is, as Lovenduski (1993: 2) has argued, divided between two dimensions of representation. There are those who argue that a 'critical mass' is sufficient as long as an assembly takes into account the interests of all its electors (Meier, 2004; Muriaas, 2011). Others advocate for a 50:50 gender balance, stressing that the composition of the elected assemblies in democracies should mirror the composition of the society it serves. Still others (Rosabeth Kanter. quoted in Grey, 2006: 494) suggest differential critical masses to achieve different purposes. For example, Kanter suggests that if the representation of women increases to 15 per cent, national policies generated would probably be in favour of women, while a 40 per cent change would ensure that policies that favour women are introduced (Grey, 2006: 494). Tremblay (2006: 502) disagrees and argues that the concept of critical mass is often 'elevated to law like status' and moreover 'quickly made the object of abusive interpretations, becoming synonymous with a relationship of cause and effect'. He blames political scientists for quickly adopting the concept and suggesting generalisations, which found their way into electoral systems. Dahlerup (2006: 517) admits that some countries may adopt the critical mass merely to appear 'modern and democratic', and that political parties also recruit women to gain votes and do not expect them to focus on women welfare.

The critical mass discourse has in recent years been discarded by demands for gender balance. Women constitute around half the population in most countries, and according to the 'mirror' notion of representation, women representatives should fill about 50 per cent of all political offices. One of the earliest international organisations to call for a 50:50 representation was the Women's Environment and Development Organization (WEDO) (Dahlerup, 2006). In Africa, the ground-breaking moment was when the African Union decided to follow up the African Charter on Human and Peoples' Rights on the Rights of Women in Africa (2003) by stating that gender equality in practice meant a 50:50 gender balance in decision-making. SADC decided to follow suit and at the Heads of

State Summit in Gaborone in 2005, a 50:50 gender target was introduced. While 13 of the 15 SADC member states signed the protocol in August 2008 (with the exception of Botswana and Mauritius), only 7 of these governments have subsequently ratified the document. Furthermore, while the Democratic Republic of Congo and South Africa have ratified the document, they have failed to submit their instruments of ratification to the SADC Secretariat (SADC Gender Protocol Alliance, 2012). Consequently, the protocol cannot be enforced in the whole SADC region until these two ratifications secure a two-thirds majority.

Malawi's 50:50 campaign

Patriarchy is the dominant social paradigm in Malawi and the single most important impediment towards achieving progress towards gender equality in the country. When Malawi's first female president came to power in 2012, there was not much enthusiasm for her ascendancy as a female leader, and several women's activists were in fact, at the forefront in criticising her policies. Indeed, the general narrative that emerged in the country – which was also echoed by one of the senior party official – was that even when Joyce Banda was Vice-President, Malawi was not ready for a female president (Kamwendo and Kamwendo, 2014).

The 50:50 campaign during the 2009 general elections

The initial target for gender representation in elected political offices in Malawi was set at 30 per cent as a result of the SADC protocol on gender discussed above. This goal was not achieved in the 2004 general elections but, rather than reducing the standards, the bar was raised by Malawi in line with SADC agreement to 50 per cent in the 2009 elections. The new dimension in the election campaign was the clear sense of organisation towards achieving the target. For instance, with assistance from various development partners, the 50:50 campaign was launched and coordinated by the newly created NGO Gender Coordinating Network (NGOGCN), established on the premise that it would function as a permanent, non-partisan committee with representation from various institutions including the Association of Progressive Women (APW), Gender Support Programme (GSP), The National Women Lobby Group (NWLG), Civil Liberties Committee (CILIC), National Election System Trust (NEST), Centre for Human Rights and Rehabilitation (CHRR) and the Society for the Advancement of Women (SAW). Some groups have questioned the principle of non-partisanship in the organisational arrangement taking into consideration the fact that the Ministry of Women and Child Development (MoWCD) initially coordinated the formation of the NGOGCN secretariat. The boundary between government and the political party in power in Malawi is often blurred. With MoWCD taking centre stage, there was a generally held view that NGOGCN was actually serving the interests of the political party in government (the Democratic People's Party). Despite the above-mentioned limitations, NGOGCN went on to develop its own ambitious strategic objectives. These included:

- improving gender equality and equity through advocacy and lobbying;
- developing the organisational and human capacities of various actors;
- effectively dealing with issues of gender equality and equity;
- ensuring efficiency in communication and information flow;
- establishing and maintaining a well-developed organisational and management structure that will act as a nerve centre for the network activities; and
- supporting and sustaining activities of the network (NGOGCN, 2009).

The organisation further laid out detailed plans for capacity building, advocacy and lobbying, community mobilisation and socio-economic empowerment (MoGCCD, 2008). Regional meetings and training sessions were organised throughout the 2009 election period.

The 50:50 campaign during the 2014 general elections

Building on the success of the 2009 elections, the 50:50 campaign started off with much vigour in 2014. Specifically, the campaign was supported by a number of development partners such as the United Nations, the Royal Norwegian Embassy, Oxfam, ActionAid, GIZ and Active Learning Centre. However, coordination was undertaken by the National Technical Working Group (NTWG), which involved all stakeholders that were implementing the campaign's activities. NTWG was a composition of diverse professional technocrats who were operating in different sub-committees created on the basis of their expertise. NGOGCN on the other hand was merely the umbrella body that brought together the committees of NTWGs. The NTWG not only identified political aspirants who were women but also realized the significance of advocacy and lobbying in its overall strategy. It pursued several avenues of engagement with political parties at the national level to ensure that political actors remained committed to fielding and supporting female candidates. Meetings with community leaders at district and grassroots level were also organised as well as media outlets in order to ensure that there was positive coverage and profiling of female political candidates. In addition, the NTWG placed considerable emphasis on capacity building through training sessions for female candidates that were conducted at regional and district levels. Apart from training, another element of capacity building included the production and distribution of T-shirts to candidates, which carried the image and slogan of their respective women candidates. About 100 T-shirts were freely distributed to each female candidate aspiring to be an MP. However, almost all the candidates complained that these T-shirts were not adequate. Most importantly, however, the organisation provided cash support – MK200,000 for every candidate for the post of MP and MK90,430.62 for every candidate for the post of a councillor. All female candidates were also provided access to free legal services offered by the Women's Lawyers Association of Malawi on a pro bono basis.

The role of the media taskforce

As part of the preparation for the 2014 general elections, one of the sub-committees of the NTWG was the 50:50 media taskforce with the specific aim of increasing publicity for female candidates and the 50:50 campaign itself. According to Chikunkhuzeni (2014), the taskforce was mandated to undertake the following tasks:

- coordinated coverage of the campaign and its activities including positive and ethically correct publicity of female candidates;
- promote coherent and coordinated messaging and information sharing regarding the campaign;
- support the NGOGCN secretariat on the appropriate modes of communication and available opportunities to ensure maximum publicity of female candidates.

In order to achieve these functions, the taskforce established an executive committee comprised of 6 journalists from all regions of Malawi, which was helped by a regular committee consisting of 17 journalists from various media houses, in addition to ex-officio members that included the NGOGCN communications officer. Some of the activities undertaken by the taskforce included training in gender-sensitive elections reporting, organisation of field visits, training of women candidates in media relations and communication skills, production of radio and television programmes, and assistance with writing op-ed pieces. Despite its enormous potential, the media task force was unfortunately unable to make significant breakthroughs in campaigning for the women representation. One of the main reasons for this failure was the huge demand for publicity by the candidates and the corresponding lack of capacity in the task force. Moreover, the task force faced considerable difficulty in negating the influence of political patronage in ensuring that several media reports appeared to be explicitly or implicitly biased against women (Chikunkhuzeni, 2014).

Impact of cultural homogenisation on gender

Despite a female president leading the country from April 2012 until March 2015, there was surprisingly no significant impact in relation to the improvement of women's political activism and participation in Malawi. Surveys by Afrobarometer conducted in the period 2002–14 on gender-related matters show that Malawi still lags considerably behind in achieving the gender parity as envisaged in its various 50:50 campaign activities. The survey results show that more men than women are interested in public affairs and political discussions, and the gap in interest of public affairs and frequency of political discussions between men and women is steadily increasing in favour of men. Additionally, the survey results indicate that women in Malawi are less likely than men to participate in political activities and activism that include attending political rallies and campaign meetings, persuading others to vote for a candidate and working for a political candidate. More importantly, although more than half of Malawians hold the view that women should have the same chance of being elected to political office as men, these numbers are steadily declining. Thus, the above results provide a relatively clear indication that efforts aimed at enhancing political participation of women in politics have not yielded much. It is no wonder therefore that women's representation in the Malawian Parliament decreased to 17 per cent in the 2014 elections, after having risen from 6 per cent in 1994 to 22 per cent in 2009. Despite having enacted several laws aimed at promoting and strengthening gender equality, most notably through the Gender Equality Act (2012), an increase in female political representation remains largely elusive.

Participation of political discussions and public affairs

Political socialisation depends on, among other things, political discussions and interest in public affairs. The Afrobarometer surveys (see Figures 10.1 and 10.2) show that women in Malawi are less likely to be involved in political discussions than their male counterparts and that their interest in public affairs is also far lesser than men. While 79 per cent of men indicate that they discuss politics, only 65 per cent of women do so. Although this gap was 14 per cent in 2002, it widened to 21 per cent in 2005. And while the gap narrowed to 11 per cent in 2008, it returned to the 2002 figure of 14 per cent in the 2012 and 2014 surveys. In relation to showing interest in public affairs, the results indicate that there is on average a 13 per cent gap between men and women. When compared to the 2012 survey, the gap has significantly widened from 6 per cent in 2002 to 13 per cent in 2014. With the exception of the 2014 results, there has thus been a downward trend in the percentage of men and women showing interest in public affairs.

Female political activism

One way of determining the potential of women taking up a more active part in politics is to analyse their political activism: attendance at campaign meetings, persuading others to vote and working for a political candidate, for example. It is quite well accepted in academic and policy circles that women in Malawi are less likely than men to participate in political activities and activism. More than half (56 per cent) of male respondents in the Afrobarometer surveys say they attended a political rally in the previous year of the survey, while only 44 per cent of female respondents did so. Similar gaps are reflected in attendance at campaign meetings (27 per cent men, 17 per cent women), persuading others to vote for a candidate (25 per cent men, 17 per cent women), and working for a political candidate (19 per cent men, 11 per cent women). Women are also somewhat less likely than men to join others to raise an issue or to participate in a demonstration or protest march. The gap between women and men who join others to raise an issue

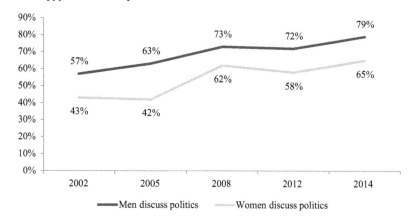

Figure 10.1 Participation in political discussion by gender, 2002–14
Source: Author's own calculation from various Afrobarometer surveys

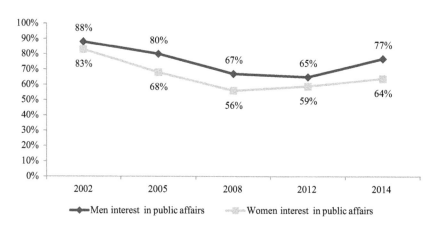

Figure 10.2 Interest in public affairs, by gender, 2002–14
Source: Author's own calculation from various Afrobarometer surveys

has not changed much (8 percentage points in 1999; 6 percentage points in 2014). Similarly, women are less likely than men to contact local officials and leaders. Only 12 per cent of women had contact with an MP in the year before the survey, compared to 18 per cent for their male counterparts. Similarly, only 8 per cent of women were in contact with government officials versus 13 per cent of men. This gap has also been fairly steady since 2002.

Support for female leadership

Women should have the same opportunities as men to take up leadership positions, according to 60 per cent of Malawians, reflecting a sharp drop from 78 per cent in 2012. Correspondingly, the proportion of respondents who agree with the statement that 'men make better political leaders than women' rose from 21 per cent in 2012 to 37 per cent in 2014. In the 2011–13 survey of 34 African countries, on average 68 per cent of respondents said that women are as capable as men of being political leaders. What is interesting with this 2014 finding is that it was at a time when Malawi had a female president in office. It would be expected that those who support women leadership should actually increase when comparing the 2012 and 2014 results, but this was not the case. As explained below, having a female president had its own disadvantage in that the expectations from the electorate were higher than usual. The revelations of increased corrupt activities in government, which were infamously termed the 'Cashgate' scandal, may have negatively affected the president's popularity as well as perceptions of female leadership in general.

The weak political performance of women in the campaign

The post 2014 general elections revealed a number of weaknesses in the 50:50 campaign which are discussed below and they include:

- narrow media coverage on gender issues;
- lack of commitment from political parties; and
- conflict among gender NGOs.

Narrow media coverage on gender issues

A Media for Southern African (MISA, 2010) study found that women as news sources in Malawi had increased to 20 per cent from the 11 per cent recorded in 2003. Despite this increase, women still lag behind in access and use of the various sources of media. There was a conscientious strategy to involve the media in the 50:50 campaign, and a media committee was set up, which aimed at propagating a positive image for women aspirants. Using advocacy and lobbying activity, the media provided much of the coverage in support of women candidates. Some of the special areas covered included advocacy meeting with party leadership, orientation meetings with journalists and sensitisation meetings with community leaders and religious leaders. Furthermore, airtime was bought by various well-wishers on radio and TV to showcase the 'women aspirants'.

Although the media may have contributed to an overall enrichment of democratisation in the country by covering the debate on female representation in parliament, the 50:50 campaign and process was based on a politically unsustainable premise. The media perspective, in relation to gender issues, was too narrow, over-simplistic and short term. It was too narrow in that the media portrayed the issue of men competing against women. The media campaign ignored the role of men in promoting women candidates and hence gave the impression that it was only a 'women's issue'. It was thus over-simplistic because it did not directly address the patriarchal system, which has perpetually undermined female political representation in the country.

Another media-related weakness of the 50:50 campaign was the fact that media messages with a gender component typically competed with other existing messages which were targeting virtually the same audience (Chikunkhuzeni, 2014). Thus publicity alone was not enough to create substantial impact. Indeed, the media strategies in the 50:50 campaign erroneously focused on publicity and not change of voter behaviour. There was little recognition or understanding of the interface between political communication and voter behaviour. Furthermore, Chikunkhuzeni (2014) observes that the campaign had a narrow focus on news media workers rather than a broader focus on including news presenters, advertisers, public relations officers, spokespersons and party campaign directors.

Lack of commitment from political parties

Although the number of independent candidates in the past two elections has been increasing, the reality is that most of these individuals were not completely independent. Rather they were previously members of a political party, but subsequently became frustrated with internal power struggles or were simply overlooked in the candidate selection process. This is evidenced by the fact that the majority of these so-called independent candidates typically return to their former parties as soon as they get elected to parliament. It has been argued that the increase in women parliamentary representatives in 2009 was mainly due to the fact that the Democratic People's Party (DPP) had more women candidates than any other political party in the country and, more importantly, the DPP also won many seats in parliament (Kayuni and Muriaas, 2014). Consequently, there is general acceptance among Malawian scholars that political parties are the most important institutions that determine success for parliamentary candidates. Due to the highly competitive nature of the first-past-the-post electoral system in Malawi, it is very difficult for aspiring female candidates to succeed. One way of addressing the issue has been the suggestion that political parties could adopt voluntary quotas. However, this option is very problematic in the current political set up of Malawi because political parties have not been able to demonstrate commitment to this end. Although all major political parties clearly outlined their commitment to gender equality in their electoral manifestos in 2009 and 2014, such promises were not translated into reality.

Conflict among gender NGOs

When Joyce Banda assumed the presidency in 2012 following the death of Bingu wa Mutharika in office, it turned out to be both a blessing and a curse for the women's political movement in Malawi. Banda's position as president as well as her candidature in the 2014 elections raised the profile of women seeking public office. However, any weakness in her office was deemed to be evidence of the failure of female leadership in general – even when such failures had nothing to do with the president's gender. The issue was further complicated by the fact that several prominent women activists at that time belonged to or supported opposition political parties, and they launched a concerted effort to protest against Joyce Banda's leadership. This resulted in a scenario whereby it was generally perceived amongst voters that women themselves had declared a 'vote of no confidence' on their female political leaders. Taking into consideration that Malawi has an entrenched patriarchal system, the role of other women activists to campaign against the female president of the country was political damaging not only to the incumbent but generally for the agenda of the entire women's movement, which was championing for an incremental increase in female representation in public office.

Short-termism in the campaign process

The electoral process is often regarded as a circle or process with each stage reinforcing the other. The 50:50 campaign in Malawi in 2009 and 2014 was limited to the electoral campaign period. This narrow view of the electoral process has had adverse implications in enhancing women's political representation. Moreover, due to disagreements among NGOGCN members as well as donors regarding the implementation plan for the 2009 and 2014 elections, the gender campaign started off very late in both electoral years. Consequently, when the 50:50 campaign was officially launched, the general national electoral campaign was already at an advanced stage. The original plan of the 50:50 campaign was largely meant to encourage aspiring women candidates through training programmes and workshops. However, due to the delay, it was too late to identify and inspire new candidates when these workshops were actually conducted.

Conclusion

This chapter has examined the strategy to promote gender equality in Malawi, primarily viewed through the lens of the 50:50 campaign launched in 2009 and 2014. I have argued that the campaign that Malawi adopted was not fully home-grown but rather a product of cultural homogenisation, which began first at the global level and was subsequently translated into the regional (SADC) and national levels. The media and the development partners (donors) played a critical role in ensuring that the global rhetoric of the 50:50 campaign was operationalised for application within Malawi. After more than a decade of the campaign, it was expected that there would be profound changes in the socio-political environments through a radical increase in the number of women elected to parliament. However, the recent elections results proved that the opposite was true. Based on Afrobarometer survey results from 2002–14 as well as a comparison of the 2002 and 2014 parliamentary electoral results, I have argued that female political participation in Malawi continues to be significantly lower than that of men. It is unlikely that women will be on an equal footing with men if the current strategies for gender equality are maintained. A deeper problem emerging from 2012 and 2014 Afrobarometer survey results is that an increasing number of women themselves are now believing the narrative that male leaders are better than their female counterparts. This is after years of the gender equality campaign, which directly propagated a message where gender quality and respect for the talents and skills of women were supposed to be highlighted. The media, which was envisaged as a major player in addressing the problem, was thus not able to directly deal with the issue of the dominant social determinant: patriarchy. It did not genuinely question the patriarchal system but simply cut and pasted the overarching international gender narrative in a local context without adequately making persuasive arguments that took into consideration local sentiments and the Malawian socio-political context. From a social-cultural perspective, the 50:50 campaign was organised in the context of cultural homogenisation and the failure of the campaign to address the gender inequality may largely allude to the failure of cultural homogenisation itself.

However, other factors beyond media may have contributed to the failure of the 50:50 campaign, the most significant being the country's electoral system. Almost all countries in Africa that have taken impressive strides in gender representation in the political arena have abandoned a pure first-past-the-post system. Even with an elaborate 50:50 campaign, it is unlikely in the near future that Malawi will make significant progress unless the electoral system is comprehensively overhauled. One might even say that the 50:50 campaign was actually misguided: it should have focused mainly on lobbying for the overhaul of the electoral system. Running the campaign in this highly constrained electoral system entailed essentially fighting a losing battle.

Note

1   The Afrobarometer (http://www.afrobarometer.org) is an independent, nonpartisan research project that measures the social, political, and economic atmosphere in Africa. Afrobarometer surveys are conducted in more than a dozen African countries and are repeated on a regular cycle. Because the instrument asks a standard set of questions, countries can be systematically compared. Trends in public attitudes are tracked over time. Results are shared with decision makers, policy advocates, civic educators, journalists, researchers, donors and investors, as well as average Africans who wish to become more informed and active citizens. In total six rounds or cycles of surveys have been conducted across Africa from 1999 up to 2015. Malawi has participated in all these rounds.

References

Ahikire, J. (2009) *Women's Engagement with Political Parties in Contemporary Africa: Reflections on Uganda's Experience* (Policy Brief 65). Johannesburg: Centre for Policy Studies.

Allanana, M. (2013) 'Patriarchy and Gender Inequality in Nigeria: The Way Forward'. *European Scientific Journal* 9(17): 115–44.

Beynon, J. and Dunkerley, D. (eds) (2000) *Globalization: The Reader*. New York: Routledge.

Castells, M. (2004) *The Power of Identity*. Oxford: Blackwell Publishing.

Chikunkhuzeni, F. (2014) 'Media, Gender and Elections'. Paper presented at the critical reflections on the 50:50 campaign and the 2014 tripartite elections – strategic forward looking towards 2019, Bingu International Conference Centre (BICC), 21 August.

Chimba, D. (2006) 'Women, Media and Democracy: News Coverage of Women in the Zambian Press'. PhD Dissertation in Mass Communication, University of Wales, College of Cardiff.

Dahlerup, D. (2006) 'The story of the theory of critical mass'. *Politics and Gender*, 2(4): 511–22.

Fotopoulos, T. (1999) 'Mass Media, Culture and Democracy', *The International Journal of Inclusive Democracy*, 5(1): 1–61.

Gallagher, M. (2002) 'Women, Media and Democratic Society: In Pursuit of Rights and Freedoms'. EGM/MEDIA/2002/BP.1, United Nations Division for the Advancement of Women (DAW) Expert Group. Beirut, Lebanon 12–15 November. Available at: http://www.un.org/womenwatch/daw/egm/media2002/reports/BP1Gallagher.PDF (accessed 28 February 2016).

Green, C. and Baden, S. (1994) 'Women and development in Malawi', Report prepared for the Commission of the European Communities Directorate-General for Development, Bridge Development-Gender Report No. 23.

Grey, S. (2006) 'Numbers and Beyond: the Relevance of Critical Mass in Gender Research', *Politics and Gender*, 2(4): 492–502.

Hassim, S. (2003) 'The gender pact and democratic consolidation: Institutionalizing gender equality in the South African state'. *Feminist Studies*, 29(3): 505–28.

Hughes, M. and Paxton, P. (2007) 'Familiar theories from a new perspective: The implications of a longitudinal approach to women in politics research'. *Politics & Gender*, 3(3): 370–78.

Inglehart, R. and Welzel, C. (2009) 'How Development Leads to Democracy. What We Know About Modernization'. *Foreign Affairs*, March/April, 88(2): 33–48. Available at: http://www.foreignaffairs.com/articles/64821/ronald-inglehart-and-christian-welzel/ how-development-leads-to-democracy (accessed 10 October 2015).

Inglehart, R., Norris, P. and Welzel, C. (2004) 'Gender Equality and Democracy'. John F. Kennedy School of Governance, Harvard University. Available at: http://www.hks. harvard.edu/fs/pnorris/Acrobat/Gender%20equality%20&%20democracy.pdf (accessed 20 October 2015).

IPU (2012) 'Women in politics: 2012', Geneva: Inter-Parliamentary Union, available at: http://www.ipu.org/pdf/publications/wmnmap12_en.pdf (accessed 10 October 2015).

Kamwendo, J. and Kamwendo, G. (2014) 'When Exploitation is Camouflaged as Women Empowerment: The case of Malawi's first female president Joyce Banda'. *Feminist Africa* 20: 77–82.

Kanyongolo, N. and Wadonda-Chirwa, P. (2009) *SADC Gender Protocol Barometer Baseline Study Malawi*. SADC, Botswana.

Kayuni, H. and Muriaas, R. (2014) 'Alternatives to Gender Quotas: Electoral Financing of Women Candidates in Malawi'. *Representation-Journal of Representative Democracy*. 50(3): 393–404.

Kramarae, C. (1992) 'The condition of Patriarchy', in Kramarae, C. and Spender, D. (eds.) *The Knowledge Explosion*. London: Athen Series, Teachers College Press.

Krook, M. (2009) *Quotas for women in politics: Gender and candidate selection reform worldwide*. Oxford: Oxford University Press.

Krook, M. (2010) 'Women's representation in parliament: A qualitative comparative analysis'. *Political Studies*, 58(12): 886–908.

Lewellen, T. C. (2002) *The anthropology of globalization: Cultural anthropology enters the 21st century.* Westport: Bergin & Garvey.

Lovenduski, J. (1993) 'Introduction: The dynamics of gender and party', in Lovenduski, J. and Norris, P. (eds.), *Gender and Party Politics.* London: Sage.

Meier, P. (2004) 'The mutual contagion effect of legal and party quotas: A Belgian perspective'. *Party Politics,* 10(5): 583–600.

Meintjes, S. (1996) 'The women's struggle for equality during South Africa's transition to democracy'. *Transformations,* 30: 47–64.

MISA (2010) *Gender and Media Baseline Study.* Harare: Media Institute of Southern Africa.

MoGCCD (2008) *Women and Political Participation in the 2009 Parliamentary and Presidential Elections.* Lilongwe: Ministry of Gender, Children and Community Development.

Muriaas, R. (2011) 'The ANC and power concentration in South Africa: Does local democracy allow for power-sharing?', *Democratization,* 18(5): 1067–86.

Muriaas, R. and Kayuni, H. (2013) 'The Reversed Contagion Effect: Explaining the Unevenness of Women's Representation Across South African Municipalities', *Women's Studies International Forum.* 40(2): 150–59.

Neyazi, T. (2010) 'Cultural imperialism or vernacular modernity? Hindi newspapers in a globalizing India'. *Media Culture Society,* 32(6): 907–24.

NGOGCN (2009) *NGOGCN Institutional Profile.* Lilongwe: Gender Coordinating Network.

Ogburn, W. F. and Nimkoff, M. F. (1964) *A Handbook of Sociology.* London: Routledge & Kegan Paul.

Ong, A. (2006) 'Mutations in Citizenship', *Theory, Culture and Society,* 23(2–3): 499–531.

Pitkin, H. (1967) *The concept of representation.* Berkeley, CA: University of California Press.

Rizzo, H., Abdel-Latif, A. and Meyer, K. (2007) 'The Relationship Between Gender Equality and Democracy: A Comparison of Arab Versus Non-Arab Muslim Societies'. *Sociology,* 41: 1151–70.

SADC Gender Protocol Alliance (2012) *Southern Africa Gender Protocol Alliance Annual meeting report* , Johannesburg, 14–15 August. Available at: http://www.genderlinks.org. za/article/sadc-gender-protocol-alliance-annual-meeting-report-august-2012-2013-06-29 (accessed 10 October 2015).

Sano, H. (2000) 'Development and Human Rights: The Necessary, but Partial Integration of Human Rights and Development'. *Human Rights Quarterly,* 22: 734–52.

Stacey, J. (1993) 'Untangling Feminist theory', in Richardson, D. and Robinson, V. (eds.) *Introducing women's Studies: Feminist Theory and Practice.* Basingstoke: Macmillan.

Strelitz, L. (2001) 'Where the Global Meets the Local: Media Studies and the Myth of Cultural Homogenization'. *Transnational Broadcasting Studies.* No. 6, available at: http://tbsjournal.arabmediasociety.com/Archives/Spring01/strelitz.html (accessed 20 October 2015).

Tengatenga, J. (2006) *Church, State and Society in Malawi: An Analysis of Anglican Ecclesiology.* Zomba: Kachere series.

Tremblay, M. (2006) 'The Substantive Representation of Women and PR: Some Reflections on the Role of Surrogate Representation and Critical Mass'. *Politics and Gender,* 4: 502–11.

United Nations (2013) 'Democracy and Gender Equality: The Role of the UN'. Report from the International Round Table on Democracy and Gender Equality: The Role of the United Nations, available at: http://www.idea.int/publications/democracy-and-gender-equality/loader.cfm?csModule=security/getfile&pageid=59108 (accessed 17 October 2015).

White, S. (2007) *Malawi: Country Gender Profile*. Lilongwe: JICA.

Yambo-Odotte, D. (1994) 'Women, Media, and Democracy Evanston, IL: Program of African Studies', Northwestern University. No. 8, pp. 21–4 Available at: http://quod.lib.umich.edu/p/passages/4761530.0008.012/ – women-media-and-democracy?rgn = main;view = fulltext (accessed 17 October 2015).

11 Major conclusions

Dan Banik and Blessings Chinsinga

While democracy provides increased voice and influence for the poor than non-democratic systems, many emerging democracies in developing countries are constantly struggling to achieve high rates of economic growth and reduce poverty. And the continued high rates of poverty not just in Malawi but also in other African countries beg the question as to whether democracies can indeed turn things around. Why is the democratic record at development and poverty reduction not better?

The chapters in this volume have offered insights on three broad sets of issues:

- democratisation and political culture;
- governance and policy implementation; and
- activism, aid and accountability.

Within these general categories, we have discussed a range of issues which, although focused on Malawi, have general implications for many countries on the African continent. These include:

- constitutional guarantees and regulatory and operational challenges and dilemmas related to enforcing fundamental rights;
- strategies to collectively organise voters and hold authorities to account through organisational behaviour and practices as well as specific awareness campaigns;
- the media as an instrument of policy influence, social awareness and political accountability;
- strategies and challenges related to the implementation of a set of crucial development and anti-poverty programmes;
- the impact of civil service motivation and demotivation on public policy implementation; and
- the growing importance and influence of aid and investments from non-Western donors through South–South cooperation on economic development and poverty reduction.

In the ensuing sections, we summarise the main findings of this volume under four broad categories:

- challenges to democratic consolidation amidst entrenched political settlements;
- the disconnect between the formal and the informal and resulting impacts on judicial and legislative oversight;
- heavy top-down public policies implemented by demotivated bureaucrats; and
- the emergence of new donors and a way out of the traditional conditionality trap.

Challenges to democratic consolidation amidst entrenched political settlements

Many Western powers and multilateral organisations have in recent decades emphasised the crucial role that free and fair elections play in promoting development and freedoms of various kinds. There is indeed general agreement that elections can pave the way for the establishment of a political culture where civil and political rights on the one hand and social, economic and cultural rights on the other are respected, protected and promoted. There have been few success stories, however, particularly in Africa, with several recent setbacks in many parts of the continent. The usual problems have been ineffective electoral arrangements and electoral malpractices, but also, most importantly, rulers not willing to relinquish power even when they lose the popular vote. Although there have been some exceptions, many African leaders continue to harbour ambitions of extending their tenures even when they are barred from doing so by their constitutions. Thus, contested elections or attempts by leaders to seek to stay on in office by manipulating the system often result in so-called 'critical junctures' during which young democracies are tested.

Transitions from authoritarian systems to democracy are not easy and there is considerable agreement in the literature that such transitions do not necessarily result in consolidated forms of democracy. Indeed, democratic transitions are typically characterised by the risk of regime collapse and a return to authoritarianism. Several chapters have in particular discussed the attitudinal views of democratic consolidation and examined the extent of anti-democratic behaviour and attitudes between political actors and the general public. We find evidence of the important role of critical junctures and their impact on the survival of young democracies. Malawi has experienced numerous critical junctures since 1994, but four events in particular stand out:

- the bid by President Muluzi for a third term in office;
- authoritarian tendencies exhibited by President Bingu wa Mutharika;
- the death of Mutharika in office in 2012 and debates over the constitutional validity of the Vice-President to assume the presidency; and

- the more recent Cashgate corruption scandal, where large sums of public money went into the pockets of ruling party politicians and their cronies.

These critical junctures have been extensively covered in this volume, and it is important to highlight that, during each crisis, there has been considerable erosion of public trust in the democratic political system.

The democratic dividend so far in Malawi appears to be modest gains on democracy together with a firm rejection of authoritarianism. Indeed, the country did not fall into the trap of reversing back to authoritarian and one-party rule. Rather, democracy in Malawi has survived despite being forced to weather the storm caused by numerous political crises. Consequently, a major conclusion is that Malawi is stuck in transition – neither consolidating its democracy nor regressing into authoritarianism. And there have been periods of progress followed by periods of regressions that have largely coincided with the critical junctures. There is nonetheless considerable evidence of strong public support for democracy, which provides an important barrier against further erosion of existing democratic institutions. Current evidence, nonetheless, suggests stagnation rather than consolidation. Democracy, in other words, is not the only game in town. Not yet, at least!

The slow pace of democratic consolidation can be partially attributed to Malawi's long history of authoritarianism. Ever since the country achieved independence from Britain in 1964 and until the elections of 1994, one man – the dictator Hastings Banda – and his Malawi Congress Party (MCP) dominated the country's politics. The three decades of Banda's rule were characterised by brutal repression of all forms of dissent. The MCP dominated virtually all aspects of social, political and economic life in the country and Banda exercised supreme control over the party. The political settlement of the time was constructed in a manner where economic benefits mainly accrued to MCP elites and their supporters: selected politicians, civil servants, traders and estate owners. Indeed, we have argued that the elites who benefited from this settlement simply extended their support to Banda's regime without necessarily looking out for the welfare of the country. The ensuing political settlement was, however, not inclusive, and resulted in widespread discontentment, which in turn required strong-arm tactics of the state to crush all forms of dissent. It was therefore inevitable that such a settlement would inevitably collapse, particularly in the face of economic hardship.

Since the transition to democracy in 1994, there has been a rapid growth in the number of political parties operating within the country. Several chapters in this volume have examined how and to what extent these parties have shaped (or placed obstacles in the way of) the country's democratic and development trajectories. The major conclusion – based on analyses of selection of leaders and their successors, electoral candidates, available funding, ideological commitments and party discipline in the legislative process – is that the political system remains fragile. The legal framework enabling the creation of political parties and their regulation – the Political Parties (Registration and Regulation) Act of 1993 – does not provide for transparency and accountability in daily operations. The

Act, moreover, is silent on how parties are financed and does not require parties to publicly declare their sources of wealth and reveal their assets.

Some have claimed that political parties, especially during the first two decades of democratic politics, contributed significantly to the evolution of a defective democracy in Malawi. Indeed, without an ideology-based platform, and often operating without a specific manifesto, parties today are unable to offer a visionary socio-economic and political agenda. Several chapters in this volume have offered various explanations of how and why parties are unable to distinguish their policies from their rivals, and how the party organisation has primarily become a vehicle for contesting state power every five years. But, once in power, parties appear incapable of charting new pathways and setting their particular stamp of public policies, largely pursuing the very same policies that they criticised while in opposition. Thus, this volume offers evidence confirming that political parties in Malawi have largely failed to create a political settlement that could result in a process of sustained social and economic development. Rather than ideology, four sets of interrelated factors appear to determine the formation and functioning of parties in Malawi like in many other African contexts. These include patronage, clientelism, ethnicity and tribalism. Party conventions are seldom held, and, even when they are occasionally held, the primary agenda is simply to confirm the inevitable: the endorsement of the party president (who is often the main financier) as the candidate for presidential elections. Moreover, very few office bearers of political parties are ever elected to their positions, which gives the party leader enormous power and unrestricted influence over the entire party apparatus. These features make it difficult for parties to successfully manage internal conflicts and develop long-term visions based on a consistent policy message.

Disconnect between the formal and the informal: Impacts on judicial and legislative oversight

Malawian courts routinely profess fidelity to formalist legal theories that advocate a strict separation between law and politics. However, we find that the highest courts often intervene in political contestations and thereby exercise a significant amount of influence on the construction of the political discourse. Such influence is evident with respect to the contribution of the country's Supreme Court and High Court towards the 'judicialisation' and 'informalisation' of the country's politics. Although there have been attempts to prevent the courts from involving themselves in political matters, the judiciary has, on occasion, adjudicated in matters that fall within the realm of politics. Some of the reasons behind this increased politicisation of the judiciary include the constitutional provisions that allow judges to adjudicate beyond 'law', in addition to provisions that authorise the court to mediate in political disputes. Thus, for example, Malawian courts have dealt with cases that relate to the succession of traditional chiefs, and have thereby reinforced contested provisions of customary law and related informal institutions that are not subject to formal constitutional provisions that guarantee and protect human rights. The actions of the courts have on occasion also resulted in the weakening of formal mechanisms of accountability. For example, the courts have ruled that a constituent has no right to force his or her MP to attend Parliament and that the party leadership need not be consulted when a party member is appointed to a Cabinet position. However, the judiciary has also on occasion constrained the informalisation of politics – for example by branding certain behaviours as corrupt even when local communities accept such actions. The main conclusion in this respect is that the judicialisation and informalisation of politics can contribute positively to inclusive development if the judiciary overtly acknowledges its political role and develops a clear legal doctrine that legitimises only those informal institutions that promote inclusive development.

While the judiciary has asserted its independence in Malawi's recent political history, the legislature has largely been dominated by the executive ever since the introduction of multiparty democracy. This is partly because of the country's choice of a political system, which provides substantial powers to the President and assigns a subservient role to the legislature. The routine presence of personalised patronage in Malawian politics has further entrenched the culture of parliamentary subservience. However, this is not unique to Malawi as most legislatures in Africa continue to face the challenge of a dominant executive. Other challenges that prevent greater legislative control of the executive relate to inadequate availability of resources, lack of technical expertise, frequent changes in the composition of its committees and various types of pressure exerted by administrative officials and party leaders. Despite these constraints, the Malawian parliament has demonstrated that it has the potential, and can be an effective mechanism, for ensuring accountable governance. A major success for Parliament, despite strained executive–legislative relations, has been the performance of committees particularly during critical junctures in the country's efforts at democratic consolidation. Such events have included the floor-crossing saga of MPs repeatedly changing party loyalty, the attempt by former President Bakili Muluzi to abolish presidential term limits, and the reluctance of the executive to publicly declare their wealth and assets. During these junctures, parliamentary committees have played a pivotal role in holding the executive to account. For example the Public Accounts Committee has been instrumental in probing corruption cases while the Public Appointments Committee has withheld crucial appointments when key officials have been suspended or appointed by the government without proper consultations with all parties concerned. Similarly, the Legal Affairs Committee has initiated impeachment proceedings against a sitting President on the basis of allegations of financial misconduct and formation of a new political unit in parliament with breakaway factions from the party that elected him to office. However, not all contributions of these committees have been adversarial in character. For example, the Budget and Finance Committee has frequently provided constructive feedback and recommendations to the government on a range of issues related to allocations on agriculture, health and education.

Heavy top-down public policies implemented by demotivated bureaucrats

A major obstacle to development efforts in poor countries, be they democracies or non-democracies, has been ineffective implementation of anti-poverty schemes. There has traditionally been an overwhelming emphasis on 'top-down' approaches where experts, often far removed from the problems faced by the poor, attempt to define what disadvantaged groups need. In contrast, there is far less emphasis on 'bottom-up' processes where the poor themselves are involved in articulating their needs.

This predominance of a heavy top-down approach together with the lack of correspondence between programme goals and implementation realities has rendered many anti-poverty schemes in developing countries ineffective. As several chapters in this volume have demonstrated – most notably the cases related to fiscal decentralisation, youth employment policy and the gender equality campaign – typical challenges to successful implementation include:

- the lack of knowledge or disinterest among policy formulators on the problems facing local communities;
- lack of communication among implementing officials; and
- lack of continuity in the top ranks of the public services as personnel are constantly shunted from one department to another either as a form of reward (e.g. promotion) or as a punishment (e.g. demotion or transfer to less attractive posting).

For example, the politics surrounding fiscal decentralisation, resource allocation and decision-making has contributed to the weak and fragmented service delivery capacity of local governments in Malawi. Indeed, a major conclusion is that the impact of the devolution policy on service delivery is largely negated when district administrations do not control key functions including staff recruitment. Thus, even though the country now has elected officials (councillors) at the local level in place, improved local governance and more efficient public service delivery will only result when further devolution of functions and funds and rationalisation of the legal framework are undertaken. Political leaders have similarly not shown much interest in finding solutions that will improve the agricultural sector. The pressing policy problems relating to youth unemployment – which have not received much political attention – is a case in point.

Similarly, when Malawi decided to initiate a gender equality campaign aimed at increasing the number of women representatives in parliament during the 2009 and 2014 parliamentary elections, the entire initiative was based on an unsustainable political premise. Indeed, the major cause of policy failure was that the dominant social paradigm of patriarchy that is entrenched in the country was never really challenged. Although the Malawian media was roped in as a major actor to spread the message of gender equality, it has consistently pursued strategies that are excessively narrow in focus, over-simplistic in their operationalisation and short-term oriented. The gender equality campaign also illustrates some of the challenges associated with implementing policies that are sometimes initiated, advocated and funded by external actors without substantial local ownership or 'buy-in'.

The successful formulation and implementation of public policy requires the presence of a well-functioning administrative apparatus. Even when a country transitions to democracy, it does not necessarily inherit a strong, stable and competent administrative infrastructure. A major challenge for most developing countries is to establish clear merit-based procedures for recruitment and training of competent civil servants. This requires a strong political will to undertake substantial administrative reforms that risk being opposed by powerful bureaucrats who fear the loss of their privileged positions.

Patrimonialism is often a major barrier in the democratic consolidation phase, and in Malawi, as in other developing countries, civil servants often complain of increasing political interference in administrative activities. Such interference, they argue, seriously undermines bureaucratic initiative and bureaucratic neutrality, and is a major source of demotivation in the public service. While ministers in Malawi do not formally have a prominent role in recruitment, promotion, demotion or transfer of public servants in the ministry, the reality is quite different. Political interference is rampant in the public service, which often negatively impacts service delivery. Excessive political interference can indeed contribute to implementation failures as dubious political interests may override the wisdom of qualified civil servants.

However, civil servants themselves also try to align themselves with selected politicians in the hope of being awarded plum postings or partaking in corrupt transactions. Consequently, the unholy nexus between corrupt politicians, private contractors and favour-seeking bureaucrats contributes to an enormous wastage of public resources and continued misery for Malawian citizens. Nonetheless, political disinterest can also be lethal in that, without sustained political support, civil servants do not possess the power and influence to implement policies or radically change or adapt policies which have inherent weaknesses. There is thus a greater need for civil servants (as implementers) to provide critical and regular feedback to politicians (as policymakers) without the fear of reprisals. It is the lack of such contact (or the fear of providing critical and honest feedback) between policymakers and implementers that often explains implementation failure in many developing countries.

Emerging donors provide flexibility and a way out of the traditional conditionality trap

Malawi has a long history of being dependent on external actors (mainly Western donors and multilateral organisations) who have traditionally made substantial contributions to the country's national budget in addition to providing support at project and programme levels. However, financial support from these donors has often come with certain strings attached: demands for good governance, tolerance of dissent, combating corruption, focus on gender equality, respect for gay rights, etc. Many African governments have, in recent years, expressed frustration over the growing list of donor demands and conditionalities. Indeed, some governments (e.g. Malawi under President Bingu wa Mutharika) have accused Western donors of pursuing a development agenda contrary to the actual needs of the nation. Accordingly, there is a feeling in many quarters that Western aid agencies do not practice what they preach and that the Western experience of development and poverty reduction does not appear very relevant to solving problems in aid recipient countries.

In recent years, however, a new set of donors – from so-called emerging countries of the South – have made their presence felt in Africa. In particular China, but also India, Brazil and many other Asian donors, are interacting in numerous ways with countries in sub-Saharan Africa, including through so-called South–South dialogues. Such developments not only provide emerging countries with access to natural resources, in addition to new and growing markets, but they also tend to reduce the dependence of African countries on traditional forms of aid from the West. Emerging countries and their policies thus represent a counterweight to the policies and development aid models of the West that have for long been promoted directly or indirectly (e.g. through multilateral institutions) in poor countries.

Although China is a new donor in Malawi, it has already made its presence felt in many sectors. Indeed, Chinese foreign aid and investments have contributed significantly to addressing macro-level national and community problems. Chinese assistance, based on principles of 'win–win' and 'mutual respect', is often very 'visible' as the emphasis has traditionally been on infrastructure projects as opposed to, for example, budget aid, which has been the preferred option for Western donors. The downside of China's activities in Malawi primarily relate to the inability of local businesses to compete with the Chinese, the quality and durability of infrastructure projects, disagreements between the Malawian and Chinese governments regarding who should cover the high costs of maintaining the Chinese-built infrastructure projects and secrecy around the Chinese aid management system. There have also been concerns in some quarters about China's 'neo-colonist' aspirations and that the Chinese tend to benefit more than African countries.

Despite some very valid concerns, an important conclusion is that despite the rhetoric often found in Western media outlets, there is very little evidence to indicate that Western donors and the Chinese are competing in Malawi. Rather, the picture that emerges is that Western donors accept that they and China are involved in very different sectors and very different types of activities. Indeed, Chinese aid in Malawi primarily focuses on the neglected and 'orphan' sectors such as infrastructure and energy. In addition, the spill-over effects of macro-oriented projects initiated by the Chinese government and private sector companies have resulted in a rapid growth of small and medium-scale business enterprises run by Chinese nationals in urban and semi-urban areas. Such enterprises are providing local communities with access to a large range of

Chinese products (albeit some of poor quality) at affordable prices. The presence of China has added a new dimension to the development agenda as many African leaders openly express their frustration over the inability of Western donors to provide aid related to infrastructure development. African governments have now greater flexibility in financing their needs, and are in a better position to play the field – requesting different types of assistance from different categories of donors and well-wishers.

The way ahead

Many democracies in the developing world appear to fulfil the procedural requirements of democracy although the actual functioning of the system is often detrimental to the needs of the large majority of the population who continue to live in poverty. Thus, the challenge for democracies is not merely to achieve economic growth but to also undertake successful interventions aimed at redistributing the benefits of growth in order to reduce poverty and address growing inequality. It is against this backdrop that this volume has revisited broad theoretical and practical assumptions on the relationship between democracy, development and poverty reduction. Democracies must re-examine the reasons that explain their limited success in providing social welfare. This not only includes revisiting the ability to formulate and implement public policy, but also how such policies are financed. For example, while a major form of accumulating public resources is through taxation, most developing countries face the problem of whom to tax (e.g. due to the presence of a large unorganised sector), the appropriate level of taxation, and how tax revenue can be collected efficiently. The general consensus for many years has been that democracy has a greater impact on development and poverty reduction in less patrimonial societies. In sub-Saharan Africa, this requires radical political and administrative reforms aimed at reducing the impact of patrimonialism and increasing the effectiveness of democratic political institutions. While it is unrealistic to expect that such reforms will be implemented overnight, recent events in Malawi as well as in many other African countries provide hope that change will indeed take place even if the pace of reforms may at first appear to be slow.

Index

For Product Safety Concerns and Information please contact our EU
representative GPSR@taylorandfrancis.com
Taylor & Francis Verlag GmbH, Kaufingerstraße 24, 80331 München, Germany